Berkmann's
Pop Miscellany

ALSO BY MARCUS BERKMANN

Rain Men: The Madness of Cricket

A Matter of Facts: The Insider's Guide to Quizzing

Fatherhood: The Truth

Zimmer Men: The Trials and Tribulations
of the Ageing Cricketer

The Prince of Wales (Highgate) Quiz Book (ed.)

Ashes to Ashes: 35 Years of Humiliation (and About 20
Minutes of Ecstasy) Watching England v Australia

A Shed of One's Own: Midlife Without the Crisis

Set Phasers to Stun: 50 Years of *Star Trek*

The *Spectator* Book of Wit, Humour and Mischief (ed.)

Berkmann's Cricketing Miscellany

Berkmann's Pop Miscellany

*Sex, Drugs and Cars in
Swimming Pools*

MARCUS BERKMANN

Little, Brown

LITTLE, BROWN

First published in Great Britain in 2021 by Little, Brown

1 3 5 7 9 10 8 6 4 2

A CIP catalogue record for this book
is available from the British Library.

ISBN 978-1-4087-1385-3

Typeset in Times by M Rules
Printed and bound in Great Britain by
Clays Ltd, Elcograf S.p.A.

Papers used by Little, Brown are from well-managed forests
and other responsible sources.

Little, Brown
An imprint of
Little, Brown Book Group
Carmelite House
50 Victoria Embankment
London EC4Y 0DZ

An Hachette UK Company
www.hachette.co.uk

www.littlebrown.co.uk

To Paula, Martha and James

Contents

Introduction

I have been obsessed with pop music for more than forty years. In my teens, when I should have been revising, or communing with my peers, or really doing anything else at all, I spent long school-holiday days lying in bed, reading trashy fiction and listening to pop radio. I listened to so much pop radio I started to look forward to the same songs rolling around again, an hour or two after they had last been played. A new song on the playlist was something to be cherished. If a song I liked went up in the charts that week, it really mattered.

Two or three years later, when small amounts of money at last came into my life, I started buying albums, often at Our Price in Charing Cross Road, where all the most popular, and therefore discounted, records cost £3.99. One day there was some tax change or other, and all the chart records immediately went up to £4.31. I listened widely, and sometimes wisely, and often bought foolishly. My friend David was obsessed with the Doors, and although they sounded pretty terrible to me, I bought a couple of their records, the first untitled album and *L. A. Woman*. Trying to like something you don't like, I discovered, actually makes you hate that music more than you could ever have thought possible. Nowadays I only have to hear the opening chords of 'Light My Fire' and I run screaming from the room.

The years from 1977, when I bought my first album (*Rattus Norvegicus*, by the Stranglers), were the brief heyday of punk and the longer hangover of post-punk, which curiously mutated into the gloss, hairstyles and synthesisers of the 1980s. Because I was young then, most of my favourite albums were released between 1977 and 1982. I should probably admit now, to get it out of the way, that I have always had rather an inconvenient taste in music. I liked clever pop tunes above all else. I adored 10cc, Steely Dan, Squeeze, the Electric Light Orchestra. I couldn't really see the point of punk, and unlike 97 per cent of all men who later became pop critics, I have always detested the Velvet Underground. In fact, I have only ever liked two things that Lou Reed has done: the album *Transformer*, famously produced by David Bowie and full of good tunes, and the track 'Street Hassle', which, unusually for Reed, has a killer string quartet riff. Inspired by these, I bought several of his other albums, only to discover that the whole of the rest of his career had been completely pointless. Of course, it's not enthusiasm that inspires a career in pop journalism, it's the reverse. No one hates more music that the person who really loves music.

So if my taste puts you off – and at least one professional musician was so appalled by the music I admitted to liking that he never spoke to me again – don't worry, because it's not a huge part of this book. I may prefer quite a lot of Wings albums to almost every Beatles album, but it's not relevant to what we are trying to do here. For this is a music book that is only marginally about the music. This is for two reasons. One, music is incredibly hard to write about; and two, it's often boring to read about. In the research for this book I opened a number of previous miscellany-type books on the subject, and one of them had six pages on amplifiers. Is that remotely interesting to anyone who isn't a musician? Given the choice of writing about Sting's records or his enormous ego and tendency to hang out on chat shows with tribesmen from the Amazon rainforest, I know which I prefer.

This book is a sequel of sorts to *Berkmann's Cricketing Miscellany*, and I realised that book would do well when more than one person told me that you don't have to like cricket to enjoy it. That wasn't the conscious intention when I was compiling it, and I still think that if you like cricket you'll love the book, but the emphasis was always on the daft stories and ridiculous punning titles of cricketers' autobiographies rather than runs and wickets. Cricket is full of eccentrics, and by extraordinary coincidence so is pop music. Some very learned pop historians will know a few of the stories within these covers, but not all of them, I hope, and as in the cricket book, I have gone for freshness above all else. If it's a story I feel I have heard a hundred times, it has not gone in – unless there's a crucial detail I hadn't heard, and which made me laugh, which is the main criterion for inclusion anyway.

The bulk of this book is formed around a list of birthdays of prominent musicians and musical personalities, from Louis Armstrong (4 August 1901) to Billie Eilish (18 December 2001). If I have forgotten (and I surely have) to include the name of someone terribly important and influential, sorry about that. After the birthdays, there follow several tiny essays about some of the people mentioned in that list. Not everyone in the list of birthdays has been written about, and not everyone written about is in the list of birthdays. The first because what went in depended utterly on the quality of the material I unearthed. There's no entry on George Harrison, for example, because I didn't find anything interesting about him that I hadn't heard a thousand times before.* The second because interesting things did happen to people not sufficiently eminent to appear in the list. Donita Sparks? Twiggs Lyndon? Crosby, Stills and Nash?† So do not regard this as in any sense a definitive history of pop; it's a pot pourri of excess, poor behaviour

---

* Other than a tree planted in his memory died after being infested by beetles.
† Only joking.

and unfortunate lifestyle decisions, such as biting the heads off bats and premature death. The entries on Ozzy Osbourne and Keith Moon are among the longest in the book, and not because of anything they have achieved as musicians. For some stories, such as Keith Moon's twenty-first birthday party at the Holiday Inn, Flint, Michigan, there are as many different versions as there were people who were there, and I have tried to filter the truth out from the guff. But if there is a genuine, verifiable mistake here, please let me know and it will be ruthlessly excised from later editions.

The other section that may require an explanation is called Records That Time Forgot. Twenty-five years ago, this was the purported title of my first solo book, but the publisher didn't want that and I wrote something about village cricket instead. Now it's the overall title for eight odd, personal essays about the records and the bands of my youth. If you are of a nervous disposition, and/or too cool to accept or even comprehend that anyone ever liked Supertramp, you are advised to give this section a miss.

Finally, as in *Berkmann's Cricketing Miscellany*, there is no index, and this is intentional. This is not a work of reference, it's an entertainment. If there's something you read last week and now can't find, I apologise, but in looking for it you might chance upon something even better and find yourself wholly distracted by that. It has been great fun to write: read a book, add something, read another book, add something else, take something away, either because it's not as good as the material surrounding it or because it turns out to be palpably false. You pick the low-hanging fruit first, then get your ladder out to pick the slightly less accessible fruit, and then when you wrench your back it's time to stop.

There's a more comprehensive list of acknowledgements at the back, but I would particularly like to thank my friends and fellow trivia trufflers Mitchell Symons and Mark Mason for their energy and ideas; my old friend Bill Matthews for Bill's Spotify the Link; my publisher Richard Beswick, who was rather muted about the whole idea until he read the sample material and saw how rude it was; Charles Peattie and Mark Warren for permission to reprint their 'Celeb' strips from *Private Eye*; Mark Ellen for his permission, given at a drinks party he has probably long forgotten, to quote liberally from his greatest achievement, *Word* magazine; and to the government of Boris Johnson for imposing lockdown just at the point when I really had to start work on this, thus leaving me with literally nothing else to do.

1901–1926

Notable Births

4 August 1901:	Louis Armstrong
3 May 1903:	Bing Crosby
30 May 1909:	Benny Goodman
27 February (or 27 April) 1910 (or 1914):	Winifred Atwell
18 May 1912:	Perry Como
22 August 1912 (or 1917):	John Lee Hooker
25 January 1915:	Ewan MacColl
7 April 1915:	Billie Holiday
9 June 1915:	Les Paul
12 December 1915:	Frank Sinatra
19 December 1915:	Edith Piaf
25 April 1917:	Ella Fitzgerald
21 October 1917:	Dizzy Gillespie
17 March 1919:	Nat 'King' Cole
3 May 1919:	Pete Seeger
7 April 1920:	Ravi Shankar
26 May 1920:	Peggy Lee
6 December 1920:	Dave Brubeck
25 May 1921:	Hal David
3 April 1922:	Doris Day
10 June 1922:	July Garland
22 May 1924:	Charles Aznavour
20 June 1924:	Chet Atkins
29 August 1924:	Dinah Washington
6 July 1925:	Bill Haley
15 August 1925:	Oscar Peterson
8 December 1925:	Sammy Davis Jr
3 January 1926:	George Martin
26 May 1926:	Miles Davis
3 August 1926:	Tony Bennett
18 October 1926:	Chuck Berry

Ed Sullivan *(28 September 1901)*

Creator and host of *The Toast of the Town*, later *The Ed Sullivan Show*, which ran on CBS from 1948 to 1971. In late 1963 Sullivan was passing though Heathrow airport on his way home, and witnessed screaming girl fans waiting to greet the Beatles, who were coming back from recording an appearance on Swedish TV. The group were as yet unknown in America, but Sullivan, who had something of a reputation as a star-maker, had missed the emergence of Elvis seven years before and had never forgiven himself. The Beatles ended up appearing on his show three times, and their debut, on 9 February 1964, was described by Bob Stanley as 'possibly the most significant cultural event in post-war America'. More people watched that show than any previous show in American TV history, and it's still one of the most-watched programmes of all time.

Bing Crosby *(3 May 1903)*

Crosby directly influenced the development of the post-war recording industry. After seeing a demonstration of a German broadcast-quality reel-to-reel tape recorder, he invested $50,000 in a California electronics company called Ampex to build copies. He then convinced ABC to allow him to tape his shows. He became the first performer to pre-record his radio shows and master his commercial recordings onto magnetic tape. He also helped to finance the development of videotape, bought television stations, bred racehorses and co-owned the Pittsburgh Pirates baseball team.

Bing Crosby was a disciplinarian father who, according to a tell-all book by his son Gary, beat his children like gongs. Crosby's will established a blind trust, in which none of his six sons received an inheritance until they had reached the age of sixty-five. Two of the six aren't there yet (born 1958 and 1961); three didn't make it (two of them shot themselves, another died of lung cancer at sixty-two), so only Philip benefited, before dying of a heart attack aged sixty-nine. That worked pretty well, then.

Winifred Atwell *(27 February or 27 April, 1910 or 1914)*

Trinidad-born honky-tonk pianist who, in the mid-1950s, became the first black artist to sell a million records in the UK. Lloyds of London insured her hands for a million dollars, with a proviso stating she should never wash dishes. She had hit after hit, had her own TV show and played three Royal Variety Performances. It was good-time music without an iota of pretension, but Winifred inspired a generation of keyboard players to come. As Keith Emerson later told *Keyboard* magazine, 'I've always been into ragtime. In England – and I'm sure Rick Wakeman would concur – we loved Winifred Atwell, a fantastic honky-tonk and ragtime player.'

There's also the sheer unlikeliness of her success. Britain in the 1950s was hardly welcoming to its West Indian immigrants, whom it regarded as little more than a necessary evil, but Winifred Atwell charmed the nation. In America, by contrast, she was tentatively booked to go on *The Ed Sullivan Show* in 1956, but producers were worried that audiences in the South would rise up against the mere idea of a female black musician, especially one with a non-American accent. The invitation was quietly rescinded.

John Hammond *(15 December 1910)*

Record man whose litany of significant musical discoveries slightly staggers the mind. In 1933 he heard Billie Holiday, then seventeen, performing in Harlem and arranged for her recording debut on a Benny Goodman session. In 1937 he heard Count Basie and his Orchestra broadcasting from Kansas City, and brought them to New York and the big time. Hammond wasn't too keen on the be-bop scene of the mid-1940s, but rejoining the Columbia label in the late 1950s, he signed Pete Seeger and discovered an eighteen-year-old gospel singer called Aretha Franklin. In 1961 he signed a young folk singer called Bob Dylan, produced his first few recordings and kept him on the label, despite the moans of fellow executives, who called him 'Hammond's folly'. He oversaw the posthumous reissues of Robert Johnson's recorded work, and in 1967 signed a thirty-two-year-old Canadian singer-songwriter called Leonard Cohen after hearing him at folk festivals. In 1972 Hammond auditioned a twenty-three-year-old New Jersey singer-songwriter called Bruce Springsteen. He retired from Columbia in 1975, but in 1983 he recommended Stevie Ray Vaughan to their Epic subsidiary. Hammond died in 1987 after a series of strokes, apparently listening to the music of Billie Holiday.

Perry Como *(18 May 1912)*

At the age of eleven he was helping out in the local barbershop to help supplement the family income. At sixteen he owned his own barbershop and sang to his customers. His voice was warm, soft and downy: listening to it was like being enveloped in a giant duvet, to the point where you could scarcely breathe. 'He communicated security and a short back and sides,' wrote Bob Stanley in *Yeah Yeah Yeah*, 'and he summed up the early fifties' friendly persuasion but also its lack of thrills, or any raw emotion. A 1956 poll claimed Como as America's ideal husband, but he was no one's ideal lover.'

Ewan MacColl *(25 January 1915)*

Grimly political folk singer who nonetheless wrote one of the finest of all love songs, 'The First Time Ever I Saw Your Face', for his third wife, the American folk singer Peggy Seeger. MacColl was forty and she was twenty when they met and fell in love. 'Things were so confused between me and Ewan that I went home,' Peggy said many years later. But Ewan could not follow her to America because the authorities there regarded him as a dangerous revolutionary and wouldn't give him a visa. So he would send tapes to her of him talking, and on one of them he sang this song. 'The intensity of it quite frightened me,' said Peggy. Six months later she returned to London and started living and performing with Ewan. In their concerts together, though, he would never sing this song. 'He didn't like baring his emotions on stage,' said Peggy. But he didn't mind Peggy having a go. When she first started singing it, she felt 'almost stripped naked' by the experience.

The song was the first track on the first album by Roberta Flack in 1969, and barely anyone noticed it. Two years later, though, Clint Eastwood shot his first film as director, *Play Misty For Me*, and put the Flack version on the soundtrack. Atlantic reissued it, and it became the biggest-selling single of the year. MacColl was now in his mid-fifties, had four children and had been struggling financially for some time, so the income was welcome. What wasn't quite so welcome was the way a surge of MOR singers turned his modest tune into a showstopping standard, generally performed in lamé suits and accompanied by swirling strings. Ewan MacColl had a special section in his record collection for these covers, which he called the 'Chamber of Horrors'. He said that Elvis Presley's version was like Romeo singing to Juliet from the bottom of the Post Office Tower. The Flack version, though, still makes the hairs tingle on the back of my neck. Ewan MacColl died in 1989, and Peggy Seeger never sang the song in public again.

Billie Holiday *(7 April 1915)*

Born Eleanora Fagan in Baltimore, Maryland, to a thirteen-year-old mother and a fifteen-year-old father, she was regularly beaten by her cousin Ida, raped by a neighbour at the age of ten, and sent to a Catholic reformatory where the Mother Superior made her spend the night in a locked room with the body of a dead girl in a coffin. At thirteen she moved to Harlem and worked as 'a twenty-dollar call girl ... more than I could make in a damn month as a maid'.

It's probably just as well, then, that she could sing.

In *She Bop*, Lucy O'Brien writes, 'In the same way that analysis has been made of Madonna's belly-button, Holiday's eyebrows are a work of art and self-definition: arch, beautifully painted black half-moons that frame her coolly intelligent, distant eyes – a shape that announces both sophistication and artifice.'

Frank Sinatra *(12 December 1915)*

A sign outside his estate in Palm Springs read 'Forget the dog. Beware of the owner.' His FBI file ran to 2403 pages.

When Sinatra heard that Woody Allen was having a relationship with Mia Farrow's adopted daughter Soon-Yi, Sinatra contacted Farrow, his ex-wife, and offered to have Allen's legs broken.

Sinatra died on 14 May 1998. His final words were 'I'm losing'. His daughter Nancy didn't quite manage to be beside his bedside as he breathed his last, as she was watching the last episode of *Seinfeld*. In his will, a provision stated that if anyone contested it, they would immediately be disinherited.

Bing Crosby, talking about Sinatra, said, 'The voice of a lifetime. Unfortunately it's my lifetime.'

Edith Piaf *(19 December 1915)*

'Like many women in pop who died young, she has been presented as a victim, hopelessly addicted to painkillers and unsuitable men,' writes Lucy O'Brien in *She Bop*. But 'Piaf was also a woman uncharacteristically in control of her career, at one time purportedly one of the highest-paid entertainers in the world, third only to Sinatra and Bing Crosby. On stage she milked and manipulated the rapport she had with an audience – in one performance shortly before her death she collapsed but the show still had to go on. In a moment of bathos someone tried to drag her off stage, but she fully surrendered herself to the melodrama, clutching hold of a piano leg, wailing that she had to finish and could not disappoint the crowd.'

It is said that Edith Piaf's funeral, in 1963, was the only time after the Second World War that Parisian traffic came to a standstill.

Vera Lynn *(20 March 1917)*

Dame Vera Lynn, according to the website Popbitch on the day of her death in 2020, outlived each member of the best-known line-ups of the Ramones, Motörhead and the Jimi Hendrix Experience.

Ella Fitzgerald *(25 April 1917)*

Marilyn Monroe was a fan, and in November 1954 saw her perform in a small jazz club in Los Angeles. The two became friends, and Ella complained to her new BFF that she couldn't get a gig at the Mocambo, a famous LA nightclub, partly because she was black (although a handful of African-American singers had sung there before) but mainly because she was too fat (or, in the euphemism of the time, 'not glamorous enough'). Marilyn went to the manager of the Mocambo and promised that if he booked Ella, she would be there to support her at a front-row table every night of the residency. So he booked her for a fortnight, and Marilyn went there every night, and the manager booked Ella for a third week, and Ella's life was changed for ever. As she told *Ms.* magazine in 1972, 'I owe Marilyn Monroe a real debt . . . After that, I never had to play a small jazz club again.'

Ella Fitzgerald never sang a note written by Stephen Sondheim. Her manager Norman Granz hated him and all his songs, and that was that.

Nat 'King' Cole *(17 March 1919)*

In 1948 Cole bought a house in the all-white Hancock Park neighbourhood of Los Angeles. The Ku Klux Klan, never shrinking violets, responded by placing a burning cross on his front lawn. Members of the property owners' association told Cole they did not want any 'undesirables' moving into the neighbourhood. Cole said, 'Neither do I. And if I see anybody undesirable coming in here, I'll be the first to complain.'

Ravi Shankar *(7 April 1920)*

In August 1971, the legendary and long-lived Indian musician Ravi Shankar was the opening act at George Harrison's Concert for Bangladesh. Shankar and his band took the stage and got to work, and after their first piece the audience clapped and cheered with great enthusiasm. 'Thank you,' said Shankar, with due modesty. 'If you appreciate the tuning so much, I hope you will enjoy the playing more.'

Judy Garland *(10 June 1922)*

Louis B. Mayer, on being shown a preview of *The Wizard of Oz*, thought that the film was slightly too long. He had the perfect solution: drop the opening song, 'Over the Rainbow'. Fortunately, the film's assistant producer Arthur Freed talked him out of it.

E. Y. 'Yip' Harburg wrote the song's lyrics. 'Judy was an unusual child with an ability to project a song and a voice that penetrated your insides,' he said later. 'She was the most unusual voice in the first half of this century ... Judy Garland was to singing what Gershwin was to music. They brought a quality and vitality that was typically and uniquely American.'

In 1960 Garland recorded the song again. 'The childlike lyrics were delivered with hopeless melancholy,' wrote Mary Harron. 'It had become a lament for her own life ... The best versions of "Over the Rainbow" come from extremes. You have to be very young or very disappointed to do this song justice.'

Bill Grundy *(18 May 1923)*

'Say something outrageous,' said Grundy to the Sex Pistols on *Today*, a local London news programme, on 1 December 1976.

'You dirty bastard.'

'Go on, again,' said Grundy, who could have had no idea that his TV presenting career was about to end.

'You dirty fucker!' said Steve Jones. There was laughter from the group.

'What a clever boy!' said Grundy, with infinite contempt.

'What a fucking rotter,' said Jones.

According to a report in the following day's *Daily Mirror*, 'lorry driver James Holmes, 47, was outraged that his eight-year-old son Lee heard the swearing ... and kicked in the screen of his TV.

'"It blew up and I was knocked backwards," he said. "But I

was so angry and disgusted with this filth that I took a swing with my boot.

'"I can swear as well as anyone, but I don't want this sort of muck coming into my home at teatime."'

The Sex Pistols only appeared on *Today* because Queen dropped out at the last minute, and EMI (with whom they were then signed) didn't want to miss a promotional TV slot. As Bob Stanley put it, 'it only happened because Freddie Mercury and Brian May were out Christmas shopping'.

Dinah Washington *(29 August 1924)*

Born Ruth Jones on the South Side of Chicago, Washington had either seven or nine husbands (but definitely not eight) and notched up twenty-seven R&B hits for Mercury Records between 1948 and 1961. 'Dinah had the ego of an ox but Ruth Jones was a sweet little girl,' said sax player Eddie Chamblee, one of the seven (or nine). Washington could sing anything and often did: according to AllMusic, her 'distinctive vocal style ... was at home in all kinds of music, be it R&B, blues, jazz, middle of the road pop – and she probably would have made a fine gospel or country singer had she the time.' She was also a notable exponent of the 'dirty blues' genre, which might explain the numerous weddings. 'Long John Blues' was supposedly about her dentist: 'He took out his trusty drill/Told me to open wide/He said he wouldn't hurt me/But he filled my whole inside.'

Washington was also a talented businesswoman, having launched her own booking agency (which handled Aretha Franklin and Sammy Davis Jr), and she owned a restaurant in Detroit. 'Though ebullient and robust, she operated from a baseline of insecurity,' writes Lucy O'Brien. 'Washington was addicted to slimming pills and tranquillizers, going through wild fluctuations in weight.' She died, aged just thirty-nine, of an overdose of pills and alcohol, weighing just five stone.

Don Arden *(4 January 1926)*

Father of Sharon Osbourne and rock 'n' roll manager with psychotic tendencies. In the mid-1960s he was managing the Small Faces, and made the mistake of telling their parents that they were always tired not because they were too busy doing gigs, but because they were too busy doing drugs. The group looked around for new representation, and Robert Stigwood paid them a visit. So Arden paid him a visit. 'There was a large ashtray on the table,' he told a TV documentary team. 'I picked it up and smashed it down with such force that the desk cracked. I pretended to go berserk. Two of my men lifted Stigwood from his chair, dragged him to the balcony and held him so he looked down to the pavement four floors below.' One of these men, so he later claimed, was Peter Grant, Led Zeppelin's equally insane manager. Later Arden adjusted his story. 'It was only one floor,' he admitted.

Miles Davis *(26 May 1926)*

Received his first trumpet at the age of thirteen; it was a gift from his dentist father. Went to the Juilliard School of Music in New York, but cut classes in order to play with Charlie Parker. When he was playing with John Coltrane, he became increasingly irritated by the length of the saxophonist's solos, and on one occasion had a go at him.

'Sorry, Miles, I just get carried away,' said Coltrane. 'I get these ideas in my head, which just keep coming and coming, and sometimes I just can't stop.'

'Try taking the motherfucker out of your mouth,' said Miles.

Many years later Miles was at a dinner in the White House, in honour of Ray Charles. A society lady asked him what he had done to be invited. 'I've changed music four or five times,' said Miles. 'What have you done of any importance except be white?'

Chuck Berry *(18 October 1926)*

'He had the look of a card sharp blessed with luck, a brown-eyed handsome man with a cherry-red Gibson and a major thing for cars and girls that he syphoned into super-detailed lyrics,' wrote Bob Stanley. But he was also 'the least charming of the original rockers, rude and incredibly tight-fisted'.

From 1957 onwards, Berry always toured alone with his guitar, insisting that promoters provide him with a back-up band and all other musical equipment. It's possible that he might not have paid too much attention to the individual members of these bands. At the Hollywood Palladium in 1972, all was going swimmingly until the lead guitarist left the stage and was replaced by A. N. Other Guitarist. The new axe-wielder turned his amp up far too loud for Berry's taste, so Berry stopped in the middle of a song, ordered the new guitarist off the stage and asked the original one back. After the gig Berry's girlfriend told him that the person he had dismissed had been 'that Rolling Stones guy', or as the rest of the world knows him, Keith Richards.

Richards and Berry were probably never destined to be soul-mates. In 1981 they bumped into each other in New York. Berry again failed to recognise Richards, and punched him in the face. In 1983, at Los Angeles International Airport, Berry dropped a lit match down Richards's shirt. 'Every time him and me got in contact, whether it's intentional or not, I end up getting wounded,' said Richards. When he played the Hollywood Palladium with the X-Pensive Winos in 1988, he welcomed the audience to 'a stage I've been thrown off many times'.

Celeb, by Charles Peattie and Mark Warren, has been running in *Private Eye* since the late 1980s. They originally envisioned Gary Bloke as a generic celebrity, but he swiftly mutated into a wrinkly old rock star who never takes off his sunglasses. The strips are presented here in chronological order and span about twenty years.

1927–1934

Notable Births

1 March 1927:	Harry Belafonte
3 December 1927:	Andy Williams
26 February 1928:	Fats Domino
2 April 1928:	Serge Gainsbourg
12 May 1928:	Burt Bacharach
30 December 1928:	Bo Diddley
5 April 1929:	Joe Meek
18 July 1929:	Screamin' Jay Hawkins
28 November 1929:	Berry Gordy
1 August 1930:	Lionel Bart
23 September 1930:	Ray Charles
22 January 1931:	Sam Cooke
29 April 1931:	Lonnie Donegan
5 November 1931:	Ike Turner
26 February 1932:	Johnny Cash
9 April 1932:	Carl Perkins
14 April 1932:	Loretta Lynn
8 September 1932:	Patsy Cline
15 November 1932:	Petula Clark
5 December 1932:	Little Richard
18 February 1933:	Yoko Ono
21 February 1933:	Nina Simone
13 March 1933:	Mike Stoller
25 April 1933:	Jerry Leiber
3 May 1933:	James Brown
29 November 1933:	John Mayall
1 December 1933:	Lou Rawls
1 June 1934:	Pat Boone
19 September 1934:	Brian Epstein
21 September 1934:	Leonard Cohen

Serge Gainsbourg *(2 April 1928)*

The heavy-lidded French singer, for whom the word 'louche' could have been specifically coined, was born Lucien Ginsburg. He changed his first name as a tribute to his Russian forebears, and he changed his last name because he was a great fan of the eighteenth-century English painter Thomas Gainsborough. And not at all because it sounded better or anything.

Bob Holness *(12 November 1928)*

In the early 1990s Stuart Maconie was editing the Thrills gossip and silliness column for the *NME*, and introduced a section called 'Believe It Or Not', in which he told ridiculous lies about famous pop stars. For instance, he alleged that 'David Bowie had invented the game Connect 4, that Neil Tennant was a fully qualified rugby league referee, and that Billy Bragg could breathe underwater'.

But one of these blatant untruths went on to be widely believed, especially by drunk men in pubs. Maconie said that the famous sax break in Gerry Rafferty's song 'Baker Street' had been played not by the eminent saxophonist Raphael Ravenscroft, as we (and indeed he) had all believed, but by Bob Holness, host of TV's *Blockbusters* quiz. This was so widely disseminated that Holness himself got to hear of it, and had to issue an official denial. Ravenscroft heard of it too, and said it was he who had made it up. Nearly thirty years later, so many people still think it's true it has surely attained the status of fully-fledged urban myth. Maconie himself has read it in newspapers, and people have assured him it's true at parties, and have not believed him when he said he invented it.*

---

* As it happens, Bob Holness did have a genuine connection with pop music. His daughter Ros was a founder member of Toto Coelo, who had a hit with 'I Eat Cannibals' in 1982.

Other urban myths, not made up by Maconie, include:

- Keith Richards goes to Switzerland every spring to have his blood changed. (No, he doesn't. Keith says he made up the story himself to impress a journalist.)
- Mama Cass Elliot choked to death on a ham sandwich. (No, she didn't. She had a heart problem and she hadn't actually eaten much on the day of her death.)
- Peter, Paul and Mary's song 'Puff the Magic Dragon' is all about illicit drug-taking. (No, it isn't. Peter Yarrow, who wrote it, says it's about lost innocence.)
- 10cc were named after the average amount of semen in a male ejaculation. (No, they weren't. Jonathan King, who oversaw their early career, had a dream in which a band called 10cc were the biggest band in the world. And the average amount of semen in a male ejaculation is 3cc.)
- Marilyn Manson had a rib removed so he could fellate himself. (No, he didn't. What an excellent and believable reason to undergo major surgery.)
- Stevie Nicks employed a roadie specifically to blow cocaine up her arse. (No, she didn't. She used her nose, like everyone else.)

Lee Hazelwood (9 July 1929)

Gravel-voiced singer-songwriter probably best known for his collaborations with Nancy Sinatra. In 1973 Hazelwood released a solo album called *Poet, Fool or Bum*. Charles Shaar Murray reviewed it in the *NME* with a single word: 'Bum'.

Screamin' Jay Hawkins *(18 July 1929)*

In the summer of 1954, Screamin' Jay Hawkins was in the middle of his set at Herman's Bar in Atlantic City when his girlfriend walked up to the stage, threw down the keys to their apartment and stomped off. When Jay returned home, all her things were gone and she had written the words 'Goodbye my love' in lipstick on the bathroom mirror. Jay emitted an unearthly scream, and then he sat down and wrote a song to get her back.

The song was 'I Put a Spell on You', which would later be covered by everyone and his horse. 'I put a spell on you,' sang Jay, 'because you're mine.' It's one of the most deranged vocals in rock history. Ben Thompson called it 'a masterpiece of tortuous simplicity'. Some of the more incoherent groans late in the song had to be cut out because radio stations deemed them to be 'cannibalistic'. Hawkins built an entire voodoo-tinged stage act around the song, with skulls held in one hand and bones stuck up his nose, and Alan Freed paid him $2000 to get out of a coffin on stage for the first time. What's remarkable, though, is that the song worked. Screamin' Jay got his girlfriend back. Apparently, she really liked the B-side.

Larry Parnes *(3 September 1929)*

Svengali-like manager of various good-looking young men in the late 1950s and early 1960s who always insisted on changing their names to something more glamorous. So Clive Powell became Georgie Fame, Reg Smith became Marty Wilde and Ronald Wycherley became Billy Fury. He wanted to change Joe Brown's name to Elmer Twitch, but sensible Joe wasn't having any of that. As Simon Napier-Bell wrote, Parnes had an instinctive feeling for the teenage boys that girls would fancy, as they were the ones he fancied himself. According to an unidentified friend of his,

Parnes's flat was always full of boys who had turned up hoping to be chosen for stardom. 'If Larry likes the look of them, he gives them a clean white T-shirt and tells them to hang around. If a boy's wearing a black T-shirt, it means Larry's had him already and his friends can have a go if they want to.'

Berry Gordy Jr *(28 November 1929)*

Autocratic leader of Motown Records from the late 1950s to the late 1980s, whose tendrils of influence extended everywhere. Mary Wells had a US number one with 'My Guy' in 1964, felt she was undervalued (and underpaid) at Motown and signed instead with 20th Century Records. That was the end of her career. She never had another hit. Wells thought Gordy had put the boot in, and whether he did or not, it undoubtedly suited Gordy for Wells and everyone else to think he had.

Lionel Bart *(1 August 1930)*

Songwriter and creator of *Oliver!*, who changed his surname from Begleiter after passing a certain London hospital on a bus, and claimed to have written 'Living Doll' for Cliff Richard in ten minutes. He made millions but spent more millions on a lavish 1960s lifestyle. At his parties there would be one bowl full of cash and another full of cocaine for guests to help themselves to.

At the height of the Oasis/Blur rivalry, Liam Gallagher referred with contempt to Blur's 'chimney sweep music'. As it happens, Damon Albarn was being interviewed soon after by Adrian Deevoy in *Q* magazine:

'Well, I do have a big *Oliver!* problem. I'm completely besotted by Lionel Bart. There's a great story about him: he'd made a fortune, he was richer than any of the pop stars, worth something like £50 million in 1964, and when he was at his most wealthy and bon vivacious he hired this château in France and flew fifty or sixty friends out there for this amazing weekend party. Then he just disappeared, and a year later he got a bill and none of the people had left the party. They'd stayed for a year and he hadn't noticed.'

Do we believe this? I have searched and I have hunted and I have not found anything to confirm it, but then again I have not found anything to refute it either. It might even have happened.

Ray Charles *(23 September 1930)*

When flying around America from gig to gig, Ray Charles would terrify members of his band by insisting on taking control of the plane when it reached cruising altitude. Bobby Womack toured with him in the 1970s and wrote this in his autobiography: 'A blind man playing chess was one thing, but flying a plane – that was different ... As soon as we hit air, the buckle was off and Ray raced up the aisle towards the cockpit. I said, "Where's he going? He never runs like that when he's going on stage to play the piano." ... I asked Ray once why he thought he could fly a plane. You know what he said? "Because it's mine."'

Ray Charles could tell whether a woman was attractive or not based on the size of her wrists. If you wanted to be a Raelette, so the story went, you had to 'let Ray'.

If he was being paid in cash, he insisted on being paid in large piles of one-dollar notes, as that way they couldn't con him.

Sam Cooke *(22 January 1931)*

Golden boy of early 1960s soul who, unusually for a black performer of the time, set up his own record company and publishing arm, and made a mint. After Cassius Clay had beaten Sonny Liston, the first person he called into the ring was Sam Cooke. Aretha Franklin and her sister Erma used to wear their best dresses just to watch him on television. On 11 December 1964 he picked up a prostitute who ran off with his clothes while he was in the bathroom. He ran around dressed in nothing but his righteous fury, and the motel owner was so shocked she shot him dead.

Lonnie Donegan *(29 April 1931)*

His 1957 single, 'Puttin' On the Style', was the last British number one to be released only on 78. John Peel called him 'the English Elvis, the man that pushed the button that started it all'. Brian May said, 'He really was at the very cornerstone of English blues and rock.'

Lonnie Donegan had heart problems for much of his life, and in the late 1980s he had a small coronary. It was probably a slow news day, because this made the front pages: 'LONNIE DONEGAN HAS HEART ATTACK!' This unexceptional piece of information filtered through to Japan, possibly by word of mouth, because on the Japanese stock exchange they all thought it was US President Ronnie Reagan who had had the heart attack. The stock market plunged. Shares in washboard manufacturers are thought to have been particularly badly affected.

John Riley *(born 1931)*

Wikipedia lists eighteen John Rileys, including a seventeenth-century portrait painter, a jazz drummer, a Scottish footballer, a botanist, a physicist and several American politicians. But there's no room for possibly the most important John Riley of them all, the thirty-four-year-old cosmetic dentist who, at a dinner party in 1965, spiked the drinks of the four Beatles and thus introduced them to LSD. The Beatles had no idea. They left the party and drove to central London in George's Mini. They went to the Ad Lib, a club off Leicester Square. On the way up they all thought the lift was on fire, and ran in screaming. After a few drinks they drove home at ten miles an hour, 'but it seemed like a thousand,' said John Lennon. George's future wife Pattie said, 'Let's jump out and play football.' Eventually they reached George's house, which John thought was a submarine, which he was driving. This experience changed their lives, their music and, eventually, everyone else's music as well. In 1970 John Lennon was asked how many times he had taken LSD since, and he said probably a thousand times. A Beatles fan on Reddit was unconvinced: 'This is almost certainly an exaggeration ... If he'd really done it a thousand times then he was dosing himself once every forty-eight hours for five years. This would mean, for all practical purposes, that he was flying on LSD whenever he was awake.'

Johnny Cash *(26 February 1932)*

Born to impoverished cotton farmers in Arkansas, he was christened J R Cash because his parents couldn't agree on a name (his mother wanted John, his father preferred Ray). He only officially became John R. Cash when he joined the US Air Force, as they wouldn't accept his initials as a name.

According to Bob Stanley, 'he had a wood-carved face and a look of resolute danger; when he sang his voice could go deeper than a coal mine'.

In the late 1950s he bought a half-share in a shopping centre in Ojai, California, which went to his first wife Vivien as part of their 1966 divorce settlement. In 1969, after the success of *Johnny Cash at San Quentin*, Cash sold more records in the US than the Beatles.

Although he cultivated a romantic outlaw image, he never actually served a prison sentence himself. He was thrown into jail seven times for misdemeanours, but on each occasion stayed only one night.

In 1983 Cash was kicked by an ostrich named Waldo and broke

five ribs. While recovering from his injuries he developed an addiction to painkillers, and had a spell at the Betty Ford Clinic, where he met and became friends with Ozzy Osbourne. The following year he wanted his label, Columbia, to drop him, so he recorded the profoundly strange 'Chicken in Black', a song in which Cash's brain is inadvertently transplanted into a farmyard bird, who then goes out on the road singing his old songs. They did drop him, but not before it had sold more copies than any of his previous few records.*

Bill Cash, the Brexiteer Conservative MP, was a distant cousin of Johnny. Jimmy Carter, the 39th President of the United States, was a distant cousin of his wife June.

Loretta Lynn *(14 April 1932)*

Born Loretta Webb in a log cabin in the backwoods of Kentucky, she met her future husband, Oliver 'Doolittle' Lynn, when she was thirteen. They married the following year, and she gave birth to her first child at the age of fourteen. Loretta had three more children before the age of twenty-one, and became a grandmother at twenty-nine. They made their own entertainment in those days.

Little Richard *(5 December 1932)*

His mother said he was more trouble than her other nine children put together. When he was twelve, he did a poo in a shoebox, presented it to an elderly woman who lived in the neighbour-hood as a birthday present, and then hid to watch her reaction

---

* Cash's biographer Robert Hilburn disputes this story, saying that Cash was presented with the song by Columbia and responded enthusiastically, having previously recorded several 'comic' songs like 'A Boy Named Sue' and done well with them. His enthusiasm only waned when his friend Waylon Jennings said he looked 'like a buffoon' in the accompanying music video.

when she opened it. His first gay experience was with a man generally known as Madame Oop, a family friend. When he was fifteen, he had a job washing dishes in the local Greyhound bus station. 'This is how he met a fifteen-year-old from South Carolina called Eskew Reeder, who styled himself Esquerita, sported a pompadour so high there was snow on top and was camp enough to make Richard seem like a longshoreman.' Although he would spend the rest of his life complaining that other performers had copied his style, Richard was himself stylistically quite light-fingered in his early days. He copied the hairdo and the hammering right hand on the piano from Esquerita, his make-up from a bandleader called Billy Wright and his nickname from a singer called Clara Hudmon, who called herself the Georgia Peach. But it was he, not they, who invented the term 'Awopbopaloobop Alopbamboom!', and it was he who would become the first bona fide star of rock 'n' roll, beating Elvis Presley by a vital few months. 'Tutti Frutti', incidentally, was originally all about anal sex, until a lyricist called Dorothy LaBostrie cleaned it up for public consumption.

Charlie Rich *(14 December 1932)*

Sun Records veteran, country singer and clearly a man of strong opinions. In 1975 he was tasked with opening an envelope and reading out the news that John Denver had won the Country Music Association's Entertainer of the Year award. Instead he set the envelope on fire.

Leonard Skinner *(11 January 1933)*

American high-school gym teacher who, in the 1960s, repeatedly sent several boys at the Robert E. Lee School in Jacksonville, Florida, to the headmaster for wearing their hair too long. These boys took their revenge by naming their band after him and changing a few letters to avoid a lawsuit. Thus came into existence Lynyrd Skynyrd.

In the early 1970s Skinner left teaching and went into real estate, and in 1975 the band asked permission to use a photo of his 'Leonard Skinner Realty' sign in the artwork of their third album. Unfortunately, the sign had his phone number on it. People started calling. 'They'd say, "Who's speaking?" and I'd say Leonard Skinner, and they'd say "Far out!" which it really wasn't at four in the morning.'

In 2010 Skinner died in a nursing home, aged seventy-seven. The *New York Times* called him 'arguably the most influential high school gym teacher in American popular culture'.

Yoko Ono *(18 February 1933)*

Before she knew John, Yoko Ono had been making avant-garde films, initially as part of a group of conceptual artists called Fluxus. *One* was a five-minute short of a match being struck in very slow motion indeed. *Four* was another five-minute short, featuring close-ups of fifteen bare bottoms in motion, as they walked along a treadmill. *Bottoms* may have been her masterpiece, featuring 364 bare bottoms of people associated with the swinging London scene, along with interviews with their owners. It premiered at the Jacey Tatler cinema in London on 8 August 1967.

Then she met and fell in love with John Lennon.

Their first collaboration was *Smile, a.k.a. Film No 5*, which featured John in his garden, sticking out his tongue and wiggling his eyebrows, in super-slow motion, for fifty-two minutes. It was premiered at the 1968 Chicago film festival, and halfway through only half the audience were still in their seats. Yoko had wanted to make a four-hour version, but tragically it was not to be.

In 1969 came *Self-Portrait*, a forty-two-minute study of John's penis, sometimes up, sometimes down, sometimes up, sometimes down . . .

In 1970 they released *Apotheosis*, in which John and Yoko, dressed in black hoods and capes, are driven to a village in Suffolk, where they watch a hot-air balloon being inflated and launched. We then cut to the balloon's eye view and see the snow-flecked East Anglian countryside below. The balloon enters a cloud and for several minutes there's nothing but a blank white screen. 'The onus is on the viewer to interpret,' wrote one critic, possibly with a beard.

Up Your Legs Forever, also in 1970, was a legs-based remake of, or maybe even sequel to, *Bottoms*, in which three hundred pairs of legs were filmed, from top to bottom, 'for peace'. The gripping dénouement featured the Lennons whipping off their clothes and displaying their own ripe and peachy arsecheeks.

Freedom, again in 1970, had an important advantage over all these films: it lasted just one minute. It featured Yoko trying to unclasp her bra, and the film is over before she can do it. Oh, the irony.

Yoko Ono was born on the same day of the same year as the former England football manager Sir Bobby Robson.

James Brown *(3 May 1933)*

As well as pretty much inventing funk, James Brown enjoyed a profusion of nicknames, only some of which he gave himself. Mr Dynamite, the Hardest Working Man in Show Business, the Minister of the New New Super Heavy Funk, Mr Please Please Please, the Godfather of Soul and, curiously, the Ambassador of Soul.

On 3 September 1987, Brown's third wife, Adrienne, was stopped in her car in Georgia and charged with driving under the influence of drugs, speeding and criminal trespass. Before the trial came to court, her lawyer tried an unusual defence: diplomatic immunity. Back in 1986, the city of Augusta had held a

James Brown Appreciation Day, and in a speech a congressman said that 'James is indeed our number-one ambassador'. This, the lawyer said, was proof of Brown's ambassadorial status, so he should have diplomatic immunity, 'and such immunity extends to his wife, the accused herein'. The lawyer withdrew the motion the following day, saying he had filed it only because he was 'pressed for time'. I'm not sure which is worse, the original deposition, or the excuse for it.

In 1988, police were called to Brown's home in Beech Island, South Carolina, after James and Adrienne had had another of their arguments. 'She had black and blue marks over her whole body – arms, legs, hips, thighs, feet,' said a police spokesman. Brown had beaten her up after shooting her car (which she was driving at the time) and, slightly more bizarrely, her fur coats. 'He had taken my Black Diamond mink, laid it outside on the ground and he shot at it,' said Adrienne. 'They're trying to fix it at Richard's Furriers right now.' The Godfather of Soul bashed her up quite regularly, she added, although 'there's only been two incidents where I was beaten so bad that I needed my teeth replaced'.

'Mr and Mrs Brown make a very exciting couple,' said one of his lawyers.

Andy Stewart *(30 December 1933)*

Wrote his biggest hit, 'Donald, Where's Your Troosers', in just ten minutes, while sitting in a recording studio lavatory with his troosers doon.

Leonard Cohen *(21 September 1934)*

When his first album came out, the *New York Times* reviewed it under the headline 'Alienated Young Man Creates Some Sad Music'.

Fortunately, there were girls. Cohen loved women, really rather a lot. In 1966 he met Nico, whom he described as 'the most beautiful woman I'd ever seen'. He followed her all over New York, but she turned him down. 'Look, I like young boys,' she explained. 'You're just too old for me.' Leonard was thirty-two, Nico twenty-eight. (Her boyfriend at the time was eighteen-year-old Jackson Browne.)

In 1967 there was a liaison with Judy Collins, who later covered 'Suzanne', which Cohen had written about Suzanne Verdal, or Suzanne #1. Some time in the late 1960s he went and lived with Joni Mitchell in Laurel Canyon for a month, as everyone was obliged to in those days. In 1969 he was in the lift at the Chelsea Hotel in New York when Janis Joplin walked in. He asked her if she was looking for someone.

'Yes,' said Janis, 'I'm looking for Kris Kristofferson.'

'Little lady,' said Leonard, 'you're in luck. I am Kris Kristofferson.'

'I thought he was bigger,' said Janis.

'I used to be bigger,' said Leonard, 'but I've been sick.' Not the greatest chat-up line in the world, but it seems to have worked. Although he didn't mention Janis by name, he wrote about sex with her rather too graphically for comfort in 'Chelsea Hotel #2' (1974). She had died several years before, but he never ceased to regret this 'indiscretion'.

Then there was Marianne Ihlen, who inspired songs like 'Bird on a Wire' and 'So Long, Marianne', and Suzanne Elrod, or Suzanne #2, with whom Cohen spent the early 1970s and who was the mother of Cohen's two children, Adam and Lorca.* In the 1980s there was French photographer Dominique Isserman, and in the early 1990s the fantastically attractive actress Rebecca De Mornay. And they're only the ones we know about.

---

* Suzanne Elrod is pictured on the far right of the cover of Leonard Cohen's 1977 album *Death of a Ladies' Man*.

In the early 1990s Cohen threw aside career, songs and women and became a Buddhist monk for nine years. No one really knows why, but one recent theory is that it was repentance, possibly even self-imposed punishment, for his brief cameo, in 1986, in the seventeenth episode of the second season of *Miami Vice*.

He did it, he said later, to impress his son, who was a big fan of the show. He was to play François Zolan, a Frenchman dressed in black who was working with Interpol to assist in the search for a rogue agent. 'I went down there and did my first scene and the assistant director rang me up and said, "You were great, truly wonderful,"' Cohen told *Q* magazine. 'And I said, "OK, thanks a lot." Then the casting director from New York called me up and said, "You were fantastic, truly wonderful!" And I said, "You mean I'm fired." And he said, "Yeah, we're cutting all your other scenes and giving them to another guy."'

What remains in the show are two very short scenes of Cohen on the phone, talking in French. At the end of the second scene he throws a fish to his pet alligator, who chews on it gratefully. If he's on screen for a whole minute, he's doing well. But in those fifty-five or so seconds you can see the problem. Poet, singer-songwriter, novelist, ladies' man, one of the coolest men who ever lived, Leonard Cohen could not act for toffee. He is as wooden as your kitchen table. He had a pet alligator, though. You can't help admiring the man.

1935–1939

Notable Births

8 January 1935:	Elvis Presley
11 February 1935:	Gene Vincent
16 February 1935:	Sonny Bono
31 March 1935:	Herb Alpert
29 September 1935:	Jerry Lee Lewis
30 September 1935:	Johnny Mathis
22 April 1936:	Glen Campbell
23 April 1936:	Roy Orbison
2 May 1936:	Englebert Humperdinck
3 June 1936:	Levi Stubbs
7 September 1936:	Buddy Holly
24 October 1936:	Bill Wyman
17 December 1936:	Tommy Steele
8 January 1937:	Shirley Bassey
6 April 1937:	Merle Haggard
15 June 1937:	Waylon Jennings
25 January 1938:	Etta James
21 August 1938:	Kenny Rogers
3 October 1938:	Eddie Cochran
16 October 1938:	Nico
6 November 1938:	P. J. Proby
13 March 1939:	Neil Sedaka
2 April 1939:	Marvin Gaye
19 August 1939:	Ginger Baker
30 August 1939:	John Peel
30 October 1939:	Grace Slick
26 November 1939:	Tina Turner
26 December 1939:	Phil Spector

Elvis Presley *(8 January 1935)*

'He was pure instinct,' wrote Bob Stanley. 'What's more, he was precisely what post-war youth had been waiting for: sex incarnate ... The low, heavy lids, the curling lip, the pelvis. Best of all, adults thought him crude, vulgar, animalistic. At a stroke, Elvis Presley created the generation gap.'

Elvis's hair was naturally blond as a child and medium brown by adulthood: he dyed it black throughout his career. By the end, according to his personal hairdresser Larry Geller, it was actually the very darkest shade of blue, preferred because it concealed the encroaching grey more efficiently.

One night in the late 1950s, Lil Thompson's Steakhouse in Tennessee held an Elvis Presley impersonator contest. The great man heard about it, turned up with his entourage and sat quietly at the back. No one recognised him, so he decided to take part. 'I'm going to mash this,' said Elvis. Lil was worried that everyone would go mental when they realised who he was, but nothing of the sort took place. Elvis sang 'Love Me Tender', the audience applauded politely, and he came third.

Elvis never toured overseas because his manager didn't have a passport. Colonel Tom Parker wasn't a Colonel, and he wasn't called Tom Parker. He was born Andreas Cornelis van Kujik in Holland in 1909 and entered America as an illegal immigrant in 1926. When Elvis was in the army in Europe between 1958 and 1960, Parker couldn't visit him, and just stayed in the US worrying that some other manager would steal him away from him.

'I don't know anything about music,' said Elvis once. 'In my line of work, you don't have to.'

Before he went to bed, Elvis liked to have his hair washed and blow-dried by one of his staff. On the night he died, his bed was shared with Ginger Alden, aged twenty and a former Miss Traffic Safety. Elvis had hated to sleep alone since early childhood. All the girls who went to bed with him had been told there would be no sex, as Elvis needed to preserve 'his bodily fluids' for his never-ending tour. The book he was reading when he died on the lavatory was *The Scientific Search for the Face of Jesus*.

After Elvis died, the demand for his records was so vast an RCA pressing plant in the UK that was about to close was reprieved and put on full capacity.

Elvis Presley never gave an encore. Hence the phrase 'Elvis has left the building', always announced after he had played his last song and left the stage.*

Peter Grant *(5 April 1935)*

Violent, cocaine-fuelled and terrifyingly bearded Led Zeppelin manager who may not have been one of the nicest people in the world. He was 6 feet 3 inches tall, a former wrestler who used the pseudonyms Count Massimo and Count Bruno Alassio of Milan, and he had form, having once worked as a heavy for the slum landlord Peter Rachman. 'Known associates' of the Kray twins hung around his office. Grant also worked for the notorious manager/promoter Don Arden, and it was from Arden that Grant said he learned 'the power of fear'. At one concert in Canada, he spotted a man operating electronic equipment and came to the not unreasonable conclusion that he was recording the concert for a bootleg. Grant and three heavies smashed the man's equipment and beat him up. Unfortunately, he turned out to be an environmental health officer monitoring decibel levels for the local council.

In 1977, on a tour of the USA, Led Zeppelin were playing some dates in Oakland, California. Grant's son Warren was there and wandered into a secure area. Jack Calmes, the head of the lighting

---

* According to *Sullivan's Music Trivia*, Elvis did play one encore, at a comeback gig in Hawaii. If this is true, a brilliant record is thus besmirched.

and sound company, said 'one of [promoter] Bill Graham's guards kind of moved him aside; he didn't hurt him or anything'. Grant and his bodyguards grabbed the guard, took him into one of the trailers and beat the shit out of him. According to Calmes, they tried to pull out one of his eyes. The band's tour manager Richard Cole stood outside the trailer with an iron bar to discourage any needless rescue attempts.

In 1979, in an attempted comeback, Led Zeppelin played two huge outdoor concerts at Knebworth House in Hertfordshire. Grant insisted on being paid in cash. He and his associates paid a visit to the promoter's house, where they drew the curtains and counted out £300,000 in used notes.

'He was always good to me,' says former professional groupie Pamela Des Barres. 'Sitting on his lap was one of the safest places in the world.'

Peter Grant died in 1995. At his funeral they played Vera Lynn singing 'We'll Meet Again'. Several of those present interpreted this as a warning.

Kit Lambert *(11 May 1935)*

Manager, with Chris Stamp, of the Who, who decided that the best way for Pete Townshend to make a mark would be to write a rock opera, possibly about a deaf, dumb and blind boy who is raped by his own uncle. After *Tommy* was produced, though, Lambert lost the plot. Here's Simon Napier-Bell, writing in *Black Vinyl White Powder*:

'He hired the *Queen Mary* for a promotion party and supplied a different drug on every deck. He holidayed for a month in Mexico and forgot the two stretch limos that were on twenty-four-hour call outside his hotel in New York. At Sardi's he set the lampshades on fire to attract the waiters' attention. He loved to walk into hustler bars with the tip of a thousand-dollar bill protruding from his half-zipped flies. Finally he bought himself a palace in Venice and renamed himself Il Baroni Lambert.'

In 1974 the Who finally gave him and Stamp the boot, and in 1981 Lambert died from a cerebral haemorrhage after falling down some stairs at home, having been beaten up by a drug dealer at a gay nightclub over an unpaid debt. Nothing suspicious there, then.

Jerry Lee Lewis *(29 September 1935)*

David Hepworth said he 'would argue with a signpost'. Jerry Lee himself said he was 'born feet-first with a hard-on'. At the end of 1956, he received a royalty cheque for $40,000, roughly ten times the average American annual wage. By March 1957 he had spent it all, and went back to his manager, asking for another $17,000. What do you need it for? asked the manager. I want to buy some cows, said Jerry Lee.

Like Elizabeth Taylor and Mike Love of the Beach Boys, Lewis enjoyed a good wedding. He was married for the first time at the age of fifteen, to the seventeen-year-old daughter of a travelling evangelist. Two years later he had hitched up with another woman, whom he got pregnant. Her brothers were keen that he should marry her, so he did, without quite having got round to divorcing the first one. After two sons had arrived, Jerry Lee's music career took off and he moved out, into his bass player's house, where he met his bass player's daughter, who was thirteen, and his cousin, and he married her, even though he hadn't quite got round to divorcing either of the previous two. This made him that rare and beautiful thing, a trigamist. (It exists: I looked it up.)

This being the southern states of America, he somehow managed to get away with it all until 1958, when he became only the second American rock 'n' roller to tour Britain after Bill Haley. The press were at Heathrow to greet him and his entourage, and someone asked the small girl besides him who she was. 'I'm Jerry Lee's wife,' she said, very possibly chewing gum. How old are you? said the journalist. 'Fifteen,' she responded, which wasn't strictly the truth.

More than sixty years later, Jerry Lee is still better known for having married an embryo than for any of his recording output, live shows or lunatic personal magnetism. His then current single, unhelpfully called 'High School Confidential', was sent back in vast quantities by the distributors, prompting his manager to say that it could be the first single in pop history to ship gold and return platinum.* Live shows became awkward. At the Granada Theatre in Tooting, teenagers shouted 'Go home, baby snatcher,' and barracked him non-stop during the twenty-seven minutes of his live performance. 'I was a young fool when I married at fifteen and sixteen,' he told the *Daily Express*. 'My father should have put his foot on my neck ... Everybody thinks I'm a ladies' man and a bad boy, but I'm not. I'm a good boy and I want everyone to know that.' His career never recovered.

Jerry Lee and Myra nonetheless remained married for more than ten years before he went on to wife number four. As his guitarist said, 'Myra grew up and I don't think he ever did.'

Johnny Mathis *(30 September 1935)*

Often described as 'the best all-around athlete to come out of the San Francisco Bay Area', Mathis was asked in 1956 to try out as a high-jumper for the US Olympic team travelling to Melbourne later that year. Unfortunately he already had an appointment in New York on the same day, to make his first recordings. His father

---

* According to Frederic Dannen, this is a very, very old music industry joke and every generation that coins it anew thinks they have thought of it for the very first time.

advised him to choose the music. Johnny Mathis remains one of relatively few multiple Grammy winners to hit nine holes-in-one.

Buddy Holly *(7 September 1936)*

The former Charles Holley was the first member of his family to graduate from high school. If he was very lucky, he thought, he might get a job as a draughtsman.

Buddy Holly died aged twenty-two – 'the day the music died' – when the Beechcraft Bonanza he had chartered between tour dates crashed into a frozen cornfield shortly after take-off. Ritchie Valens, the Big Bopper and pilot Roger Peterson also copped their lot. Holly had hired the plane because the tour bus was unheated, and he wanted time to do his laundry before the next gig.

Bill Wyman *(24 October 1936)*

As *Word* magazine said, 'it's always the funny-looking ones'. The Rolling Stones bassist, unfettered by good looks, identifiable charm or even a reasonable speaking voice, was nonetheless his band's most prolific shagmeister for many years. Keith Richards called him 'a man who thinks with his dick', and Wyman was frequently seen to mouth the number of his hotel room on stage to pretty girls in the audience. Even his only solo hit '(Si Si) Je Suis Un Rock Star' was just about his attempts to get a girl into bed for 'horizontal jogging'. All of this became public when, at the tender age of forty-seven, he hooked up with the thirteen-year-old Mandy Smith, who he'd met at the Lyceum in London. When she was eighteen they married. Her hair was dyed blonde and his was a weird sort of purple. They separated two years later. Bill's son Stephen, aged thirty, then married Mandy's mother Patsy, aged forty-six, which meant that Bill's former mother-in-law was now also his daughter-in law, a sort of familial Moebius strip. Mandy later married a footballer and discovered God, and really, who can blame her?

In 1990 Wyman published a rather Pooter-ish memoir, *Stone Alone*, based on his diaries, in which he recounted the tale of a band meeting in 1965. 'Since the band had started two years earlier, I'd had 278 girls, Brian (Jones) 130, Mick (Jagger) about thirty, Keith (Richards) six, and Charlie (Watts) none.' He also claimed in the book to have had a fling with the youthful Linda Eastman, before she met and married Paul McCartney. At the inaugural *Q* Awards later that year, Mark Ellen, who had just read the book, could not resist introducing them. 'There was a brief, very sixties, flicker of recognition – did we or didn't we? – before she gave him a squeeze and announced they were "old friends".'

Tommy Steele *(17 December 1936)*

The former Tommy Hicks (renamed by Larry Parnes) was the first rock 'n' roll star to be made into a waxwork at Madame Tussaud's. As Dorothy Parker said when told that Calvin Coolidge had died: how can they tell?

Don Everly *(1 February 1937)* and Phil Everly *(19 January 1939)*

In 1960 the brothers left the small Cadence label, with whom they had had a string of hits, and signed with Warner Brothers. A year later they split with the writing and production team who had supplied them with those hits. They began to argue. They would travel separately to gigs and stay in different hotels. Eventually they hired different agents, managers and lawyers. In 1973 Phil smashed his guitar on stage and walked out on the partnership. Don wasn't fazed. He said the act had 'died ten years ago'. Bob Stanley saw it differently: 'In the whole fourteen-year period from "Bye Bye Love" to 1970 single "Yves", they hardly ever cut a bad record and are maybe the most underrated act of their era.'

In 1981 Phil said this: 'Everyone has the feeling that all you have to do is to achieve stardom and once you're there you can relax. It's just the opposite. Once you get there, then the war really starts. The pressures get larger because getting hit records is a miracle.'

Phil died in 2014 of lung disease, having smoked like a beagle for decades and latterly gone everywhere with an oxygen tank. Don, interviewed by the *Los Angeles Times*, said he had lived 'a very difficult life' with his brother and that they had become estranged again in their latter years, mainly because of their 'vastly different views on politics and life'. But he also said, 'I always thought about him every day, even when we were not speaking to each other. It still just shocks me that he's gone.'

Kenny Lynch *(18 March 1938)*

Later better known as a light entertainer (and one of the six celebrities larking about on the cover of Wings's 1973 album *Band on the Run*), Lynch also took part in the 1962 Song For Europe heats, had two top-ten hits in 1963, became the first British songwriter to be hired to work in the Brill Building in New York (where he collaborated with Mort Schuman), owned a record shop in Soho that specialised in soul imports, had his songs performed by Cilla Black and the Small Faces ('Sha-La-La-La-Lee' was one of his), and oversaw the production of Hylda Baker and Arthur Mullard's version of 'You're the One That I Want'. Perhaps most remarkably of all, for the time, his real name actually was Kenny Lynch.

Tam Paton *(5 August 1938)*

Hard-as-nails, slow-to-cough-up manager of the Bay City Rollers, who are, I believe, the only band in recorded history to choose their name by throwing a dart at a map of America. It landed on Bay City, Michigan, and not on Fries, Virginia, Dinosaur, Colorado, or Placentia, California, which was a relief to everyone. The 'classic' line-up of the Rollers had numerous hits in 1974 and generated something inevitably called Rollermania. When Ken Russell released his film about Franz Liszt the following year, he was swift to call it *Lisztomania*.*

According to Stuart Maconie, Paton exerted 'an almost monstrous level of control over the band', and two of them accused him of sexually assaulting them. In 1982 he was convicted of gross indecency with two teenage boys, and served one year of a three-year prison sentence. According to the Rollers' bassist Alan Longmuir, he was 'a powerful and vindictive man not to be taken lightly'. When Alan's brother Derek, who was the group's drummer, was convicted of possessing child pornography in 2000, he believed he was 'the victim of a set-up vindictively orchestrated by Tam Paton', who was becoming 'increasingly threatening' after Derek's legal action to recover missing royalties. After Paton died in 2009, Les McKeown couldn't have been any clearer: 'I'm delighted he's dead. He ruined a lot of people's lives, including mine. I've planned a nice day of celebration with my wife and mates. We will rejoice. It's been a long time coming and it's closure for me. Tam Paton is dead; long live the future; the future's bright.'

Kenny Rogers *(21 August 1938)*

Bearded, whispering country singer whose first big solo hit, 'Ruby, Don't Take Your Love to Town', reached number two in the UK in 1969, pipped to the top slot by the manifestly superior 'Two Little Boys' by Rolf Harris.

---

* Roger Daltrey starred as Liszt. Obvious casting, when you think about it.

Jet Black *(26 August 1938)*

Drummer for punkish ne'er-do-wells the Stranglers, who was nearly forty when they broke through in 1977, which to us at the time made him seem older than Methuselah (lived to the age of 969), Noah (950) and Adam (930) all rolled into one. It's worth pointing out, though, that not only was he older than all the Beatles, he was a year older than Jet Harris, the Shadows' bass guitarist between 1958 and 1962. The older Jet's music career therefore started nearly ten years after the younger Jet's had ended. (Jet Black was really called Brian Duffy. Jet Harris's real first name was Terry.)

Eddie Cochran *(3 October 1938)*

When Cochran died in a car crash in England, aged just twenty-one, the policeman who attended the scene was Dave Dee of Dave Dee, Dozy, Beaky, Mick & Tich.

Nico *(16 October 1938)*

The Velvet Underground's occasional chanteuse was, according to Richard Goldstein in *New York Magazine*, 'half goddess, half icicle'. 'If you say bad things about her singing, she doesn't talk to you. If you say nice things, she doesn't talk to you either.'

Morrissey described her singing voice, rather wonderfully, as 'the sound of a body falling downstairs'.

Dusty Springfield *(16 April 1939)*

When she was eleven, Mary O'Brien's convent-school teacher asked the class what they wanted to do when they were older. 'I want to be a blues singer,' piped up Mary.

In her biography *Dusty*, Lucy O'Brien (no relation) quotes Jerry Wexler, who co-produced *Dusty in Memphis*, talking about the uniqueness of her sound. 'There were no traces of black in her singing, she's not mimetic . . . she has a pure silvery stream.' Dusty Springfield is many people's favourite singer, but she wasn't her own. 'All I know is that I have a distinctive voice I don't particularly like listening to.'

Simon Napier-Bell described her as 'reclusive, lazy, petulant and totally charming'. 'I was being called a star, but to me, I was still me,' she told him. 'To be the star they wanted, I had to hide behind a mask, and I chose mascara. And it was so difficult to get off, I sometimes left it three weeks or more, adding more as it was needed.'

Ian Hunter *(3 June 1939)*

As a student in London in the early 1970s, the future president of Pakistan Benazir Bhutto was a dedicated fan of Mott the Hoople.

John Walters *(11 July 1939)*

Long-time producer of John Peel's Radio 1 show and a considerable broadcaster in his own right, Walters described his complex relationship with Peel as 'a bit like a master and his dog, each believing the other to be the dog'. A former schoolteacher and trumpeter for the Alan Price Set, he once turned down the Sex Pistols for a Peel session, saying that Johnny Rotten 'didn't look like the kind of boy you would trust to give out the scissors'.

John Peel *(30 August 1939)*

In 1998 the journalist Simon Garfield published a wonderful book called *The Nation's Favourite*, about the ructions at Radio 1.

He interviewed all the principals and many of the secondaries, revealing, among many other things, that Dave Lee Travis owned no records at all, because they would need dusting.* Most of the funniest things in the book, though, were said by John Peel.

'People like Mike Read and DLT would often complain that they couldn't go anywhere without being recognised, but of course would go everywhere in a tartan suit carrying a guitar, so they would have attracted attention in a lunatic asylum. In the streets of London people would go, "Who the fuck is that? Isn't that that Mike Read bloke?"'

'When Radio 1 started it was genuinely regarded as rather unhealthy for presenters to show any interest in music, as it was believed that this would lay us open to unscrupulous promotions people offering fast cars and women. Of course these things never happened, but you did have to keep your interest in music very much to yourself.'

'The most appalling event in the Radio 1 year – and it required something pretty special to take that accolade – was always the Radio 1 DJ Christmas Party ... Always the first thing that people did when they came into the room was look anxiously at the seating plan, and you could tell by the look on their faces whether they had found themselves anywhere in the vicinity of Simon Bates. General rejoicing, quite clearly, if they found they were not.

'On one occasion Kid Jensen, Paul Burnett and myself – not a carefully honed fighting team, but nevertheless filled with drink – we went down and waited in the underground carpark at the BBC for the opportunity to beat up Simon Bates. Fortunately he didn't turn up, or we might have suffered an embarrassing reverse, as he's probably stronger than us.'

[After Simon Bates left the station.] 'You have to say he was a

---

* Stuart Maconie also heard a rumour that Noel Edmonds had no records at his own home.

remarkable man. I was always given to understand that when Bates launched into 'Our Tune' it was when the station had its biggest audience of the day. At eleven in the morning every layby on every major road in the country was full of weeping truckdrivers.'

'One controller, Derek Chinnery, disliked me intensely, and took every opportunity to let me know that this was the case. He was persuaded to keep me on largely by John Walters, who was my producer for about twenty years. Walters was a brilliant debater, or rather arguer. He could see through all the bollocks to the core of any argument, and would fix his teeth into it and never let go. There have been times in the history of Radio 1, and this will no doubt surprise you, when the controllers have not been people of enormous intellectual stature. And these men would just get so fed up with arguing with Walters that they would just roll over.

'Once Derek Chinnery called Walters into his office after he had read something in the papers about singers with spiky hair who were spat on by their adoring audience. He said something like, "We're not playing any of this punk rock, are we?" and Walters gleefully replied that the last four programmes had consisted of nothing but. No doubt Walters will be able to tell the story far better than me, and at far greater length, and in a way that reflects far more glamour on himself.'

Peel said he very rarely saw bands play live, partly because of where he lived (outside Stowmarket in Suffolk) and partly because he was usually broadcasting when they were playing. So occasionally bands would come down and see him. One such was Blur, whose visit Peel managed to keep a secret from everyone. He called up the parents of five friends of his daughter Flossie. 'Your daughter must not go to school today,' he told each of them. 'She must come to our house, but I can't tell you why.'

Steve Lamacq said of him, 'There is always some speculation that John will one day introduce a band on stage, and he'll put them on at the wrong speed.'

Walters had this to say: 'I think that a very strong case could be made for John Peel being the single most important individual in the history of British rock music. People say, "Oh, but what about Lennon?" but over the years I think it holds true.'

Grace Slick *(30 October 1939)*

Lead singer of Jefferson Airplane and, later, Jefferson Starship. 'Benign, sarcastic, confident, she cut a graceful figure with her curiously long face, striking eyes and keen, commanding voice.' Grace Slick was already in her late twenties when her song 'White Rabbit' became an enormous hit; forty years later, it still earned her $30,000 every time it was used in a film. She named her daughter god (lower case) before coming to her senses and rechristening her China. Having once attended the same finishing school as Richard Nixon's daughter Tricia, she was invited to the White House in the early 1970s, took chief Yippie Abbie Hoffman as her plus-one and had on her person a substantial dose of LSD, with which she hoped to blow the president's mind. The two of them were quickly chucked out. In the early 1990s she became one of the first rock performers to retire, saying 'I don't like old people on a rock and roll stage, including myself.' In 1993, welders fitted a sign outside her house in Marin County that read 'Danger: Fire Area'. In doing so, they caused a fire which burned her house down. In 2005 she told Andy Gill of *Word* magazine that she had shagged everyone in the band except fellow singer and guitarist Marty Balin. In 2018 Balin died aged seventy-six, a broken man.

Phil Spector *(26 December 1939)*

Spector's father Ben committed suicide when Phil was just nine, and the inscription on his grave was 'To know him is to love him', hence the title of the Spector song, his first number one, sung by him for his group the Teddy Bears.

Spector produced Leonard Cohen's 1977 album *Death of a Ladies' Man*: they shared a lawyer, who introduced them. That same evening Spector invited Cohen back to his home, which was freezing cold because of the air-conditioning, and locked the door. 'As long as we are locked up, we might as well write some songs together,' said Cohen. They went to the piano, started that night, and ended up working together for a month, which Cohen remembered as enjoyable, although he had to wear an overcoat every day. But the record was a disaster. Cohen was low on confidence: 'I wasn't in the right kind of condition to resist Phil's very strong influence on and eventual takeover of the record.' There were lots of guns in the studio, some of them held by Phil's personal bodyguards. At one point Spector held a loaded gun to Leonard's throat.

'I love you, Leonard,' he said.

'I *hope* you love me, Phil,' said Leonard.

In 1979, Spector produced the Ramones' album *End of the Century*. Dee Dee Ramone claimed he once pulled a gun on him when he tried to leave a session. Marky Ramone confirmed that guns were there, 'but he had a licence to carry. He never held us hostage. We could have left at any time.'

Spector did almost nothing at all for the next quarter century, before emerging from retirement in 2003 to shoot his girlfriend Lana Clarkson in the mouth. He was sentenced to nineteen years to life and died in prison in January 2021 of Covid-19.

BILL'S SPOTIFY THE LINK

My friend Bill, who should know a thing or two about pop quizzes, as one of the creators of *Never Mind the Buzzcocks*, had a lovely idea which he put up on social media during the coronavirus lockdown. Each week, on Thursday, he would list four or five songs which shared a connection. Your job was not to identify the link, but to add another song to which the link also applied. So, if the list was this:

- 'Baker Street' by Gerry Rafferty;
- 'Warwick Avenue' by Adele;
- 'Waterloo' by ABBA; and
- 'Mornington Crescent' by Belle and Sebastian,

then you might add 'Mile End' by Pulp, 'Angel' by Massive Attack, 'Kentish Town' by Tracey Thorn or 'Bond Street' by Burt Bacharach. The link is 'songs that have the same names as Tube stations', and Bill was very precise about his links. So, for example, 'Waterloo Sunset' by the Kinks would not qualify, as the title merely *contains* the name of a Tube station. The arguments thus generated would take the entire day to resolve, as quarantined pop nerds of every stripe argued the hours away. Bill got so tired of all the bickering that he stopped doing them after a few weeks. I have this vague memory that he actually had some work to do.

I wondered, though, whether his idea might be adaptable for this book, so we talked and this is what we came up with. I shall give three lists of four songs for each link, on consecutive pages. Look at the first list, decide what the link is, and write it down. Move to the second list, go through a similar process, and write that down. Then turn over the page and do the third and final list. The answer will be on the page after that. If you got it right with the first link, give yourself three points; if you got it with the second, it's two points; and with the third, it's one point. You must be rigorous, and you must not cheat. Some of the links will be between the songs, some will be between the artists, some will be between what's actually in the song, and to make it slightly harder I won't tell you which. There will be six such quizzes spread throughout the book, for a maximum of eighteen points. If you get double figures you're doing well. If you get full marks you are probably Bill himself, or a member of the Trump family.

Here, then, is the first. Good luck, and no peeking.

1.1

'Birdhouse in Your Soul'
by They Might Be Giants

'She Drives Me Crazy'
by Fine Young Cannibals

'Fields of Fire'
by Big Country

'Needles and Pins'
by the Searchers

1.2

'Forever Young'
by Alphaville

'My Sharona'
by the Knack

'Martha's Harbour'
by All About Eve

'Mary's Prayer'
by Danny Wilson

1.3

'Paranoid'
by Black Sabbath

'Beautiful Day'
by 3 Colours Red

'Bang Bang You're Dead'
by Dirty Pretty Things

'5 Years Time'
by Noah and the Whale

Answer

They're all artists who took their names from film titles, or from part of a film title. Noah and the Whale, for instance, named themselves after *The Squid and the Whale* (2005) and its writer-director Noah Baumbach. Danny Wilson comes from *Meet Danny Wilson* (1952). There's no connection between the songs.

1940–1941

Notable Births

17 February 1940:	Gene Pitney
17 April 1940:	Billy Fury
7 June 1940:	Tom Jones
8 June 1940:	Nancy Sinatra
23 June 1940:	Adam Faith, Stu Sutcliffe
7 July 1940:	Ringo Starr
9 October 1940:	John Lennon
14 October 1940:	Cliff Richard
21 October 1940:	Manfred Mann
12 December 1940:	Dionne Warwick
9 January 1941:	Joan Baez
15 January 1941:	Captain Beefheart
24 January 1941:	Neil Diamond
15 March 1941:	Mike Love
18 March 1941:	Wilson Pickett
11 May 1941:	Eric Burdon
24 May 1941:	Bob Dylan
2 June 1941:	Charlie Watts
9 June 1941:	Jon Lord
12 June 1941:	Reg Presley
16 July 1941:	Desmond Dekker
30 July 1941:	Paul Anka
14 August 1941:	David Crosby
9 September 1941:	Otis Redding
19 September 1941:	Cass Elliot
3 October 1941:	Chubby Checker
13 October 1941:	Paul Simon
28 October 1941:	Hank Marvin
5 November 1941:	Art Garfunkel
20 November 1941:	Dr John
24 November 1941:	Pete Best
25 November 1941:	Percy Sledge
17 December 1941:	Dave Dee

Tom Jones *(7 June 1940)*

Recorded 'It's Not Unusual' as a demo for Sandie Shaw. She passed, but suggested he release it himself. He must have sung it tens of thousands of times since.

Many years later, Jones would grow a short goatee beard to conceal an unsightly scar left by some unfortunate plastic surgery, when he had some fat removed from under his chin.

Ringo Starr *(7 July 1940)*

When John Lennon rang up Ringo to offer him the drum stool in the Beatles, the former Richard Starkey was doing a residency at Butlin's in Skegness. First things first, said John. The sideburns will have to go. And you'll have to stop quiffing your hair back like a greasy rocker. OK, said Ringo, without demur.

David Hepworth wrote this in *Nothing Is Real*: '[Brian] Epstein said it was only when Ringo joined that the picture seemed complete, which was a shrewd observation to make. If you go back and listen to those pre- and post-Ringo recordings you can hear how even within the limitations of a rudimentary rock 'n' roll style Ringo sends the blood coursing through the band's veins in a way his predecessor [Pete Best] would never have done if he'd remained on that drum chair for the next ten years.'

I think I'd put it more bluntly: whenever anyone tells you what a lousy drummer Ringo was and how he was the luckiest man in the world to join the Beatles, it's a surefire sign that this person doesn't have the smallest fucking clue what he is talking about.

In 1967 Ringo gave his wife Maureen one of the best birthday presents anyone can ever have received. It was Apple's first ever single, called 'Maureen is a Champ', to the tune of 'The Lady is a Tramp', and it had been specially recorded as a favour by Frank Sinatra, with new lyrics written by Sammy Cahn. The company pressed just one copy.

John Lennon *(9 October 1940)*

John Lennon's first girlfriend was called Thelma Pickles.

In 1966 Maureen Cleave of the *Evening Standard* conducted a fascinating and in-depth interview with the twenty-five-year-old Lennon, then living at Weybridge in Surrey with his wife Cynthia, very near to Ringo and Maureen and George and Pattie. (Paul still lived in London.) 'The fans are still at the gates but the Beatles see only each other.'

They watched films, played rowdy games of Buccaneer, whiled away the small hours of the morning making mad tapes. '"We've never had time before to do anything but just be Beatles," said John.

'He is much the same as he was before. He still peers down his nose, arrogant as an eagle, although contact lenses have righted the short sight that originally caused the expression. He looks like Henry VIII more than ever now that his face has filled out – he is just as imperious, just as unpredictable, indolent, disorganised, childish, vague, charming and quick-witted. He is still easy-going, still tough as hell.'

It was in this interview that John said the words that would make the next couple of years of his life rather less pleasant than they might have been. '"Christianity will go," he said. "It will vanish and shrink. I needn't argue about that; I'm right and I will be proved right. We're more popular than Jesus now ... Jesus was all right but his disciples were thick and ordinary. It's them twisting it that ruins it for me."'

In the US, the Bible Belt went mad and burned Beatles albums, which presumably they had had to buy in order to burn. When the Beatles played Memphis later that year, they became the first band, as far as is known, to be picketed by the Ku Klux Klan, in their full white-sheet regalia.

'Imagine no possessions' was a line in John Lennon's 1971 song 'Imagine', which was recorded in a huge house called

Tittenhurst Park near Sunninghill in Berkshire, which John and Yoko had bought for just £145,000 in 1969. (My parents bought a really nice flat in Hampstead for £11,000 two years later.) For the song's video, John and Yoko sat dressed in white at a white piano in a white room that was about the size of Basingstoke. Go on, it's easy if you try.

John Lennon left the UK after recording the *Imagine* album, and never came back.

Cliff Richard *(14 October 1940)*

After he had been on ITV's *Oh Boy!* in 1957, the *NME* wrote this about seventeen-year-old Cliff: 'His violent hip-swinging was revolting, hardly the kind of performance any parent would wish their children to see. He was wearing so much eye-liner he looked like Jayne Mansfield.'

Frank Zappa *(21 December 1940)*

Frank Zappa was often sick as a child, with asthma, earaches and chronic sinusitis. To cure the last, a doctor inserted a pellet of radium into each of the boy's nostrils. Zappa died, aged fifty-three, of prostate cancer.

For his fifteenth birthday, his parents gave him $5. Frank used the money to make an international call to one of his heroes, the French avant-garde musician Edgard Varèse. But he wasn't at home.

In 1965, after one of his shows, a used car salesman approached Zappa and offered him $100 for an audiotape of the musician making love, ostensibly for a stag party. Zappa was on his uppers at the time, and so took up the offer. He spent the night with one of his go-go dancers, faking the whole thing, with bedsprings, grunts, sighs and squeaks. He said he spent hours cutting the laughs out of the recording.

The following day Zappa delivered the tape but the used car sales-man turned out to be an undercover cop from the vice squad. Zappa was arrested and charged with conspiracy to commit pornography. He served ten days in jail, and would later say, 'You can't appreci-ate what a jail is and what goes on there unless someone sticks you in one. In a way, I guess I have to thank Detective Willis and the evil machinery of the San Bernardino legal system for giving me a chance to see, from that perspective, what the penal system is like in this country, and ... how ineffectual and how stupid it is.'

But there was an unforeseen bonus to this small adventure. His criminal record from this entrapment exempted him from being drafted, so Frank Zappa never had to go to Vietnam.

In 1971 Zappa embarked upon a disastrous European tour with his band, the Mothers of Invention. In Montreux, where they were playing a casino, a fan set off a flare, the casino burnt down and all their equipment was destroyed. On the other side of the Lake Geneva were members of Deep Purple, who watched the fire rage and were inspired to write their song 'Smoke on the Water'.

Don Van Vliet/Captain Beefheart *(15 January 1941)*

For a brief period in 1956, Don Van Vliet was in the same class at school (the Antelope Valley Union High School in Lancaster, California) as Frank Zappa.

In 1975 Viv Albertine, later the guitarist in the Slits and much later a gifted memoirist, was sitting in a café in the Portobello Road and spotted the Captain across the room. As he left he passed her table, stopped and said 'I love your hat.' (She was 'wearing a giant shocking pink silk beret with white polka dots on it that my mum had made for me'.) She looked back at him with a serious expres-sion and said, 'I love your music.' 'He looked surprised. He wasn't a very well-known musician, not the sort who got recognised. He nodded and left.'

In 1980, the British post-punk group XTC were staying in New York's Gramercy Park Hotel, and Andy Partridge heard that the Captain, who was one of his heroes, was also staying there. Sadly they never bumped into each other, but the group's bass player Colin Moulding did think he spotted a certain Beefheart the following morning, 'buying porn from the little concession stand in the hotel'. 'I quite like that,' said Partridge. 'It's good to know he has earthly needs.'

Neil Diamond *(24 January 1941)*

In the mid-1970s Neil Diamond had a roadie called Larry E. Williams, who wrote a song called 'Let Your Love Flow' that Diamond's company Bicycle Music published. Diamond didn't want to record the song himself and it eventually found its way to the Bellamy Brothers, who recorded it and took it to number one in the US, number seven in the UK and into the top ten in most other countries. It was the only song of Williams's that was ever recorded.

Neil Diamond once walked around Australia wearing a T-shirt that said 'I Am Not Neil Diamond'.

Mike Love *(15 March 1941)*

How many times has Mike Love of the Beach Boys been married? According to Wikipedia, five, but in his book about Laurel Canyon bands, David McGowan says he'd already been married and divorced six times by 1981. Current estimates put him on nine spouses, equal with the occasional actress Zsa Zsa Gabor and the Mexican revolutionary Pancho Villa. No famous person has yet made it to double figures.

Bob Dylan *(24 May 1941)*

Legendary mumbling troubadour who has been famous for longer
than most of us have been alive. For a short time in his youth Bob
Dylan was actually 'Bob Dillon', named after Matt Dillon, the
US Marshall in TV's *Gunsmoke*. At the age of nineteen, while
travelling to New York to make his name, he broke his journey
in Madison, Wisconsin, and told a perfect stranger, 'I'm going to
be bigger than Elvis Presley.' He told people in the big city that
he had run away with the circus as a child, that he had learned
to play guitar from an old bluesman called Wigglefoot. It was all
completely made up. He was obsessed by Woody Guthrie and went
to visit him when he was in hospital. According to '60s figure
Wavy Gravy (born Hugh Nanton Romney Jr), Dylan stole a pair
of Guthrie's underpants and would wear them on special occasions. On the covers of *Blonde on Blonde*, *John Wesley Harding*,
Nashville Skyline and his first *Greatest Hits* set, Dylan wore
exactly the same suede jacket.

Bob Stanley talks of his 'scything misanthropy'. In 1966
Dylan's limo was cruising the streets of New York and his fellow
passenger was the protest singer Phil Ochs, who may have suggested, *en passant*, that Dylan's current single wasn't the best
work he had ever done. Dylan ordered the driver to stop, opened
the door and said, 'Get out of the car, Ochs.' They didn't speak
for nearly ten years.

In 1974 Dylan enrolled in an art class taken by Norman Raeben,
who was unaware of his new student's fame and, worried about his
trampish demeanour, offered to let him sleep on the studio floor in
exchange for some light janitorial duties.

Joni Mitchell has said of him, 'Bobby invented a character
to deliver his songs.' In *Nothing is Real*, David Hepworth goes
further: 'I would argue that Dylan's single most creative act was
to invent Bob Dylan and then to remain behind that mask, never

once letting it slip, for over fifty years.' Or as Dylan himself put it, 'Just because you like my stuff doesn't mean I owe you anything.'

In 2004, possibly for the money, Dylan appeared in a TV ad for the women's lingerie brand Victoria's Secret, playing his song 'Love Sick' in a Venetian palazzo as luscious young lovelies wandered around in negligées.

Dylan keeps a count of how many times he has played each song live and puts it on his website. Current leader is 'All Along the Watchtower', with 2268 live performances (up to November 2018).

Jon Lord *(9 June 1941)*

Lantern-jawed hairbag keyboardist for Deep Purple, who in 1969 wrote a Concerto for Group and Orchestra and hired the Royal Philharmonic Orchestra and its conductor Malcolm Arnold to play on the recording. It wasn't a success, and Deep Purple swiftly reverted to the ferocious unorchestrated heavy metal for which they would become globally renowned. At one point in rehearsals, Arnold told his orchestra that they were 'playing like a bunch of cunts'.

Reg Presley *(12 June 1941)*

Leader and main songwriter for the Troggs, born Reg Ball, who may not have written 'Wild Thing' (that was the work of Chip Taylor*) but did pen many others that sounded a bit like it. In 1994 the Glaswegian group Wet Wet Wet recorded Presley's song 'Love is All Around' for the soundtrack of the film *Four Weddings and a Funeral*. It spent fifteen weeks at number one and made Presley an enormous pile of money, which he spent on crop circle research.

---

* 'Chip Taylor' was the radio-friendly pseudonym of James Voight, the younger brother of actor Jon Voight. Who, it turns out, was the first person ever to hear 'Wild Thing'. 'He didn't think much of it,' said Chip ruefully.

David Crosby *(14 August 1941)*

In early 1969, David Crosby, Stephen Stills and Graham Nash had their photograph taken for the cover of their first album together. They sat in a line on an old sofa, in Richard Williams's words 'radiating hippie allure and authenticity', outside a deserted house on a West Hollywood side street.

That evening they were looking at the photographs and they suddenly realised they had posed in the wrong order: Nash, Stills, Crosby. So they went back the following day for a reshoot, only to find that the house had been knocked down overnight. Williams says, 'As a metaphor for the destiny of what was, for a short time, the most popular rock group in the world, that would be hard to beat.' Peter Doggett, the band's biographer, would write, 'Crosby, Stills, Nash and Young have spent approximately two of the past fifty years as a functioning band and the other forty-eight fending off questions about why they are no longer together.'

Still, it's been a half-century packed with incident, if not particularly good records. Crosby, Stills and Nash haven't had a huge public argument since a Christmas tree-lighting ceremony at the White House in 2015, where they had performed 'Silent Night' very badly to an audience that included Barack and Michelle Obama, and Miss Piggy from *The Muppet Show*.

Otis Redding *(9 September 1941)*

Redding never heard the waves crashing on the beach in his hit 'Sitting on the Dock of the Bay', as he died in a plane crash just a few days after recording the song, before the effect had been dubbed on. The record became the first posthumous number one in US chart history.

Hank Marvin *(28 October 1941)*

The ever-smiling Shadows lead guitarist's real name is Brian Rankin. His bandmate Bruce Welch was born Bruce Cripps. Rankin and Cripps sounds like a firm of Sheffield undertakers. In the spring of 1959, Hank's Fender Stratocaster guitar cost him £120, which was about eight weeks' wages for the average Englishman at the time. It was the first one Leo Fender's company had ever exported to Europe. David Hepworth said 'he was the guitar hero of the boys who would grow up to be guitar heroes'. Bob Stanley said 'it's impossible to overstate the Shadows' importance'. Brian May taped 'Foot Tapper' off the radio and had learned to play it before the record was in the shops. Pete Townshend called them 'a living myth ... frozen in my mind as one of the great passions of my life'.

Art Garfunkel *(5 November 1941)*

Like the writer of this book, Art Garfunkel read maths at university. 'I'm precise. I think in proportions. I play games with numbers and I proportionalise. I imagine we have now done one-eighth of our interview,' he told the *Daily Telegraph*'s Nigel Farndale. Unlike the writer of this book, Garfunkel briefly took a job as a maths teacher in the early 1970s. 'I'd just got married and moved to Connecticut, and there was a nearby preparatory school and so I taught math there. It was a weird stage of my life, to leave Simon and Garfunkel at the height of our success and become a math teacher. I would talk them through a math problem and ask if anyone had any questions and they would say: "What were the Beatles like?"'

Pete Best *(24 November 1941)*

By mid-1962, Pete Best had been the Beatles' drummer for two years. According to David Hepworth, 'he was recruited because drummers are hard to find, he was good-looking, and he lived in a house big enough for them to play in'. But his drumming was timid, and George Martin, the group's new producer, was swift to spot their weakest link. He told them that when they came to his studio to record, he would have to hire a proper drummer to play with them.

The Beatles hadn't fired anybody before, so they delegated the job to their manager Brian Epstein, who had. Brian invited Pete along to his office and asked him how he thought it was going. Pete said he thought it was going fine. Brian said, that's a shame because we've decided to sack you. Pete asked why. Because you aren't good enough, said Brian. Pete Best never spoke to any of his former bandmates ever again.

Peter Sarstedt *(10 December 1941)*

When I was a teenager in the 1970s I used to listen to Capital Radio in London. Each spring, the station would dedicate its airwaves for a day or two to a charity telethon called Help a London Child. People would ring in to pay money for favoured records to be played, and occasionally someone famous would come in and play a song live in the studio. One year that someone was Peter Sarstedt, who had had a hit a few years before with that most mannered and, let's face it, fatuous of songs, 'Where Do You Go To (My Lovely)?' The single version lasted 4 minutes and 42 seconds, which was long enough, but Sarstedt said there was actually a longer version with several more verses that were very rarely played. So he started singing it. And he carried on singing it. Time goes more slowly when you are younger, and the longer version may have only lasted fifteen or twenty minutes, but for me it was an intense, drawn-out kind of agony that seemed to go on for several hours. One verse would end and another would begin. He barely paused for breath. It never even occurred to me that I could have switched the radio off and gone and done something else instead. I had to sit there next to the radio and wait for this caterwauling disgrace of a song to end. And that was the point. Only by listening to it could you be absolutely sure that it wouldn't go on for ever. If I had switched off the radio he could still be singing the song now, years after he died. It felt like a glimpse, possibly my first, into the limitless horror of true insanity. Stephen King would have written a cracking novel about it.

Songstories

'Blowin' in the Wind'
(Bob Dylan, August 1963)

Just as the world divides neatly into the left-handed and right-handed, or people who adore peanut butter and people who detest peanut butter, so pop fans divide very neatly into those who hear the first line of the chorus of 'Blowin' in the Wind' as 'the ants are my friend', and those who do not.*

'I Want to Hold Your Hand'
(The Beatles, November 1963)

In January 1964 the Beatles flew to Paris to play a ten-day residency there. They were staying at the Hotel George V, and they had that time to write enough songs for the soundtrack to what would become *A Hard Day's Night*. On their only day off, they had to record German language versions of their two biggest hits,

---

* This is known technically as a 'mondegreen'. The term was coined in 1954 by the American writer Sylvia Wright, who said that when she was a child, her mother used to read to her from the Scottish ballad 'The Bonny Earl of Murray' and she heard the line 'layd him on the green' as 'Lady Mondegreen'. The word mondegreen first appeared in the *OED* in 2002.

'She Loves You' and 'I Want to Hold Your Hand'. At the end of the session they had an hour to spare, so they swiftly recorded a new Paul McCartney composition, 'Can't Buy Me Love'.

To aid their labours, Lennon and McCartney had a piano installed in their suite. Within those ten days they had written thirteen new songs, and flew back to London for a single day, before going on to New York, where they needed to put in an appearance, as 'I Want to Hold Your Hand' has just risen from seventy-three on the chart to number one in a fortnight. John Lennon was twenty-three years old, Paul McCartney was twenty-one.

Bob Stanley believes the Beatles to have been 'literally miraculous'. As evidence he cites the extraordinary fact that, in all the thousands of photos that were taken of them in their seven years at the top, not one of them featured a single Beatle with his eyes closed.

'House of the Rising Sun'
(The Animals, May 1964)

According to Mickie Most, who produced it, the Animals recorded 'House of the Rising Sun' in fifteen minutes.

'You've Lost That Lovin' Feelin''
(The Righteous Brothers, November 1964)

In early 1965 'You've Lost That Lovin' Feelin'' was played on *Juke Box Jury*. All four members of the jury voted it a miss. One of them asked whether it had been played at the right speed.

Phil Spector produced the song and co-wrote it with Barry Mann and Cynthia Weil. Bobby Hatfield was annoyed that Bill Medley would start the first verse by himself and that Hatfield wouldn't join the song until the first chorus. Hatfield asked Spector what he was supposed to do during Medley's solo. 'You can go directly to the bank,' Spector replied.

On the suggestion of his engineer, Spector put the time on the single as 3:05, even though it was actually 3 minutes and 45 seconds long. Radio stations at the time rarely played songs longer than 3 minutes, but it took programme directors a while to work out why their playlists were running long. By then the song was a hit.

In 1999 the performing rights organisation BMI ranked 'You've Lost That Lovin' Feelin'' as the most played song on American radio and television in the twentieth century, with more than eight million plays.

'A Whiter Shade of Pale'
(Procul Harum, May 1967)

The first ever single by Procul Harum became one of the best-known pop songs of all time. *Melody Maker* of 3 June 1967 contained this account of the song's genesis. 'It was "sixth member" Keith Reid who had the idea for the song, at a "gathering". "Some guy looked at a chick and said to her, 'You've gone a whiter shade of pale.' That phrase stuck in my mind. It was a beautiful thing for someone to say. I wish I'd said it," laughed Keith.' A few months later a woman called Diane Stevens wrote to the magazine to put the record straight. She was the 'chick' who had gone a whiter shade of pale, and the person who had used the phrase was her then husband Guy Stevens, Procul Harum's then manager, who would go on to produce Mott the Hoople and the Clash.

The song was an instant worldwide hit. Brian Wilson, whose mental health may not have been at its best, said he thought the song was his personal funeral march, and that whenever he heard it he momentarily thought he was at his own funeral.

When lead singer and co-writer Gary Brooker married his wife Frankie, 'A White Shade of Pale' was played at the wedding, by Procul Harum's Matthew Fisher up in the organ loft.

'Carrie Anne'

(The Hollies, May 1967)

Hollies lead singer Allan Clarke, though married, was having an affair with Marianne Faithfull, and Graham Nash fancied her too. With Tony Hicks the pair of them wrote this song apparently during a concert with Tom Jones. They recorded it live in two takes. Only in 1995 did Nash admit that, instead of using her real name, Marianne, he had changed a few letters and that, in all those years, not a single person had ever spotted the connection.

The Records That Time Forgot

Bob Dylan: 'Make You Feel My Love'

We all try to be as objective as possible around music, especially when we graduate from being mere fans to writing about it for a living. But you can't ignore the role of early trauma. When I was a teenager my friends and I used to go round to a particular house which was large and shambling and had several rooms that seemed to serve no obvious purpose. One of these had a record player in it, and on many Saturday nights we would have a 'party', which would involve strong drink, thousands of cigarettes (the family who lived there were heavy smokers, almost from birth) and records played on the record player. Unfortunately, the record player belonged to my friend William, and William recognised no music beyond the mighty Bob Dylan. Every Saturday, when I wanted to dance to Chic and Earth, Wind & Fire, we had to listen to this terrible stuff that barely qualified as music at all, sung in Dylan's uniquely atrocious voice.

I came to hate Bob Dylan.

In fact, I came to hate all music that thought lyrics were more important than tunes. To this day I can tolerate good music with dreadful lyrics (the Electric Light Orchestra) but not the reverse. I have not the slightest idea what the Bee Gees are singing half the time, but I don't care. But when Dylan starts doing his stuff, every song sounding basically the same, some with eighty-three verses, others with just forty-six, I want to scream and shout and break things, like record players and maybe records as well. If I did ever embark on a course of intensive psychotherapy, I feel sure this is where we'd start.

Enter Bryan Ferry, one of my favourite artists, most of whose impossibly polished records I still own in some form or other. Ferry was seventeen when Dylan released *The Freewheelin' Bob Dylan*, an impressionable age, and has clearly held him in the highest esteem ever since. On his 2002 album *Frantic* he recorded two Dylan songs that I am not sure I had ever consciously heard before, 'It's All Over Now, Baby Blue' and 'Don't Think Twice, It's All Right'. Both are mesmerisingly good. Five years later (a moment in Ferry time) he made a complete album of Dylan covers, on which he recorded several familiar tunes and one more I hadn't heard, 'Make You Feel My Love', which I am beginning to believe is one of the greatest songs ever written. Having only heard Dylan songs sung by Dylan, it had never occurred to me that he was a tunesmith of rare gifts. 'Make You Feel My Love' was, of course, most famously covered by Adele, with all her melismatic excess and lack of taste, but even she couldn't ruin it.

I started buying albums that covered Dylan's songs, just to see what people did with them. Ben Sidran's jazzy, low-key *Dylan Different* is probably the best. I started buying Dylan's own albums, especially the later ones which at least had more going on in them than the early ones, but it was no use. His voice is unbearable. I cannot overcome my deep-seated prejudice, and now I know I never shall.*

---

* In a blog post called 'Eight Voices of Bob Dylan', the writer Rob Jones said that when people say they don't like his voice, he always wonders which voice they don't like, because he has more than one. He goes on to give a detailed description of them, from the early folk voice, 'The Young Man in Old Man's Clothes', through 'The Nasal-Voiced Youth', 'The Braying Beatnik' of 'Maggie's Farm' and 'The Country Crooner' of Nashville Skyline, to 'The Grizzled Troubadour' of the present day. Eight voices, and I hate them all.

Music fans tend to define themselves by the music they love, but what they hate is often more interesting. Ferry and I were both in our late teens when we first heard Dylan, and he made an ineradicable impression on us both. It also makes me realise that most people's music tastes don't really change very much. Occasionally something comes along that we weren't expecting, and our horizons shift. But I was in my mid-twenties when hip-hop arrived, and in my late twenties when dance music took over, and I still don't really care for either. (Not that I have worked that hard at it, you understand.) Why did Oasis become so successful? Because they reminded us all so forcibly of all the guitar music we had loved when we were young. Their lack of originality was their strength, although it obviously turned out to be their weakness as well. If Noel Gallagher had ever written a song even a tenth as good as 'Make You Feel My Love', some of us might have more respect for him. I should probably add here that I have never knowingly heard Dylan's original version, and have no desire to hear it. That ship has sailed.

BILL'S SPOTIFY THE LINK

Remember the rules: I shall give three lists of four songs for each link, on consecutive pages. Look at the first list, decide what the link is, and write it down. Move to the second list, go through a similar process, and write that down. Then do the third and final list. The answer will be on the page after that. If you got it right with the first link, give yourself three points; if you got it with the second, it's two points; and with the third, one point. You must be rigorous, and you must not cheat. Some of the links will be between the songs, some will be between the artists, some will be between what's actually in the song, and to make it slightly harder I won't tell you which.

2.1

'Born This Way'
by Lady Gaga

'Liberian Girl'
by Michael Jackson

'Jennifer Juniper'
by Donovan

'Hit Me with Your Rhythm Stick'
by Ian Dury and the Blockheads

2.2

'Should I Stay or Should I Go?'
by the Clash

'Hold on Tight'
by Electric Light Orchestra

'Spanish Stroll'
by Mink Deville

'Carmen'
by Lana del Ray

2.3

'7 Seconds'
by Youssou N'Dour and Neneh Cherry

'Denis'
by Blondie

'Lady Marmalade'
by Labelle

'Psycho Killer'
by Talking Heads

Answer

Every song is sung in English but has foreign words in the lyrics. 'Voulez-vous coucher avec moi?' in Lady Marmalade. 'Psycho Killer qu'est-ce que c'est', and so on.

1942–1943

Notable Births

2 February 1942:	Graham Nash
9 February 1942:	Carole King
13 February 1942:	Peter Tork
24 February 1942:	Paul Jones
28 February 1942:	Brian Jones
2 March 1942:	Lou Reed
9 March 1942:	John Cale
25 March 1942:	Aretha Franklin
19 April 1942:	Alan Price
24 April 1942:	Barbra Streisand
5 May 1942:	Tammy Wynette
12 May 1942:	Ian Dury
18 June 1942:	Paul McCartney
20 June 1942:	Brian Wilson
13 July 1942:	Roger McGuinn
27 July 1942:	Bobbie Gentry
1 August 1942:	Jerry Garcia
3 September 1942:	Al Jardine
24 September 1942:	Gerry Marsden
27 November 1942:	Jimi Hendrix
30 December 1942:	Michael Nesmith
9 January 1943:	Scott Walker
19 January 1943:	Janis Joplin
25 February 1943:	George Harrison
21 March 1943:	Viv Stanshall
14 May 1943:	Jack Bruce
27 May 1943:	Cilla Black
15 June 1943:	Johnny Halliday
17 June 1943:	Barry Manilow
26 June 1943:	Georgie Fame
26 July 1943:	Mick Jagger
10 August 1943:	Ronnie Spector

19 August 1943:	Billy J. Kramer
6 September 1943:	Roger Waters
23 September 1943:	Julio Iglesias
28 November 1943:	Randy Newman
8 December 1943:	Jim Morrison
18 December 1943:	Keith Richards
31 December 1943:	John Denver

Carole King *(9 February 1942)*

Carol Joan Klein was born on the day that soap rationing began in Britain.*

Neil Sedaka's 1958 single 'Oh! Carol' was about Carole King, whom he had known at Abraham Lincoln High School in Brooklyn. Gerry Goffin, who had just married King (he was twenty, she was seventeen and not unpregnant), took the tune and wrote a playful response, sung by Carole, entitled 'Oh! Neil!' It wasn't a hit, but this was the song that got Goffin and King their contract to write songs for Don Kirshner's company in the Brill Building and thus launched their careers.

Brian Jones *(28 February 1942)*

Jones could seemingly play any musical instrument. At the age of thirteen he was already a gifted clarinettist, but sold his instrument to buy an alto saxophone, which he played in several groups in his home town of Cheltenham. (One of these, the Ramrods, split

---

* By the same token, Alice Cooper was born on the day that Ceylon gained its independence, Robbie Williams on the day that Alexander Solzhenitsyn was expelled from the Soviet Union, and Natalie Imbruglia on the day that Edward Heath resigned as leader of the Conservative Party.

up after their lead singer choked to death on a chip while on his honeymoon.) In the Rolling Stones, Jones taught Mick Jagger how to play the harmonica, gave guitar lessons to Keith Richards, was the first English musician to play the slide guitar and (allegedly) mastered the sitar in thirty minutes. But there were, shall we say, problems of temperament.

By 1965 Jones had already fathered three illegitimate baby boys by three different women. Indeed, two paternity suits were filed at the same time. Pat Andrew, Jones's girlfriend in the Stones' early days, had a boy called Mark Julian. Linda Lawrence sought a lump sum for her son, Julian Mark. Pat Andrews said, 'I would never have gone public about Mark until I read in the papers about Linda, and their calling the baby Julian Mark.' Both boys were named after the alto-saxophonist Julian 'Cannonball' Adderley. In the last four years of his life, Jones and his never-say-die spermatozoa would sire three more sons.

On tour in America, he once hit a groupie, and his bandmates got a roadie to beat him up to teach him a lesson. In Morocco he tried to punch Anita Pallenberg but missed and broke his wrist on a metal window frame. On that same trip, Jones returned from a night out on acid with two prostitutes and woke up Pallenberg to demand she join them in a foursome. She packed her bags and moved in with Keith Richards, never to return.

On a visit to Sri Lanka, six months before he died, Jones had his astrological chart done. 'Be careful swimming in the coming year,' he was told. 'Don't go in the water without a friend.'

Lou Reed (2 March 1942)

He's in Stockholm, in 1977, and he's talking to Allan Jones, then of *Melody Maker*:

'We're in Sweden, right, and they can't get me some *ice*. Good Christ! Sweden's almost in the goddamn *Arctic Circle* and they can't get me some miserable fucking *ice*. There must be ice *every-where*. I told this guy to get his wife or whoever to fill her mouth with water. Then I told him to send her out into the street with her mouth open, wait for the water to freeze and then come up to my room and spit in my fucking drink.'

That might be the most rock star paragraph ever spoken.

Lou Reed turns up again and again in Jones's book, *Can't Stand Up for Falling Down*, and you can see why: he's excellent copy. (He's also dead, so he can't sue for libel.) In April 1979 Jones comes across Reed having dinner with David Bowie in a Kensington restaurant. They're having a lovely time, old friends sharing memories, making toasts to each other, that sort of thing. Then Bowie clearly says the wrong thing. Lou Reed smacks Bowie around the chops.

'Don't you EVER say that to me!' he shouts. 'Don't you EVER fucking say that to me!'

Fists are flying and most of them are Lou's. According to Jones, 'about nine people pile on Lou and wrestle him away from Bowie ... There's a terrible silence, a heavy-hanging thing, omi-nous. People are watching, open-mouthed, frozen in mute surprise. Lou sits down next to Bowie, whispers something. They embrace. There's a collective sigh of relief.' Dinner is resumed. But the next thing Jones knows, Lou is dragging Bowie across the table and punching him in the face.

'I told you NEVER to say that!' shouts Lou. Is it a new thing that Bowie shouldn't have said, or is it the previous one accidentally repeated? Lou is finally dragged out of the restaurant by his mind-ers and Jones, profoundly curious, asks Bowie what happened.

'Fuck off!' shouts Bowie. 'If you want to know what fucking happened, you'll have to ask fucking Lou! He knows what fucking happened!'

Bowie leaves in a massive temper, kicking unoccupied chairs out of the way.

'Goodnight, then, Dave!' shouts Jones. 'There's a kind of anguished howl from above,' he wrote, 'followed by a plant pot that sails over my head and shatters against the wall behind me.'

Jones never did find out what the argument was about.

Lou Reed died in 2013. The London free newspaper *Metro* published an obituary the following day, and the day after they published this in their Corrections and Clarifications column: 'Yesterday's Lou Reed obituary should have referred to his collaboration with Metallica on the album *Lulu*, rather than collaborations with Metallica and Lulu.'

John Cale *(9 March 1942)*

The Velvet Underground's co-founder studied viola and piano at the London Conservatory of Music and initially went to the United States as a Leonard Bernstein fellow. He was sponsored by Aaron Copland, but reluctantly, it would seem. Copland wouldn't let him play his work at the Tanglewood Music Center. 'It was too destructive,' said Cale. 'He didn't want his piano wrecked.'

Aretha Franklin *(25 March 1942)*

'Franklin is as adamantine in the history of black American music as Duke Ellington, Miles Davis and James Brown. She is a fundamental. A big boulder. If they ever get round to carving an African American music Rushmore, she'll be up there for keeps, in all weathers, her nose throwing out rain like a flume. She has earned her formal title, the Queen of Soul, and will never have to face a succession crisis.' (Nick Coleman in *Voices*.)

Brian Wilson *(20 June 1942)*

In 1970, after retiring from playing live with the Beach Boys, Brian Wilson briefly ran a health food store in Los Angeles called the Radiant Radish. He wanted to expand the franchise by opening a twenty-four-hour table tennis shop, but was talked out of it.

Paul Williams, writing for *Crawdaddy!*, once summed up the Beach Boys' music in three words: warmness, serenity, friendship. It's for this reason, says Bob Stanley in his mammoth tome *Yeah Yeah Yeah*, that 'there is more love directed at Brian Wilson than anyone else in this book'.

Jerry Garcia *(1 August 1942)*

Bearded guitarist for the Grateful Dead, who died aged just fifty-three, roughly eighteen years of which he had spent playing guitar solos. The rest of the band decided not to continue after his death. '[The band] had been our home for our whole adult lives,' said Mickey Hart, one of their two drummers. 'It served us all well – us, the audience and, hopefully, humanity. We did it with everything we had. It was a magnificent creation. We thought we should go out with dignity.'

Alvin Stardust *(27 September 1942)*

In *Cider with Roadies*, Stuart Maconie describes the early 1970s hitmaker as 'a man who you could well believe had enjoyed a previous career as a rock 'n' roller called Shane Fenton. I could have believed that he'd enjoyed a previous career as someone who sent children up chimneys, such was his air of great antiquity and malevolence.'

Twiggs Lyndon *(26 October 1942)*

In 1969 the Allman Brothers Band needed a road manager, and they found the resourceful but excitable Twiggs Lyndon, who had done the same job for Percy Sledge and other R&B acts. Twiggs quickly became an indispensable part of the operation, overseeing gear procurement and rehearsal space, and carefully curating a list of the ages of consent in each state they would be travelling through.

In April 1970, the Allman Brothers were supposed to be playing a gig in Buffalo, New York, for $1000. But they were fifteen minutes late on stage and the club owner gave them only $500. Twiggs stabbed him three times with a ten-inch fishing knife, killing him. In court, his lawyer, John Condon Jr, argued that life on the road with the Allman Brothers had essentially driven him round the bend. He called the Allman Brothers' bassist Berry Oakley to the stand.

'Did you take any dope in the last month?' asked Condon.

'Uh-huh,' said Oakley.

'In the last week?'

'Oh yeah,' said Oakley.

'What about the last hour?'

'You bet,' said Oakley.

Twiggs was found not guilty by reason of temporary insanity. He was transferred from jail, where he had already served eighteen months, to a psych ward, from which he was released after six months.

Twiggs died in 1979 while skydiving, when his parachute didn't open.

Billy Connolly *(24 November 1942)*

At Live Aid in London in 1985, we had just seen some stark footage of starving Ethiopian children, set to the Cars' song 'Drive'. Back to the studio with David Hepworth, and Billy Connolly and Pamela Stephenson on the sofa next to him, all of them clearly moved. Hepworth then announced the Pretenders, who were starting their set in Philadelphia. Chrissie Hynde had a new guitarist and a new bassist, after the drug-related deaths of James Honeyman-Scott and Pete Farndon. The red light went off and Hepworth, Connolly and Stephenson were off air.

'The Pretenders,' said Connolly, shaking his head. 'You wouldn't want to join *that* group.'

'Why not?' said Hepworth.

'Nobody leaves.'

Jimi Hendrix *(27 November 1942)*

After he first heard Hendrix play live, Jeff Beck said, 'I think I'll go and get a job in the post office.'

In 1967 the Jimi Hendrix Experience played 255 shows. In one of the more bizarre misbookings in rock history, a few of those were as support act to the Monkees. That didn't go well. 'Finally in New York,' wrote Michael Nesmith, 'the yelling for us got so bad during Jimi's set that he walked off the stage. He was in the middle of a number. He threw the guitar down, flipped everyone the bird, said, "Fuck you," and walked off the stage. I was standing with Mickey Dolenz, and I turned to Mickey and I said, "Good for him."'

Janis Joplin *(19 January 1943)*

One of her conquests was Peter Tork, later of the Monkees. 'Every time I saw Janis, she was happy to see me, hugged me, gave me that great big old laugh, and the next thing I knew we were rolling in the hay together,' he told Pamela Des Barres. 'Then one day I caught up with her at a Who concert and she wasn't friendly to me at all, and I said, "Okay, I get it, she's after one of these *other* guys!" That was that.'

In 1970 Janis Joplin changed her will to provide $2500 'so my friends can get blasted after I'm gone'. She even appended a guest list. Was this some sort of premonition? Two days later she was dead of an accidental heroin overdose, possibly compounded by alcohol. She died just sixteen days after Jimi Hendrix popped his clogs, also at the age of twenty-seven. The party took place at a Californian tavern and lasted all night.

Viv Stanshall *(21 March 1943)*

One-time leader of the Bonzo Dog Doo-Dah Band and thoroughly rackety individual by any standards. 'If I had all the money I've spent on drink,' he once said, 'I'd spend it on drink.'

Mick Jagger *(26 July 1943)*

'Of course we're doing it for the money as well,' Mick once told an interviewer. 'We've always done it for the money.'

Mick Jagger was once described by *Word* magazine as 'the good time that's been had by all'. 'He's always looking for it,' explains Keith Richards. A brief rundown of his lovelies would include Chrissie Shrimpton between 1963 and 1966, and Marianne Faithfull up until 1970, overlapping briefly with Marsha Hunt in 1969. He married Bianca Morena de Macías in 1971, but nicked Jerry Hall off

Bryan Ferry in 1977 and divorced Bianca in 1980. He married Jerry in 1990 and she divorced him in 1999 after DNA tests showed he had fathered a child with Luciana Morad. In the early 1990s there was a fling with Carla Bruni, who later said 'there were maybe ten other women' in Jagger's life when they were together. Others seen on his arm include Sophie Dahl, Michelle Phillips of the Mamas and the Papas and, a few years later, Michelle's daughter Chynna. In 2014 L'Wren Scott, who had recently ended their engagement, killed herself, and Mick was consoled by the attentions of Melanie Hamrick, a dancer with the American Ballet Theatre. Two years later she gave birth to his eighth child, Deveraux.

Rolling Stones tribute bands include the Stones, the Counterfeit Stones, Not the Rolling Stones, the Rollin' Clones, the Rolling Stones Now, the Strolling Bones, the Stony Rollers, the Railing Stains and the Rollin' Stoned.*

Ronnie Spector *(10 August 1943)*

For a long time, Brian Wilson thought the Ronettes' 'Be My Baby', sung by Ronnie and produced by future husband Phil, was the best single ever made. (He played it more than a thousand times.) Unfortunately, Phil turned out to be madder than a box of frogs, as jealous as a Turk and rather too fond of guns for comfort. In her autobiography, Ronnie claims that after they were married in 1968, he kept her locked up in their twenty-three-room house for several years. He surrounded the house with barbed wire, installed guard dogs in the grounds, hid her shoes to stop her leaving, wore a hat in bed to hide his baldness, played *Citizen Kane* on a loop

---

* There's a Scottish dance band who call themselves Ceilidh Minogue, a bagpipe band called the Red Hot Chili Pipers, an American country band called Rodeohead, and, for nearly twenty years, there has been a Neil Finn tribute band from Liverpool called Crowded Scouse.

to demonstrate his power over her, and kept a gold coffin with a glass top in the basement, promising that he would kill her and display her corpse if she ever left him. On the rare occasions she was allowed out by herself, she had to drive the car with a blow-up plastic man in the passenger seat to deter potential suitors. After he beat her to the ground and called her a 'nigger cunt', she finally escaped with the help of her mother, in bare feet. In their 1974 divorce settlement, Ronnie forfeited all future record earnings from the Ronettes because Phil threatened to have a hitman kill her. She made several attempts at a solo comeback, but was stymied by poor material and what Lucy O'Brien calls her 'own failure of nerve'. O'Brien continues, 'her story echoes the familiar girl-group tale of brief meteoric success, followed by lack of career development and crushing ignominy'.

Billy J. Kramer *(19 August 1943)*

Brian Epstein bought Kramer from his previous manager for £25.

One day in 1965, Kramer went up to Paul McCartney and asked him if he had written anything good recently, something suitable for him to release as a single. Yes, actually, said McCartney, who picked up his guitar and played a little tune he'd recently knocked together. 'Yesterday,' he sang, 'all my troubles seemed so far away.' Kramer thought about it for a minute, and said no.*

---

* Funnily enough, in *Black Vinyl White Powder*, Simon Napier-Bell tells a similar story about Chris Farlowe, who is said to have rejected the song because it was 'too soft'. Maybe, depending on who you talk to, McCartney offered this song to every pop singer in England during 1965, only to be turned down by them all. But somehow I doubt it.

Roger Waters *(6 September 1943)*

For their 1977 album *Animals*, Pink Floyd lofted a giant inflatable pig over Battersea Power Station and took photos of it to put on the cover. Their stadium shows thereafter were almost always accompanied by this pig, floating irrelevantly above the stage. In 1985 Roger Waters left the band not altogether amicably, and insisted on a payment of $800 per show for use of the pig. The remainder of the group consulted lawyers and found that they could surpass all copyright problems by changing the pig slightly. For this reason, the Pink Floyd pig was always seen thereafter with huge inflatable testicles, where none had been before.

'My father was a schoolteacher before the war,' said Waters in 1988. 'He taught physical education and religious instruction, strangely enough. He was a deeply committed Christian who was killed when I was three months old. A wrenching waste. I concede that awful loss has coloured much of my writing and worldview.'

Randy Newman *(28 November 1943)*

One of the greatest American singer-songwriters, whose lack of popular appeal may be down to the fact that his singing voice sounds like a cat chewing a wasp. But I would say that *Good Old Boys* (1974) and *Little Criminals* (1977) are as good as any albums made by anyone, ever, and the late work *Harps and Angels* (2008) isn't bad at all. 'If I had written "I Love You Just the Way You Are", I probably would have added "You Little Shit" – I throw in something to blow it out of the water every time,' he said in 1995. 'Billy Joel has a track record of reinventing himself, and that's very difficult. It's a talent to have. I have a track record too, which includes almost no hits.'

Jim Morrison *(8 December 1943)*

Steve Morrison, his father, had been a captain in the navy and ran the parental home as he might have run a ship. When Jim escaped to Los Angeles and started putting together the Doors, he wrote to his father to tell him of these exciting new developments. Steve wrote back in the purest rage, saying that what Jim was up to was 'a crock'. Jim never wrote or spoke to his father again.

On 9 December 1967, the Doors were about to play at New Haven, Connecticut. Jim Morrison was, in Ray Manzarek's words, 'making out' with a girl in the shower backstage when a local police officer who was providing security for the band, and clearly didn't know what Morrison looked like, told them to vacate the area.

'Eat it,' said Morrison.

'Last chance,' said the policeman, brandishing a can of mace.

'Last chance to eat it,' said Morrison, and got a face full of mace for his trouble.

The policeman apologised profusely when he was told he had just maced the lead singer of the very band he had been hired to protect. Morrison, though, was incensed. When he had finally recovered enough to get on stage, he told the audience what had happened and did not exactly mince his words.

'The whole fucking world hates me!' he yelled, before calling his assailant 'a little blue man in a little blue hat' and 'a little blue pig'. He went on, 'I'm just like you guys, man! He did it to me, they'll do it to you!' The cops responded by leaping onto the stage and stopping the show. Morrison was arrested, and the mini-riot that followed this in the streets outside led to thirteen more arrests. Morrison was charged with inciting a riot, indecency and public obscenity, although the charges were later dropped. But it was in this way that Jim Morrison became, as far as anyone knows, the first rock star ever to be arrested on stage in the middle of a performance.

'We had this group which we all knew had the potential to be something really big,' said guitarist Robby Krieger much later, 'and Jim was trying to sabotage it by fucking up at every turn. We would call a rehearsal, Jim wouldn't show, and we'd get a call from Blythe, Arizona, telling us that he was in jail.'

When he died, aged twenty-seven, Jim left all his money to Pam Courson, his 'common-law widow', but she was also a heroin addict and before she could get hold of it she also died of an overdose. In a 1975 court ruling, Jim's estate was shared equally between his parents and Pam's parents, all of whom had outlived their wayward children.

Keith Richards *(18 December 1943)*

On 6 May 1965, the Rolling Stones were on their third US tour and staying in a motel in Clearwater, Florida. Keith Richards called Mick Jagger to his room and played him a guitar riff that had come to him in a dream. He had woken up in the middle of the night, switched on the tape machine he kept next to his bed and recorded it. On the tape you could hear him drop the plectrum and the rest of the tape was Keith snoring. Something else had come to him in the dream as well.

'The words that go with this are "I can't get no satisfaction",' said Keith.

The record was in the shops exactly three weeks later.

In later years, interviewers would always ask the old reprobate about drugs, for some reason.

In 1978: 'I must say, in fairness to the poppy, that never once did I have a cold. The cure for the common cold is there, but they daren't tell anybody because they would have a nation full of drug addicts.'

In 1980: 'I don't know if I've been lucky ... but I've never turned blue in someone's bathroom. I consider that the height of bad manners.'

In 1982: 'There was a knock on our dressing-room door. Our manager shouted, "Keith! Ron! The police are here!" Oh man, we panicked. Flushed everything down the john. Then the door opened and it was Sting and Stewart Copeland.'

In his 2000 memoir *All the Rage*, the Small Faces and Faces keyboardist Ian McLagan tells of a session he was due to play on a new song of Keith's. Before they started, Keith decided it would be a good moment to introduce Ian to some Iranian opium he had acquired. He cooked it on the gas ring, inhaled the smoke through the cardboard tube from a loo roll, and passed it on.

At some point in all this, though, Keith managed to drop an ice pick through his foot.

They started recording the backing track but Keith's foot was now beginning to throb. He took painkillers and tried to sing sitting down, but the painkillers were so powerful they put him to sleep. When he woke up the song had gone clean out of his mind, and the session had to be abandoned.

Chas *(28 December 1943)* and Dave *(24 May 1945)*

Chas Hodges and Dave Peacock first met in 1963 but only started writing songs together in 1972. Before they started their own recording career, they were prolific session musicians who played on a huge multiplicity of recordings. One such was Labi Siffre's *Remember My Song* album of 1975, on which Chas played piano and Dave played bass. Many years later one of the tracks off this album, 'I Got The', was sampled by Eminem on his breakthrough hit 'My Name Is' and is the main musical refrain of the track. Which means that if anyone ever wonders if it's true that Chas and Dave played on an Eminem track, the answer is a firm YES.*

John Denver *(31 December 1943)*

Wildly successful purveyor of MOR mush in the early 1970s, born Henry John Deutschendorf Jr in Roswell, New Mexico, where aliens are supposed to have landed.† He wrote his most successful song, 'Annie's Song', about his wife, in ten minutes on a Colorado ski-lift after the couple had had an argument. In 1982 John and Annie were divorced, and their battles over property distribution became so antagonistic that John took a chainsaw to their marital bed and cut it in half. He died in 1997 while piloting an experimental aircraft, which crashed into Monterey Bay near Pacific Grove, California. The subsequent inquiry heard the slightly disturbing news that the plane had been built by someone else, from a kit.‡

---

* My thanks for this magnificent piece of information to the trivialist Mark Mason, who also told me that as a child the rugby star Lawrence Dallaglio was one of the singers on 'We Don't Need Another Hero' by Tina Turner, and that on their way to the Moon, the astronauts of Apollo 12 danced weightlessly to 'Sugar Sugar' by the Archies, which one of them had brought along on cassette.
† He would have been three-and-a-half when they arrived, or failed to arrive. Maybe he arrived with them.
‡ See previous footnote.

Band Names

Well, I thought I knew all of these. I knew that Duran Duran called themselves after a character (Dr Durand-Durand) in the film *Barbarella*. I knew that Steely Dan were named after a giant dildo from the works of William S. Burroughs. But I didn't know that Jane's Addiction were named after Perry Farrell's flatmate, and were originally going to be called 'Jane's Heroin Experience', but Farrell thought that was too on the nose. And I had no idea at all that Perry Farrell (born Peretz Bernstein) named himself after the word 'peripheral'.

So it was what we might call a Donald Rumsfeld situation. There were lots of known knowns but, as I did my research for this book, an increasing number of known unknowns. It required a little more work to unearth some unknown knowns, and I realised I was keen to leave the unknown unknowns cupboard completely bare. Here's what I found out:

Alt-J

The spoken form of the band whose real name is Δ. Alt+j is the keyboard shortcut used to type Δ on an Apple Mac computer. Δ is a symbol used to denote change in mathematical equations (as well as being the letter delta in Ancient Greek). I was typing this out on an Apple Mac computer just now and I wondered, how do you get Δ? So I typed Alt+j and it worked.

The B-52s

Named after the beehive hairstyle of the same name, which was itself named after the Boeing B-52 Stratofortress aeroplane. Cindy Wilson and Kate Pierson initially affected vertiginous beehives.

Badfinger

Derived from 'Bad Finger Boogie', the working title of the Beatles' 'With a Little Help from My Friends'.

Bastille

Lead singer Dan Smith was born on 14 July, Bastille Day. (So was I, but I don't go shouting about it.)

The Beautiful South

Partly a sarcastic reflection of Paul Heaton's dislike of the south of England, and partly an attempt to force macho men to utter the word 'beautiful'. (They're probably the only band who have ever broken up because of 'musical similarities'.)

Black Sabbath

Originally called Earth, but they then discovered there was another British band of that name. Fortunately, they spotted a cinema over the road from their rehearsal rooms playing the 1963 Boris Karloff shocker *Black Sabbath*. Other 1963 films they might conceivably have named themselves after were *Cleopatra*, *Charade*, *Come Blow Your Horn* and *It's a Mad, Mad, Mad, Mad World*.

Blur

Originally called Circus, they renamed themselves Seymour after J. D. Salinger's *Seymour: An Introduction*. Their record company, understandably, rejected this pathetically mimsy name outright, and gave them a list from which to choose. Record companies compile lists of potential band names? That sounds a fun job.

The Boomtown Rats

The name of Woody Guthrie's boyhood gang in Oklahoma City. (Which was known as 'Boomtown' during the oil boom.)

Buzzcocks

In 1976 *Time Out* magazine reviewed an ITV series called *Rock Follies* under the headline 'It's a Buzz, Cock!' (Cock meaning 'mate' rather than 'penis'.) They just liked the sound of it.

B*witched

As the humorist and critic David Quantick has pointed out, what does the asterisk stand for? Is it supposed to be B-fuck-witched? They were previously toying with calling themselves D'Zire, so punctuation was clearly not their strong point. (See also Hear'Say, Godspeed You! Black Emperor, Therapy?, !!!, M/A/R/R/S, Sunn O))) and the oddly compelling Giraffes? Giraffes!)

Chvrches

Pronounced 'churches', the band decided on the spelling to distinguish themselves in internet searches. This may be one of the dullest pieces of information you have ever encountered.

Deacon Blue

Scottish band who tempted fate by naming themselves after one of the best songs from Steely Dan's monumental album *Aja*. Needless to say, they never recorded anything even a fraction as good themselves.

The Dead Kennedys

Not an insult to the assassinated Kennedy brothers, according to lead singer Jello Biafra, but intended 'to bring attention to the end of the American dream'. (Jello Biafra might not be his real name.)

Death Cab for Cutie

After the Bonzo Dog Doo-Dah Band's song of the same name, itself named after a tabloid headline when a woman was killed in a taxi accident.

Deep Purple

Named after guitarist Ritchie Blackmore's grandmother's favourite song. The next most popular suggestion among the band was Concrete God, which might have been fun.

Everything but the Girl

From a slogan used by a shop in Hull called Turner's Furniture, which claimed that 'for your bedroom needs, we sell everything but the girl'.

The Foo Fighters

After a term used by Allied pilots in World War Two to denote unexplained aerial phenomena, such as UFOs.

Fountains of Wayne

Adam Schlesinger got his driver's licence at the DMV office in a town called Wayne, New Jersey. Next door was a lawn ornament store called Fountains of Wayne. 'We just thought it was funny,' he said.

Green Day

A slang term for an entire day spent smoking weed.

Haircut One Hundred

I haven't a clue how this band name came about, but I have included it here because it was the fifth name the band had had. They started as Rugby, then became the Boat Party, then Captain Pennyworth, then Moving England before finally settling on Haircut One Hundred. Which explains rather a lot, because if you think that Haircut One Hundred is the worst band name of all time, it's not actually as appalling as the four names that preceded it.

Hawkwind

Founder member Nik Turner spat and farted all the time.

Heaven 17

Taken from a fictional band mentioned in passing in Anthony Burgess's dystopian novel *A Clockwork Orange*. 'The Heaven Seventeen' are at number four in the charts with 'Inside', a song that the real Heaven 17 have never written, recorded or released. (Yet.)

The Human League

In the science fiction board game *Starforce: Alpha Centauri*, the Human League were a political grouping that arose in ad 2415 and were a frontier-oriented society that desired more independence from earth. As opposed to a tatty grouping of synthesiser geeks from Sheffield fronted by a man with the silliest hairstyle known to humankind. Even so, it was better than their previous name, the Dead Daughters.

Imagine Dragons

An anagram of 'a phrase that meant something to all of us', according to lead singer Dan Reynolds. 'I haven't even told my mum, and she's bothered me about it since day one.' You can bet that this will eventually turn out to be something incredibly disappointing, like 'Dragons Imagine'.

Iron Maiden

Named after a torture device Steve Harris had seen in the 1939 film *The Man in the Iron Mask*. Quite appropriate, really, if you have listened to any of their records.

Kasabian

After Linda Kasabian, a former member of the Manson Family and a key witness in the prosecution of Charles Manson and his followers for the murders of Sharon Tate and others in 1969. Also the Armenian word for butcher.

King Crimson

Coined by lyricist Peter Sinfield as a synonym for Beelzebub, prince of demons. He went on to write songs for Bucks Fizz, which sounds to me like the repayment of a Faustian pact.

The Lilac Time

Stephen Duffy's inestimable folk-rock band named themselves after a lyric in Nick Drake's 'River Man'.

Moby Grape

Named after a punchline. What's big and purple and lives in the ocean?

Mogwai

After the creatures in the film *Gremlins*.

Morcheeba

'Mor', as in MOR, middle of the road. And 'cheeba', slang for cannabis.

Ned's Atomic Dustbin

Title of an episode of *The Goon Show*, which was much loved by singer Jonn Penney's mother.

Oasis

Inspired by the Oasis Leisure Centre in Swindon, where the Inspiral Carpets had once played. Strange that so utterly northern a band should have named themselves after something so quintessentially softy southern. (See also The Beautiful South.)

Pearl Jam

Another term for sperm. You didn't need to know that. I apologise.

Pink Floyd

Named after two blues musicians, Pink Anderson and Floyd Council. If they had used the surnames, they could have been the Anderson Council.

Pixies

Unaccountably shortened from the obviously superior Pixies in Panoply.

Prefab Sprout

Meaningless. Paddy McAloon just liked the sounds of the words.

Radiohead

Previously called On a Friday, which may be the worst band name of all time (see also Haircut One Hundred). After signing with Parlophone, they were given two weeks to dream up a new name. At the time, someone was listening a lot to Talking Heads' 1986 album *True Stories*, and they decided that 'Radio Head' was 'the least annoying' track on that album. How very cool they must have considered themselves.

R.E.M.

Not the abbreviation for Rapid Eye Movement, as we had all assumed for thirty years. Michael Stipe just opened his dictionary at random and took the first initialism he saw.

Röyksopp

From 'røyksopp', the Norwegian word for a puffball mushroom. They then substituted a Swedish ö for the Norwegian ø.

Scissor Sisters

Named after a lesbian sex position. Other bands possibly named after sex positions include Sham 69, the Ruts, Butthole Surfers, the

Flaming Lips, Tenpole Tudor, Mister Fister, Arab Strap,* Kenny Rogers and the Teardrop Explodes.†

Simple Minds

From a line in David Bowie's song 'The Jean Genie'.

Simply Red

Originally called just Red, because of Mick Hucknall's unruly russet locks. The manager of a local venue was confused by this name, so he asked Hucknall to clarify. 'Red, simply Red,' said the potato-faced one, irritably. That's what went up on the posters, and the name stuck.

Spandau Ballet

It was Robert Elms's suggestion: he said he had seen it written on a wall on a weekend trip to Berlin. Later they found out that it describes the twitching feet of Nazi war criminals being hanged at Spandau Prison in West Berlin, but by then it was too late. *Word* magazine declared this to be the worst band name of all time (see also Haircut One Hundred, Radiohead). One of their rejected earlier names was Gentry.

Starsailor

The literal meaning of the word astronaut.

---

* To be fair, named after a sex toy.
† Actually taken from a panel caption in the Marvel comic strip *Daredevil* (no. 77).

Super Furry Animals

Derived from a clothing range set up by singer Gruff Rhys's sister.

Tangerine Dream

In an interview in *Let It Rock* magazine, Edgar Froese explained that they named themselves 'after the line in the Beatles song "Lucy in the Sky with Diamonds"'. Unfortunately, the actual line is 'tangerine trees'. English was not Froese's first language.

Thin Lizzy

In the 1950s (when the members of Thin Lizzy were but small lads) there was a robot character in the *Dandy* called Tin Lizzie. They adjusted this to Thin Lizzy, because in their local Dublin accent it would be pronounced 'Tin Lizzy' anyway. For some of their early gigs, the band was actually billed as Tin Lizzy.

Thompson Twins

After Thompson and Thomson, the bumbling and moustachioed twin detectives in the *Tintin* adventures. Otherwise known as Schultze and Schulze in German, Hernández and Fernández in Spanish, Parry-Williams and Williams-Parry in Welsh and জনসন and রনসন in Bengali.

Three Dog Night

According to their biography, vocalist Danny Hutton's then girl-friend suggested the name after reading a magazine article about indigenous Australians. On cold nights, it seems, they would cus-tomarily sleep in a hole in the ground wrapped around a dingo. On colder nights they would sleep with two dogs, and if it was really freezing ...

My friend Andrew Mueller, who claims to be Australian, says he has never heard such a lot of tripe in his life.

Toad the Wet Sprocket

On *Monty Python's Contractual Obligation Album*, Eric Idle has a monologue called 'Rock Notes' in which he plays a rock journalist. 'Rex Stardust,' he reports, 'lead electric triangle with Toad the Wet Sprocket, has had to have an elbow removed after their recent successful worldwide tour of Finland.'

Toploader

Probably the first band in history, and almost certainly the last, to name themselves after a type of washing machine.

Westlife

Were going to be called Westside, after a stage school in Dublin, but there was already another band of that name, so they opted for what *Word* called a 'nonsensical near-homophone'. At the same time Brian McFadden changed his first name to Bryan because 'it would be easier to sign autographs'. You want them all shot, don't you?

The Records That Time Forgot

Supertramp: *Brother Where You Bound*

The first pop album I ever heard, when I was about sixteen, was Supertramp's *Crime of the Century* (1974), and because I didn't speak the musical language, I didn't think much of it. That record belonged to my girlfriend at the time, and the second Supertramp album I heard, *Even in the Quietest Moments* (1977), belonged to my second girlfriend. Supertramp were a band much loved by girl-friends, as well as Frenchmen, for some reason. Critics invariably detested them, and it was for this reason, and maybe one or two others, that the band, four-fifths of whom were British, moved to California in the mid-1970s, never to return.

The band was based around two dissimilar but complementary songwriters, Roger Hodgson and Rick Davies. (Such 1970s names.) Hodgson sang most of the singles. His songs were simple, catchy and often yearning for some greater spiritual truth, and he sang them in a high tenor voice whose sincerity could never be doubted but whose tone created problems for passing dogs. 'Dreamer' was one of his, as was 'The Logical Song' and 'It's Raining Again', which features one of the worst couplets ever written in rock his-tory: 'Come on you little fighter/No need to get uptighter'.

I preferred Davies's songs, which were bluesier, more varied and sung in a slightly tortured growl that I liked. The band were a real band in these early days, and *Breakfast in America* (1979) was a huge smash hit all over the world, although the plinky-plonk Wurlitzer electric piano that dominates it quickly became a little wearing. But by the time of . . . *famous last words* . . . (1982), egos had expanded to fill the space available, which was where the songs should have been. Hodgson, after insisting that their latest single be credited to 'Supertramp featuring Roger Hodgson', left in a huff.

When bands break up in bad blood, one of two things can happen. Either you swiftly realise that the band was greater than the sum of its parts (the Smiths being the perfect example) or all the bickering actually inspires the people concerned to greater heights individually than they would have been capable of together. I think the latter happened to Supertramp. Hodgson went off and finished his first solo album, which he had clearly been saving up all his best songs for,* and Supertramp carried on as a four-piece and recorded a strikingly ambitious affair called *Brother Where You Bound* (1985). Producer David Kershenbaum modified the band's sound, pushing Davies's acoustic piano well back in the mix and not going too heavily into the electronics that then dominated pop music and made it all sound the same. The centrepiece of the album was the title track, which had been about ten minutes long when it had been demoed for the previous record, and was now sixteen and a half minutes long, a wild, woolly prog monster of a song about Cold War tensions in America, full of fear, special effects, a sound clip from *Nineteen Eighty-Four* and some scorching guitar solos from David Gilmour, no less. As usual with Davies, the lyrics weren't up to much, and the theme has dated just a little, but the music's

---

* George Harrison had clearly been doing something similar towards the end of the Beatles. *All Things Must Pass* is a huge triple-album splurge of creativity, after which it turned out that he had almost nothing else to offer at all.

inventiveness was extraordinary, a spit in the eye for Hodgson and anyone else who had doubted his abilities. Unfortunately, this included most record buyers. Sales were modest.

I was exhilarated by this album, though, and I imagined a bright future for the Davies-led Supertramp. As always, I was completely wrong. The next album had one of his best-ever songs, 'Free as a Bird', but the public had moved on and the band split up. Hodgson, too, lost the plot and recorded an utterly generic session-musician-based album called *Hai Hai*. (I wanted to review it with just the sentence 'Low Low' but wasn't allowed to.) In the subsequent thirty years Davies has managed to produce only two albums of new material and Hodgson one. Creatively, they were both done before their forty-fifth birthdays.

Success and failure are, of course, endemic to the pop process, but the seeds of this failure, I believe, are to be found in the success of *Breakfast in America*, which sold eighteen million copies despite not being particularly good. Where do you go from that? Down the dumper, essentially, very, very slowly.

Quiz 1

1. After Queen Elizabeth the Queen Mother died her body lay in state in Westminster Hall in London, guarded by members of the Household Cavalry, one of whom was which future pop star?
2. Every Beatle, of the four main Beatles, has been married twice, but only one went down the aisle for a third time. Which one?
3. Which number child in his family was Michael Jackson?
4. What do the bands Brinsley Schwartz, Fleetwood Mac, Van Halen and Manfred Mann's Earth Band have in common?
5. Who came last in the final of the Eurovision Song Contest in 2003, 2008, 2010 and 2019?
6. Which solo artist won the Grammy for Album of the Year in 1974, 1975 and 1977? (In each case we are looking at albums that were released in the previous year.)
7. Whose first three albums add up to sixty-five?
8. What links the waltz, the fandango, the minuet, the mazurka, the polonaise and the saraband? Beyond the fact that they are all dances.
9. Which legendary band's stage clothes were reportedly

influenced by Swedish tax law, which stated that they could be tax-deductible only if they could not reasonably be worn in public?

10. Which 1985 song, written by Bernie Taupin, Martin Page, Dennis Lambert and Peter Wolf, and recorded by a well-known San Franciscan band, was named Worst Song of the 1980s in a *Rolling Stone* readers' poll of 2011, Worst Song Ever by *Blender* magazine, and the Worst Song of All Time by *GQ* in 2016, which referred to it as 'the most detested song in human history'?

Answers on page 185.

1944–1945

Notable Births

9 January 1944:	Jimmy Page
27 January 1944:	Nick Mason
29 January 1944:	Andrew Loog Oldham
1 March 1944:	Roger Daltrey
26 March 1944:	Diana Ross
20 May 1944:	Joe Cocker
21 June 1944:	Ray Davies
12 September 1944:	Barry White
9 October 1944:	John Entwistle
12 November 1944:	Booker T. Jones
4 December 1944:	Dennis Wilson
11 December 1944:	Brenda Lee
3 January 1945:	Stephen Stills
10 January 1945:	Rod Stewart
28 January 1945:	Robert Wyatt
6 February 1945:	Bob Marley
8 March 1945:	Mickey Dolenz
30 March 1945:	Eric Clapton
25 April 1945:	Björn Ulvaeus
19 May 1945:	Pete Townshend
28 May 1945:	John Fogerty
25 June 1945:	Carly Simon
31 August 1945:	Van Morrison
26 September 1945:	Bryan Ferry
2 October 1945:	Don McLean
12 November 1945:	Neil Young
15 November 1945:	Anni-Frid Lyngstad
24 December 1945:	Lemmy
30 December 1945:	Davy Jones

Jimmy Page *(9 January 1944)*

When he was thirteen, Jimmy Page was playing in a skiffle group who appeared on the children's TV show *All Your Own* and were interviewed by Huw Wheldon, later to become Sir Huw and a formidable managing director of BBC TV.

'What are you going to do when you grow up?' asked Huw with a patrician smirk. 'Play skiffle?'

'No,' said Jimmy, 'I want to do biological research.'

Mike d'Abo *(1 March 1944)*

Singer who replaced Paul Jones in Manfred Mann in July 1966, when I was six, and I was genuinely outraged that one of my favourite singers could be superseded by this different man with a different face. He sang 'Ha Ha Said the Clown', 'Mighty Quinn' and many others, but quietly wrote killer tunes on the side. It was Mike d'Abo who wrote 'Handbags and Gladrags' for Chris Farlowe, later covered by Rod Stewart, the Stereophonics and many others. With Tony Macauley he wrote 'Build Me Up Buttercup' for the Foundations, which sold more than four million copies worldwide. And, best of all, it was he who wrote the tune for the Cadbury's Fudge jingle that was used between the 1970s and early 1990s, that anyone who was a child then can still repeat verbatim. 'A finger of Fudge is just enough to give the kids a treat/A finger of Fudge is just enough until it's time to eat ... '

Diana Ross *(26 March 1944)*

Bob Stanley says that Ross had the most radio-friendly voice of the whole Motown roster. 'No matter how muted or quiet the radio may be in a café or a taxi, Ross's voice cuts through like a laser. It's uncanny. It also explains how the Supremes amassed eleven US number ones in the sixties, more than anyone except the Beatles. Ross's voice aside, it probably helped that she was dating [Motown boss] Berry Gordy – writers and producers worked that little bit harder on a Supremes 45, and it paid off for everybody.'

Ray Davies *(21 June 1944)*

Ray and his younger brother Dave were the last of their parents' eight children, and the only boys. As young men, they had complicated relationships with the world and each other. There were so many arguments and fights on the Kinks' first tour of America in 1965 – money not paid, concerts abbreviated, punches thrown, officials told to fuck off – that the American Federation of Musicians subsequently withheld the band's work permits until 1969, effectively banning them from the US for four crucial years. In 1971 Ray and Dave were dining in Manhattan. Dave tried to steal one of Ray's French fries. Ray stabbed his brother in the chest with a fork. At Dave's fiftieth birthday party, Ray stamped on his cake.

Ray once tried to emulate Keith Moon and lay waste to his hotel room. 'I threw a Guinness bottle against the wall,' he explained. 'It bounced back and hit me on the head and knocked me out.'

The original title of 'Sunny Afternoon' was 'The Taxman's Taken All My Dough'.

Dennis Wilson *(4 December 1944)*

Often described as 'the essence' or 'the spirit' of the Beach Boys, possibly because he was the only one of them who could surf, the youngest Wilson brother was also a lifelong boozehound and drugs hoover who married five times and took part in orgies arranged by his old mate Charles Manson.* 'Whatever he did,' said one friend, 'he did in excess.' His former manager put it more bluntly: 'Dennis was a sex fiend, plain and simple.' He was frequently heard to refer to himself as 'the Wood', and he wasn't talking about golf clubs. Not only did he boff one of fellow Beach Boy Mike Love's many wives, but later married Love's illegitimate daughter. Dennis and Mike didn't get on. Once, on their way to a concert date, Dennis walked up to the area on their private jet where Mike was meditating, pulled open the door and threw up. Mike eventually issued a restraining order to keep them apart. On the day he died, aged thirty-nine, Dennis had been drinking vodka and red wine for seven straight hours and swam underneath his boat, apparently to recover a stash of drugs he thought he had hidden there. He didn't come back.

Mick Jones *(27 December 1944)*

No, not that one, the other one, who played guitar for Spooky Tooth and Foreigner. My mother put her flat up for sale in 1984, and Mick Jones of Foreigner came round with his wife to have a look. They didn't buy it. When Foreigner started, their USP was that they were half Englishmen, half Americans. The three Americans were called Lou, Al and Ed. The three Englishmen were called Mick, Ian and Dennis.

Vashti Bunyan *(born 1945)*

English folk singer-songwriter who released one album, *Just Another Diamond Day*, to such deafening silence that she gave

---

* When Manson wanted to unsettle Dennis, he instructed his gang to break into Dennis's house, move a few things around the living room, and then leave.

up her music career for thirty-five years. But there's no doubting she was of an unusually sensitive disposition. As she travelled the English countryside in the early 1970s, she once apologised to a piece of broccoli after she had picked it.

Stephen Stills *(3 January 1945)*

More than four hundred young actors and musicians auditioned for the four roles in *The Monkees*. Stephen Stills was one of them. Harry Nilsson was another. According to a widely disseminated urban myth, Charles Manson also auditioned, but he couldn't have done: he was in prison at the time.*

Rod Stewart *(10 January 1945)*

One of the greatest achievements of the pioneering music magazine *Word* (2003–12) was its fervent use of the word 'crumpeteer' to describe some of the more sexually motivated rock stars of their day. None more so, of course, than Sir Rod Stewart, who in between setting up enormous model railway systems (a lifelong interest of his), has rarely been seen in public without a tall blonde hanging off his arm. Mark Ellen says he has 'seen more sex than a policeman's torch'.

First up was model Dee Harrington, who he met in 1971, and whose knickers he wore on their first night together. Then it was on to Britt Ekland for several years after her marriage to Peter Sellers foundered. That ended less than amicably after Rod had a *tendresse* with Joanna Lumley. 'He was always a very selfish lover,' spat Britt. In 1979 he married Alana Hamilton (tall, blonde, six months younger), had a son and a daughter and split up when Rod

---

* Many years later the actor Colin Farrell would audition for Boyzone, while Russell Brand once auditioned for the boyband 5ive.

fell madly in bed with Kelly Emberg (no relation to Bella). Kelly (tall, blonde, fifteen years younger) had a daughter and they stayed together for seven years. Things start to get a little vague here. 'Sex at one point was beginning to be boring, late eighties, early nineties,' says Rod. 'Always flying in models left, right and centre. One would arrive, the other would leave.' You imagine something like a luggage carousel at an airport, with girls sitting there instead of suitcases. Rachel Hunter (tall, blonde, twenty-five years younger) arrived in 1991, they had two children and Rod claims he was completely faithful to her throughout their marriage (*strokes chin thoughtfully*), but by 1999 that was over too. In that year, though, Rod met Penny Lancaster (tall, blonde, twenty-six years younger), who appears to be his match, as they are still together. Maybe you just get too tired and old to keep going. Maybe it's the call of the chuff-chuffs from the attic room in his Los Angeles house. Maybe she just locked him in there.

Bob Marley *(6 February 1945)*

Bob Marley's father Norval was white, originally from Sussex, of Syrian Jewish origins, claimed to have been a captain in the Royal Marines and was sixty when Bob was born.

Mickey Dolenz *(8 March 1945)*

Former child actor (*Circus Boy*) who in 1965 auditioned for one of the four leading roles in *The Monkees*. At the audition, the show's producers Bob Rafelson and Bert Schneider sat behind a desk and in front of them was a line of Coke bottles. According to Bob Stanley, 'Dolenz looked at the producers, raised an eyebrow, then carefully, slowly, moved one of the bottles along the table. "Checkmate," he said, and got the job.'

Eric Clapton *(30 March 1945)*

In his youth, played briefly but not terribly productively with the Yardbirds. Their manager Simon Napier-Bell described him as 'a gloomy, troubled person who told people he expected to die before he was thirty'.

After his grandmother died, Clapton took possession of her parrot, Maurice. The bird had only ever learned to say one thing: 'Where's Eric?'

Björn Ulvaeus *(25 April 1945)*

Songwriter, producer and, with Benny Andersson, the creative core of the Swedish group ABBA (always upper case). When he was a boy, the rock critic Pete Paphides used to listen to the 'The Winner Takes It All', a surprisingly personal song for a global smash hit, and wonder whether Björn hadn't been slightly drunk when he wrote the lyrics. As he put it in his memoir *Broken Greek*, 'spillage on this scale almost never happens without the aid of a corkscrew'. Years later he interviewed Björn and asked him, bluntly, whether or not he had had a few on the night in question. Björn confirmed that he had.

Carly Simon *(25 June 1945)*

In late 1972 Simon released 'You're So Vain', a brutal takedown of an unnamed former lover, or maybe several lovers rolled into one. Who was it? Mick Jagger? David Geffen? Cat Stevens? Warren Beatty? Kris Kristofferson? Simon wouldn't say. Beatty clearly thought it was about him: he rang up Simon and thanked her. In 1983 she said it was definitely not about Mick Jagger, who actually contributes backing vocals (uncredited) from the second chorus on. In 2004 she told Regis Philbin that one of the subjects of the song had the letters 'a', 'e' and 'r' in his name. In the same year she sold the truth for $50,000 at a charity auction to the then-head of NBC Sports, on the condition that he told no one. We now know that it's about three men, and in November 2015 Simon confirmed that the second verse is about Beatty, but only the second verse. 'I didn't take the song as seriously as all that,' she told *Uncut* in 2010. 'It wasn't vengeance; it wasn't *Anna Karenina*. It was, "From this point of view, you don't necessarily look as good as you think you look." There's not an iota of hate in it.' In her long career Simon has recorded many songs on many albums, but to this day, if anyone mentions her name in conversation, one of the other people there is sure to say, 'Who was "You're So Vain" all about?' Those words will probably go on her gravestone.

During the 1970s Carly filled her albums with glutinous encomia to her lovely husband James Taylor. It was no great shock when, in 1981, they separated, and later divorced in terrible acrimony. 'Our needs are different,' she explained. 'James needs a lot more space around him – aloneness, remoteness, more privacy. I need more closeness, more communication. He's more abstract in our relationship. I'm more concrete. He's more of a . . . poet, and I'm more of a . . . reporter.'

Van Morrison *(31 August 1945)*

In his history of the *New Musical Express*, Pat Long tells of Keith Altham, sent to Belfast to interview up-and-coming group Them in 1966. Arriving at their rehearsal studios, Altham spotted their lead singer, 'a slightly chubby red-headed twenty-year-old called Van Morrison', leaning against a wall outside reading a newspaper. Altham approached him to introduce himself. 'Fuck off,' said Van. 'Can't you see I'm busy?'

Don McLean *(2 October 1945)*

Not to be confused with Don MacLean, the goofy British come-dian who appeared on the BBC TV series *Crackerjack* in the 1970s with Michael Aspel and Peter Glaze.

McLean has always refused to explain the lyrics of his mega-hit 'American Pie'. 'When people ask me what "American Pie" means, I tell them it means I don't ever have to work again if I don't want to.' I have friends who are Don McLean fans, and they say he has repeated this joke at every one of his live gigs they have ever attended.

Neil Young *(12 November 1945)*

Although Neil himself is Canadian, his mother Rassy is a Daughter of the American Revolution, which means she can trace her lineage back to people who were directly involved in the War of Independence.

In 1966 Young briefly shared a flat in Toronto with lunatic funkster Rick James. 'It's all very hazy to me now,' he told Howard Stern. 'There were some drugs going on. I remember singing one song for about a day and a half.'

In 1969, Young attached himself to Crosby, Stills and Nash, but swiftly outgrew his bandmates owing to a slightly embarrassing excess of talent. At one point C, S and N would be offered $60,000 for a concert, which would climb to $600,000 if Young were involved. Which is obviously why he wasn't.*

---

* There's a nice story about this in Frederic Dannen's book about the grimy side of the record business, *Hit Men*. It's 1988 and Ahmet Ertegun is planning a one-off CSNY album, to be released on his label Atlantic. But Young is signed to David Geffen's label, and Geffen wants 50 per cent of the proceeds. Ertegun thinks only 25 per cent. They're on the phone to each other. 'Listen, Ahmet,' says Geffen. 'Crosby, Stills and Nash are OLD FAT FARTS! The only one with any TALENT is Neil Young! I can't believe we're arguing about this! It's too silly to argue about!'

In 1976, Young performed with Bob Dylan, Joni Mitchell and many others in *The Last Waltz*, the last concert by the Band. Martin Scorsese directed the film of the concert, but its release was delayed when someone noticed that Young had sung 'Helpless' with a lump of cocaine hanging from his nose. Scorsese had to go back into the cutting room and artfully conceal it.

Neil Young has written more than thirty songs that mention the moon.

His name is listed on twenty-two patents for model railway technology.

Lemmy *(24 December 1945)*

Lemmy lost his virginity on a beach in Anglesey. 'Just starting to rain, it was,' he told John Harris in 2000. 'I didn't realise how much moisture you'd create, and how you'd pick up all that sand. It took me weeks to get it out. It must have been hell for her.'

Davy Jones *(30 December 1945)*

Moptop English shortie whose big break as an actor was as Ena Sharples's young nephew on *Coronation Street*. From there it was to the West End and Lionel Bart's *Oliver!*, in which he was cast as the Artful Dodger, and from there it was to Broadway, where Jones was nominated for a Tony award. On 9 February 1964, the *Oliver!* cast were on a special all-British edition of *The Ed Sullivan Show*, with 'Two-Ton' Tessie O'Shea and a band called the Beatles. Seventy-five million Americans tuned in that night. 'I watched the Beatles from the side of the stage,' said Jones. 'I saw the girls going crazy, and I said to myself, "This is it, I want a piece of that."'

Having acquired his berth on *The Monkees*, Jones missed filming only one episode, because he had to attend his sister's wedding. David Bowie (born Jones) had to rename himself after a knife because there was already a Davy Jones. Pavel Chekov, the moptop Russian shortie added to the cast of *Star Trek* in its second season to appeal to teenagers, was directly inspired by Davy Jones.

Songstories

'I am the Walrus'
(The Beatles, November 1967)

This begins with a tale told by Eric Burdon of the Animals in his 2002 autobiography, *Don't Let Me Be Misunderstood*. He had a wild Jamaican girlfriend called Sylvia. 'I was up early one morning cooking breakfast, naked except for my socks, and she slid up beside me and slipped an amyl nitrate capsule under my nose. As the fumes set my brain alight and I slid to the kitchen floor, she reached to the counter and grabbed an egg, which she cracked into the pit of my belly.' They then engaged in albumen-rich sexual relations as she showed him 'one Jamaican trick after another'. Later, at a party in Mayfair, Burdon told the story to John Lennon, who was highly amused and christened Burdon 'the Eggman'. Hence the lyric 'I am the Eggman / I am the walrus', and also hence Burdon's nickname of fifty years, 'Eggman', or simply 'Eggs'.

'Wichita Lineman'
(Glen Campbell, August 1968)

Bob Stanley believes that this Jimmy Webb song has 'the most beautiful line in the whole pop canon, one that makes me stop whatever I'm doing every single time I hear it: "I need you more than want you, and I want you for all time".'

'Lily the Pink'
(The Scaffold, November 1968)

The Scaffold's biggest hit was the second single my friend Tim ever bought (after Mary Hopkin's 'Those Were the Days'), although it was subsequently so overplayed that, more than fifty years later, he still says he'd be happy never to hear it again. The Scaffold were made up of Roger McGough (later an eminent poet), John Gorman (later an eminent co-presenter of *Tiswas*) and Mike McGear, really Mike McCartney, who had an older brother who played bass and sang in another Liverpool band. Less well known is that Jack Bruce played bass on the track, Elton John played the piano, and the backing vocalists included Elton, Tim Rice and Graham Nash. The song was based on a bawdy old American folk song called 'The Ballad of Lydia Pinkham', about a prominent female abolitionist and anti-segregationist who invented a herbal remedy to relieve period pains. In the Scaffold's version this became a 'medicinal compound', which has several magical properties, such as bringing about a sex change as a cure for freckles. The line 'Mr Frears has sticky-out ears' is a direct reference to the film director Stephen Frears, whom they all knew. My friend Tim says he's often wondered whether there was a subliminal connection between the song that set him on the road to a lifetime of record collecting, and his and his wife's decision to name their first child Lily. 'She was, and is, quite pink.'*

---

* Mat Snow and his wife called their child Lola. '"You named me after a tranny?" was her indignant enquiry around eight years later.'

'Bridge Over Troubled Water'
(Simon and Garfunkel, January 1970)

Simon and Garfunkel were asked if they would like to play at
Woodstock, but they had to say no, as they were too busy recording
'Bridge Over Troubled Water'. Paul Simon eventually released his
demo of the song on a 1993 box set, with just him picking away
at his acoustic guitar and singing in a high and not entirely com-
fortable falsetto. As Giles Smith wrote, 'What Garfunkel made
from the bones of the demo is something Simon is in awe of and,
at the same time, something he has never quite forgiven him for.'
By the time the record had come out, they had already agreed to
split up. Or rather, Simon had told Garfunkel they were splitting
up, and Garfunkel had taken it on the chin. When they performed
the song live at the 1993 reunion concerts, Garfunkel stole the
show night after night. Interviewed by BBC1's *Omnibus*, Simon
admitted that witnessing these extraordinary ovations cheesed
him off somewhat. He would sit to one side, completely ignored,
thinking 'Author! Author!'

The irony is that Garfunkel's great vocal triumph effectively
ended his career. He did very little after the split. Simon did more.
His revenge would be complete.

I have to admit that I have always hated the song, and it remains
one of the very few that, if played on the radio, will make me leap
across the room like a salmon to switch it off.*

---

* Others include 'Wonderwall' by Oasis, 'Imagine' by John Lennon,
'Stairway to Heaven' by Led Zeppelin and 'Bohemian Rhapsody' by Queen.
Andrew Mueller believes 'Imagine' to be the worst single of all time, although
personally I think 'Wonderwall' shades it.

'I Don't Want to Talk About It'
(Rod Stewart, August 1975)

This song, written by Danny Whitten of Neil Young's backing band Crazy Horse, was pretty much the sole flowering of what might have turned into a singular talent. But Whitten acquired a heroin addiction (mainly because he found the drug mitigated his rheumatoid arthritis), was kicked out of the band soon after they recorded this song, and died of an overdose in 1972, aged just twenty-nine. Some time in or around 1973 Tony Blair (*qv*) suggested his band Ugly Rumours play the song at their gigs, and in 1975 Rod Stewart recorded a memorable cover for his album Atlantic Crossing. It was the Everything but the Girl version, though, released in 1988, that alerted me to the song's profound wonder and strength. Subtly arranged by Ben Watt and beautifully sung by Tracey Thorn, it gave the duo their first big hit and, curiously, has become one of those songs you never tire of hearing. In fact, I have heard several other covers of it and I haven't heard a duff one yet. It may just be one of those songs it's impossible to ruin.

It's actually astonishing how few of these there are. In 1973 Harry Nilsson released possibly his best album, *A Little Touch of Schmilsson in the Night*, a trawl through the American songbook with exceptional orchestrations from Gordon Jenkins, one of Sinatra's main collaborators. The sleeve notes were written in fine style by Derek Taylor, the Beatles' celebrated PR man, who said that the last song on the album, 'As Time Goes By', was the best song ever written. I was a teenager when I first read this, and I was very impressed by his certainty, never having encountered a PR man before. But I have also never forgotten what he said, for as the years have passed, I have realised what he was getting at. 'As Time Goes By' is one of those songs that has been covered by everyone and also seems impossible to ruin.

Whoever sings it, you only have to hear the song's first couple of lines to know you're in safe hands. The makers of *Casablanca* were lucky people. Harry Nilsson was clever to recognise its power and right to put it at the end of the album, for where can you go from there? Best song of all time may be an exaggeration, but it's not much of one. 'I Don't Want to Talk About It' is in eminent company.

'Heroes'
(David Bowie, September 1977)

There's a superb documentary on YouTube about the making of 'Heroes', a song that blew my slippers and socks off when I first heard it and hasn't faded with time. Tony Visconti sits behind his mixing desk and tells some wonderful tales, one of which is about the recording of Robert Fripp's guitar. The track, they realised, needed a little something, so they called up Fripp, who was in New York, and asked him to fly into Berlin for the afternoon. Fripp's guitar sound is unique and easily identifiable, and that long weird guitarish noise on top of the actual song is his. He recorded one version, then he recorded a second version, then he recorded a third version. And Visconti had a bright idea. He thought, let's play all three tracks together.

'We played it, and you know, I must reiterate Fripp did not hear the other two tracks when he was doing the third one so he had no way of being in sync. But he was strangely in sync. And all his little out-of-tune wiggles suddenly worked with the other previously recorded guitars. It seemed to tune up. It got a quality that none of us anticipated. It was this dreamy, wailing quality, almost crying sound in the background. And we were just flabbergasted.

'So we all looked at each other. It was just Fripp, myself, and Brian Eno in the studio, and David, of course. We just looked at each other and we just couldn't believe our luck, how beautiful it sounded and how well it worked out.'

Upon such small, apparently random decisions is greatness made. Imagine life without 'Heroes'. It's not much of a life, is it?

The Records That Time Forgot

Kraftwerk: *Computer World*

Most of the bands written about in this section remain bywords for uncoolness, whose only thing in common is that they are liked by me. The exception is Kraftwerk, the German band who are to modern electronic music what the Beatles are to guitar rock. Paul Morley once said they were 'in the area of being the greatest pop group ever', which is not wrong (unlike almost everything else he said). Although they started in the late 1960s, Kraftwerk's reputation rests on five albums they recorded in a surge of creativity in the mid to late 1970s. *Autobahn* (1974), *Radio-Activity* (1975), *Trans-Europe Express* (1977), *The Man Machine* (1978) and *Computer World* (1981) coincided with swift improvements in recording technology, and in particular the ferociously fast development and refinement of synthesisers, so their timing was perfect. But Kraftwerk's precipitous growth in these years does seem to mirror that of the Merseyside moptops a decade earlier. After their own seven-year rise to brilliance, the Beatles grew their hair, argued and wisely split up. Kraftwerk didn't. In the subsequent forty years they have given us just two albums of original material, neither of them up to much.

I have often wondered about this. Inspiration isn't controllable.

It comes, it goes, and when it goes, it often goes for good. I recently read Uwe Shütte's adoring book, *Kraftwerk: Future Music from Germany*, but he is too busy worshipping at the shrine to answer any useful questions, such as, what happened there then? But when co-founder Florian Schneider died in 2020, I went back and listened to all the albums again in chronological order to try to work it out for myself. It made for an interesting few days. Each album is an enormous improvement on its predecessor, both technically and creatively, so that while *Autobahn* now feels weedy and insubstantial, *Computer World* may be the band's masterpiece, a record that feels as alive and exciting now as it did in 1981. It's everything they had wanted to be, intended to be, in seven tracks and thirty-four minutes. No wonder they struggled to top it, and indeed failed completely, over an incredibly long time.

I think there are three reasons for Kraftwerk's success, three apexes to the creative triangle, each as important as the other two. One was their love of high concept, and this, I think, is where leader and co-founder Ralf Hütter excelled. Every album had a coherent theme, rigorously adhered to. The second is technological innovation: the rapidly improving sounds of those synthesisers, with a human touch, as they weren't yet being programmed; they were being played by real people. (Every percussive sound you hear is someone hitting something.) The third is tunes. At their best, Kraftwerk wrote and performed wonderful melodies that stick in your mind. 'The Model' may have been a bit daft, but it wasn't number one for nothing.

By the late 1970s the group comprised Hütter and Schneider, long-time conspirators and rather similar-looking, in their square-faced Mitteleuropean way, as well as electronic percussionists Karl Bartos and Wolfgang Flur. The songs on early albums are usually credited to Hütter (music) and Hütter/Schneider (lyrics), but by *The Man Machine*, music is generally by Hütter/Bartos, although Schneider gets a few credits on *Computer World*. On

YouTube I saw them perform (or rather mime) one of the songs from this album on German television. Hütter and Bartos were playing keyboards, Flur was playing drums and Schneider was doing ... well ... nothing at all. This seemed a bit strange. But it really looked to all the world as though Bartos was now Hütter's number two and Schneider had been sidelined. Kraftwerk may turn out to have been like every other band, full of jealousies and power struggles and all-too-human interactions that ended up derailing the entire project.

Bartos left the band in 1990, bored by their slow progress in having an idea, any idea, on how to extend their shelf life. His solo releases since have been sporadic but they have been fresher and more tuneful than Kraftwerk's releases in the same time. What they have lacked is decent lyrics and Hütter's concepts, which have still brought a certain discipline to proceedings. 'Seven years of startling achievement followed by forty years of failure' isn't exactly what you'd like on your gravestone, but it's a surprisingly common tale in pop. They should probably have split up in the early 1980s, when they had the chance.

BILL'S SPOTIFY THE LINK

3.1

'The Scientist'
by Coldplay

'Positively 4th Street'
by Bob Dylan

'Scenes from an Italian Restaurant'
by Billy Joel

'True Faith'
by New Order

3.2

'Song for Whoever'
by the Beautiful South

'Annie's Song'
by John Denver

'Space Oddity'
by David Bowie

'The Last Resort'
by Eagles

3.3

'Unchained Melody'
by the Righteous Brothers

'Bohemian Rhapsody'
by Queen

'Song 2'
by Blur

'A Day in the Life'
by the Beatles

Answer

The titles of the songs do not appear in the lyrics. By which we mean that the entire phrase doesn't appear; the odd word might.

1946–1947

Notable Births

3 January 1946:	John Paul Jones
6 January 1946:	Syd Barrett
19 January 1946:	Dolly Parton
6 March 1946:	David Gilmour
1 April 1946:	Ronnie Lane
13 April 1946:	Al Green
10 May 1946:	Donovan
20 May 1946:	Cher
15 June 1946:	Noddy Holder, Demis Roussos
15 July 1946:	Linda Ronstadt
23 August 1946:	Keith Moon
1 September 1946:	Barry Gibb
5 September 1946:	Freddie Mercury
29 October 1946:	Peter Green
5 November 1946:	Gram Parsons
16 December 1946:	Benny Andersson
21 December 1946:	Carl Wilson
29 December 1946:	Marianne Faithfull
30 December 1946:	Patti Smith
6 January 1947:	Sandy Denny
8 January 1947:	David Bowie
24 January 1947:	Warren Zevon
30 January 1947:	Steve Marriott
28 February 1947:	Sandie Shaw
25 March 1947:	Elton John
2 April 1947:	Emmylou Harris
21 April 1947:	Iggy Pop
1 June 1947:	Ronnie Wood
24 June 1947:	Mick Fleetwood
12 July 1947:	Wilko Johnson
19 July 1947:	Brian May
20 July 1947:	Carlos Santana

22 July 1947:	Don Henley
27 September 1947:	Meat Loaf
30 September 1947:	Marc Bolan
6 October 1947:	Millie Small

Nik Cohn *(born 1946)*

A lot of rock writing is sloppy, self-indulgent, pseudo-intellectual bilge. Then there's this description by Nik Cohn of touring with the Who:

'You sleep in sunlight and soak in brandy for breakfast, Bloody Marys for elevenses, tequila for lunch; swallow uppers by the handful, downers by the tub, smoke and suck and sniff on whatever comes to hand ... Thus the tour is littered with numberless corpses. Roadies fall down elevator shafts, groupies suffocate in the shower. Promoters go bankrupt, security guards run amok with their nightsticks, the warm-up group blow themselves up. Journalists, almost always, are shipped home under sedation.'

Syd Barrett *(6 January 1946)*

With hindsight it's remarkable how quickly Pink Floyd's first frontman unravelled. After *The Piper at the Gates of Dawn* was released, Syd would appear to be in control for several weeks, and then suddenly he would snap like an overstretched rubber band. Once he kept his girlfriend locked in a room for three days, feeding her crackers under the door while she begged to be let out. Eventually some friends found her and released her, whereupon Syd locked himself in the same room for a week. As well as all the acid he was taking, Pamela Des Barres says that 'sycophantic friends would dose his drinks just to watch him shatter into interesting fragments.' At a gig in July 1967, Syd just stood on stage with his guitar dangling, unable to sing, play, even speak. In San Francisco he bought a pink Cadillac, and gave it away to a stranger a few days later. He bashed up another girlfriend with a mandolin. At one point he was tripping for three months solid. 'We staggered on thinking we couldn't manage without Syd,' said Nick Mason, 'so we put up with what can only be described as a fucking maniac.' Jonathon Green attempted to interview him for *Rolling Stone*. Syd spent most the time staring up into the corner of the room. 'Now look up there,' he said. 'Can you see the people on the ceiling?'

So Pink Floyd quietly replaced him in early 1968 with his old friend David Gilmour, who felt sufficiently abashed that he volunteered to help Syd make some solo recordings. Syd's instructions to his musicians could be gnomic. 'Perhaps we could make the middle darker and maybe the end a bit middle-afternoonish,' he said one day. 'At the moment it's too windy and icy.' In summer 1970 Roger Waters saw him in Harrods carrying two large plastic bags. On seeing Roger, Syd dropped the bags and fled. Roger looked inside the bags, to find they were full of sweets. In 1971 a second *Rolling Stone* writer came to interview him. Syd said he felt 'full of dust and guitars'.

My younger brother had a friend who liked acid. One day, when he was twenty, he had what was euphemistically called 'a bad trip', from which he never returned. He spent the next thirty years in a lunatic asylum before dying at the age of fifty. It's all such a diabolical waste.

David Gilmour *(6 March 1946)*

Some time in the early 1980s, David Gilmour bought Hook End Manor, a sixteenth-century Elizabethan house in rural Oxfordshire that boasted its own recording studio, built by a previous occupant, Ten Years After's Alvin Lee. Before he sold it on to the producers Clive Langer and Alan Winstanley (who later sold it to Trevor Horn), Gilmour kept Pink Floyd's giant inflatable pig in an outhouse.

Ray Dorset *(21 March 1946)*

Lead singer of Mungo Jerry and one of the very few mixed-race people in British pop in the early 1970s. When 'In the Summertime' was released, Ray was working in a laboratory for Timex and had to ask his boss for a day off in order to appear on *Top of the Pops*. Thanks to his exuberant performance, and the ferocious catchiness of the song, the single leapt straight to number one the following week.*

Al Green *(13 April 1946)*

Like so many future pop stars, little Al was something of a misfit as a child. He was a sensitive boy, 'the kid under the tree by himself'. And he was surrounded by macho males, his father and his brothers. 'His brothers were real manly,' said a friend of his. 'The kind of guys you don't want to be on the bad side of. Real tough guys with processed hair.'

His father Robert presented different problems. Al had a pet goat called Billy, which kept getting loose. Robert decided that both boy and goat needed to be taught a lesson. 'We were having dinner one night,' says Al, 'and I'm thinking, "This stew tastes good, not like anything I've ever tasted before."' Al asked his mother what kind of meat was in the stew. She wouldn't answer. In fact, no one said anything until Robert collapsed with laughter. 'At that moment I knew it was Billy I was eating ... I've never eaten goat since.'

---

* Thanks to Tim Cooper for this.

Noddy Holder *(15 June 1946)*

When Chuck Berry recorded 'My Ding-a-Ling' at the Locarno ballroom in Coventry in February 1972, Slade were supporting and Noddy Holder was in the audience, singing along with the rest of them. It's therefore his first ever performance on a number-one single.

Noddy Holder would often take the stage in a top hat, on which someone had glued an array of small circular mirrors. Stuart Maconie asked him if he still had the hat. Oh yes, said Noddy. He said he kept it on a shelf in the garage, between the half-empty tin of creosote and the Rawlplugs.*

My friend Jon Hotten used to know Noddy Holder's PR man, who told him that when Noddy had known him for long enough, he turned to him one day and said, 'You can call me Nod.'

Demis Roussos *(15 June 1946)*

On 14 June 1985, Roussos boarded TWA flight 847 from Athens to Rome. Unfortunately, so did two hijackers, who managed to smuggle a pistol and grenades through airport security. They demanded the release of seventeen members of Hezbollah and the Iraqi Islamic Daawa Party. The plane was diverted to Beirut, and from there to Algeria, and a US Navy petty officer was killed. Roussos spent five days on the plane, but got off lightly, because another forty or so passengers, mainly American, remained captive for another fortnight. Maybe he threatened to sing.

---

* Maconie also said that Noddy was one of the nicest people in show business he had ever met.

Keith Moon *(23 August 1946)*

His school report gave a small clue of what was to come. 'Retarded artistically. Idiotic in other respects,' wrote his art teacher. 'Great ability,' wrote his music teacher, 'but must guard against tendency to "show off".'

When the Who recorded 'Substitute', Keith was so out of it he forgot he'd played on it. As the band's manager Kit Lambert told Simon Napier-Bell, 'Later, he heard the record and presumed someone else must have been on drums. For weeks he was worried about being replaced.'

On 23 August 1967, Keith Moon turned twenty-one. The Who were touring the US for the first time, opening for Herman's Hermits, and the tour schedule meant that Moon could only celebrate his birthday the following day, at the Holiday Inn in Flint, Michigan. The management put up a 'Happy Birthday Keith' message on their roadside sign and the party began. Drugs were plentiful, girls were involved and clothes appear to have been optional. At some point between eleven and midnight, most of the hotel's fire extinguishers were emptied, and the lavatory in Moon's room appears to have exploded. To celebrate their wildest client, a drum company presented Moon with a giant cake, and as everyone gathered around to sing 'Happy Birthday', a naked girl jumped out of it. Instead of eating the cake, Moon thought it would be more fun to throw it at people, and the largest food fight in the Flint, Michigan, Holiday Inn's history now took place. The fight soon spilled out of the hotel ballroom into the lobby, and at around this time Moon seems to have lost the rest of his clothes. As he ran through the lobby completely naked, covered in birthday cake, the police arrived, and everyone legged it. Moon ran out of the hotel and, to avoid arrest, got into an unlocked Lincoln Continental. He released the handbrake, but before he could start the car it rolled back, crushing a fence and straight into the hotel pool, where it instantly sank. Moon managed to escape, but when he rose to the top of the pool he was surrounded by policemen pointing guns at him. Foolish to the point of insanity, Moon decided to make a run for it, but slipped on a piece of cake and crashed to the ground, knocking out one of his front teeth. The cops arrested him, but in an admirable demonstration of mercy stopped at an emergency dentist on the way to the jail to get his tooth fixed. The following morning, he was bailed out by his manager and put on a plane to Philadelphia for the next gig.

Keith Moon met Oliver Reed when they were filming *Tommy* in 1974. Although Reed already had something of a reputation as a hellraiser, he told Moon's biographer that 'Keith showed me the way to insanity'. The following year, Reed was at a film premiere in Hollywood when suddenly he was hit in the face by a lemon curd pie. As he wiped the sludge from his eyes, a man walked up and handed him a card. 'Pie in the Face International,' said the card. 'You have been selected by Mr Keith Moon to become a member.'

Unlike his fellow bandmates and, indeed, most sane people, Moon had no off switch. One of his favourite pranks was to drive through a sleepy English village with a Tannoy attached to the roof of his car, and announce to locals that their village was about to be attacked by poisonous snakes, or overwhelmed by a tidal wave.*

As Pamela Des Barres wrote, 'Nothing seemed to quell the fact that he was lonely and mad.'

Keith Moon died of an overdose of a drug prescribed to him to help him come off alcohol. He washed it down with a bottle of champagne laced with cocaine.

---

* Except that, according to David Hepworth, Keith Moon couldn't drive. So is this true? Is any of it?

Barry Gibb *(1 September 1946),* **Robin and Maurice Gibb** *(22 December 1949)*

The Bee Gees were not involved in *Saturday Night Fever* until a very late stage. John Travolta says that during filming, he was dancing to Stevie Wonder and Boz Scaggs. When they got the call, the brothers Gibb hotfooted it to a château in France, where they wrote and recorded demos for four new songs – 'Stayin' Alive', 'Night Fever', 'How Deep Is Your Love' and 'More Than A Woman' – in little more than a weekend. Their manager Robert Stigwood and Bill Oakes from the record company came to hear the demos. 'They flipped out and said these will be great,' said Barry Gibb. 'We still had no concept of the movie, except some kind of rough script that they'd brought with them ... You've got to remember, we were fairly dead in the water at that point. The Bee Gees' sound was basically tired. We needed something new. We felt, "Oh Jeez, that's it. That's our life span." Like most groups in the late sixties. So we had to find something. We didn't know what was going to happen.'

Freddie Mercury *(5 September 1946)*

In the early days of Queen, Freddie met a woman called Mary Austin in Biba, and they lived together for the next seven years. Eventually his unequivocal gayness asserted itself and the relationship came to a natural end, but Freddie and Mary remained close for the rest of his life. He bought her a flat round the corner from his, and when he lay dying, it was Mary who maintained a bedside vigil, and who told his parents of Freddie's death.*

At Live Aid, Elton John had an area backstage reserved for all

---

* His parents had no idea he was gay. He had never told them.

the acts who were playing. Freddie came over after Queen had stolen the show.

'Freddie, nobody should go on after you. You were magnificent,' said Elton.

'You're absolutely right, darling, we were. We killed them,' said Freddie. 'You, on the other hand, dear – you looked like the fucking Queen Mother when you were on stage. Where did you get that absolutely awful hat?'

Elton went to see Freddie in his final days. 'He was hilarious. Even when he was dying, he was exactly the same. He was lying in bed, too weak to stand, losing his sight, going, "Have you heard Mrs Bowie's new album, darling? What does she think she's doing?"'

Gram Parsons *(5 November 1946)*

Remarkably, Gram was his real name – short for Ingram, his second forename. First name: Cecil.

Simon Bates *(17 December 1946)*

For a few years in the late 1980s I wrote a pop music column for the *Daily Mail*, taking the piss out of pop stars for money. This caught the attention of Simon Bates, a blow-dried old turd who, despite being over forty, had the prestigious weekday mid-morning slot on wonderful Radio 1. Bates hated me. 'What rock has he crawled out from under?' he shouted pompously. His point was that, as neither he nor anyone else had heard of me, I had no right to be making jokes about his personal friends Bono, Sting and little Phil Collins. Needless to say, his ceaseless fury made me very popular with my bosses at the *Mail*, who immediately gave me a pay rise.

While this was going on, I went to a *Private Eye* lunch, where I met John Walters, John Peel's garrulous producer. Walters told me a story. Peel had gone into the Radio 1 offices to meet an old friend of his, an Austrian psychoanalyst who was in the country for a few days. The psychoanalyst showed up and Peel said, Before we go for lunch, would you like a quick tour of the studios? Why not, said the loony doctor, and the pair of them wandered around the drab corridors of Egton House. At which point they bumped into Simon Bates, who stopped for a quick chat with Peel. After the usual pleasantries Bates went on his way. The psychoanalyst, meanwhile, had gone white.

'What's wrong?' asked Peel.

'That man,' said the psychoanalyst. 'Do you work with him?'

'Yes,' said Peel. 'In a manner of speaking.'

'That,' said the psychoanalyst, 'is the most dangerous man I have ever met.'

Marianne Faithfull *(29 December 1946)*

Amazingly beautiful, photogenic girl singer of the late 1960s, whose mother was a descendant of the original masochist (Leopold, Baron von Sacher-Masoch, author of *Venus in Furs*), while her paternal grandfather was an eccentric sexologist who invented a device called the Frigidity Machine. She turned down Roy Orbison, aborted a child conceived with Gene Pitney and resisted the attentions of Bob Dylan, who wrote a poem for her. Of the Rolling Stones she said, 'I slept with three and then I decided the lead singer was the best bet.' Mick Jagger seduced her in a Bristol hotel after the pair of them had seen Roman Polanski's *Repulsion* on acid. They split in 1970, at the start of her heroin decade. Ten years later Marianne re-emerged, clean-ish, with a singing voice so ruined she made Tom Waits sound like Judy Collins. Who would have bet in 1965, when she released 'As Tears Go By', that she would enjoy a fifty-five-year musical career? 'She walked through the whole thing on her own terms,' said Nick Cave's confrère Warren Ellis, who was born in the year of that first hit. 'I've got all the stories,' said Faithfull herself with a knowing grin.

Patti Smith *(30 December 1946)*

In 1975 Viv Albertine is reading the *NME* when she sees a photo of Patti Smith, of whom she has never heard. It's the cover of Smith's forthcoming album *Horses*. 'I have never seen a girl who looks like this,' she says in her memoir. 'She is my soul made visible, all the things I hide deep inside of myself that can't come out.' On the day *Horses* is released, Viv cuts college to go down to HMV Records in Oxford Street. 'I'm so excited I feel sick.' She's also half-dreading it in case the music doesn't live up to the boldness of the cover.

When she arrives she sees Mick Jones, later of the Clash, loitering outside the shop. She had met him the previous year.

'What are you doing here?' she asks.

'Getting the Patti Smith record,' he replies.

She races home and puts the record on. 'It hurls through stream of consciousness, careers through poetry and dissolves into sex . . . She's a private person who dares to let go in front of everyone, puts herself out there and risks falling flat on her face . . . Listening to *Horses* unlocks an idea for me – girls' sexuality can be on their own terms, for their own pleasure or creative work, not just for exploitation or to get a man . . . If I can take a quarter or even an eighth of what she has and not give a shit about making a fool of myself, maybe I can still do something with my life.'

Sandy Denny *(6 January 1947)*

'There's an authority to her singing, an almost regal detachment,' writes Tracey Thorn. 'She is all dynamic range and power – almost as though her voice is plugged directly into a volume pedal. Even at her most gentle there is an extraordinary sense of control, so that her pitch and vibrato are sure and steady even when she's singing very softly – and then she can ramp up the volume quite suddenly and dramatically.'

Clinton Heylin, in his biography *No More Sad Refrains*, quotes her as saying, 'I do appreciate being slightly well known, because I've got a bit of an ego. But I never want to reach the top. It's such a long way down.'

David Bowie *(8 January 1947)*

David Bowie was the first person to write English lyrics to the French tune that eventually became Frank Sinatra's global megahit 'My Way'. Claude François had written and performed the original, called 'Comme D'Habitude', which means 'As Usual'.* Bowie was, at the time, a jobbing songwriter working in Denmark Street, and his version was called 'Even a Fool Learns to Love'. He even recorded it, but Sinatra rejected it and Paul Anka rewrote it as 'My Way'. But Bowie had his revenge. 'Life on Mars?' was written as a gentle pastiche of Sinatra's song style, and particularly 'My Way'.

In 1977 Bowie duetted with Marc Bolan on TV a week before his death, and with Bing Crosby a month before his.

In 1982 Talking Heads were playing the Montreux Jazz Festival and Bowie, who lived near by, knocked on their dressing-room door before the gig. Chris Frantz, their drummer, tells the story in his autobiography *Remain in Love*: 'There was a lovely assortment of backstage munchies on the table and Bowie zeroed in on

---

* Claude François was a successful and dashingly handsome French pop star who had many hits in the 1960s and 1970s and squired all the local lovelies. In March 1978 he was having a shower in his Paris apartment when he noticed that the light fixture wasn't straight on the wall. He tried to straighten it, forgot he was having a shower at the time, and was electrocuted.

that. He asked politely, "Are you going to be eating those nuts?"
I said, "Please, help yourself." He filled up one big pocket of his
jacket with nuts. Then he asked, "How about those cheeses? Are
you going to be eating those nice cheeses?" Again, I said, "Please,
help yourself." Bowie neatly wrapped up most of the cheeses in
a napkin and put them in his other pocket. Then he said, "Well,
have a great show. Break a leg." And with that he was off. [David]
Byrne looked burnt.'

Once, on stage in Sunderland, Bowie yelled to the audience,
'Hello, Newcastle!'*

Warren Zevon *(24 January 1947)*

I have always liked Hunter S. Thompson's 2001 description of his
old friend and fellow raiser-of-hell: 'Warren Zevon is a poet. He
has written more classics than any other musician of our time, with
the possible exception of Bob Dylan. He is also a crack shot with a
.44 Magnum and an expert on lacrosse . . . Warren is a profoundly
mysterious man and I have learned not to argue with him, about
hockey or anything else. He is a dangerous drinker and a whole
different person when he's afraid.'

Sandie Shaw *(26 February 1947)*

The former Sandra Goodrich became a star in her teens and always
sang in bare feet. As she told Simon Napier-Bell, 'I was so short-
sighted I couldn't see the edge of the stage without my glasses. So

---

* Kanye West greeted an audience in Sacramento with 'Hello, Seattle!' Usher
was in Maidstone when he shouted 'Hello, Manchester!' Patti Smith forgot the
words halfway through singing 'A Hard Rain's A-Gonna Fall' at Bob Dylan's
Nobel Prize for Literature ceremony. Mick Jagger forgot he had written
seventy-five thousand words of an autobiography in the early 1980s. Ozzy
Osbourne claims to have completely forgotten the 1990s.

I took off my shoes. That way, while I was looking at the audience, I could feel the edge of the stage with my toes.'

Sandie Shaw was by far the most successful British girl singer in Europe in the 1960s, mainly because she recorded songs in French, German, Spanish, Italian and Portuguese. Some of her best songs she only released in those countries.

Elton John *(25 March 1947)*

At Live Aid in July 1985, Elton John put on his pinny, brandished some tongs and fired up the backstage barbecue of steak and sausages. He added a veggie burger for his old friend Freddie Mercury.

Most pop stars sign into hotels under pseudonyms, mainly to deter fans from following them and sleeping outside their door. Elton John's pseudonyms may be the best, though. They include Sir Humphrey Handbag, Lilian Lollipop, Lord Choc Ice, Sir Tarquin Budgerigar, Bobo Latrine Jr, Binky Poodleclip, Chlamydia Schiffer and the Marquis of Minge. One the person on reception wouldn't use was Fanny Beaver Snatchclit. Of one occasion, his mother said, 'I can't believe you asked me to ring and ask for Sir Horace Pussy.'*

In October 2019 the *Guardian* asked various celebrities to ask Sir Elton a question, and because he always answered so candidly, it was one of the most fascinating pieces you could hope to read. 'The challenges I had were my shyness and my sexuality,' he said in answer to a Lewis Hamilton question. Bob Dylan asked him, 'In the song "Tiny Dancer", did you work your way up to the cathartic chorus gradually, spontaneously, or did you have it thought out from the start?' 'This is a very good question,' said Elton, as you would say to any question Bob Dylan had asked. 'Bernie's lyric

---

* Eric Clapton has used Mr W. B. Albion. Paul McCartney used to use Paul Ramon, which is where the Ramones got their name from.

took such a long time to get to the chorus, I thought, "Fuck, the chorus had better be something special when it finally arrives."'

The principal of the Royal Academy of Music, where the young Reg Dwight studied, asked him, 'If you had your time again, would you still go through it?' 'In a heartbeat,' said Elton. 'I'd advise anyone to get formal training, because it teaches you the rudiments – chord structure, melody. It introduces you to music that's beautiful and miles away from what you might do. It fills your mind with options.'

When Elton and David Furnish were married, Eminem bought them matching cock rings as a wedding present.

Iggy Pop *(21 April 1947)*

It's possible that there exist unschooled natives in the dense jungles of Papua New Guinea, and Japanese soldiers still fighting World War Two, who don't know that Iggy Pop has a ginormous penis. But, personally, I doubt it.

One of his live shows was witnessed by Jim Kerr of Simple Minds. 'At the end of the show, of course, he pulled out his penis. He'd been singing about it the whole night and I was just thinking, "Let's see it." And there it was.'

'Thirteen inches long,' said Danny Sugarman, who used to manage Iggy, 'and his proudest possession.'

In his autobiography *I Need More, I Need More*, Iggy admits to a more modest 11 inches, when erect.

The strange thing is that Iggy Pop is only 5 feet 6½ inches tall, and as skinny as a French bean. It must be about a fifth of his body weight.

Pete Ham *(24 April 1947)* and Tom Evans (5 June 1947)

The creative duo at the heart of power-poppers Badfinger, a formidably accomplished and unlucky British group of the late 1960s and early 1970s. Badfinger were the first band signed to Apple Records, and Paul McCartney wrote and produced their first single, 'Come and Get It', which reached number four in 1970. Ham and Evans co-wrote 'Without You', a vast global hit for Harry Nilsson the following year, and they were managed by the father of Lewis Collins, who later played Bodie on *The Professionals*. But success was short-lived, Apple Records started to crumble, poor decisions were made and their US manager, Stan Polley, was a crook who ran off with their money. In 1975, Ham hanged himself, three days before his twenty-eighth birthday. He left a message that said, 'Stan Polley is a soulless bastard.' Badfinger split up, re-formed, split up again, made more poor management decisions and toured in two separate bands, and in 1983, after an argument over royalties, Evans, aged thirty-six, hanged himself in his garden. Pop can be a brutal business, and its casualties are everywhere.

Cynthia Plaster Caster *(24 May 1947)*

Born Cynthia Albritton, Cynthia Plaster Caster is an American artist and 'recovering groupie' who for many years created plaster casts of famous musicians' erect penises. Each artwork was numbered. In 2001 a film documentary, *Plaster Caster*, was made about her, and she also contributed to the 2005 BBC documentary *My Penis and I.* In 2010 she ran unsuccessfully for the mayoralty of Chicago, on the Hard Party ticket.

Some of her clients include: Jimi Hendrix (0004), Wayne Kramer of the MC5 (0011), Anthony Newley (0016), session guitarist Harvey Mandel (0020), Zal Yanovsky of the Lovin' Spoonful (0028), Jello Biafra of the Dead Kennedys (0047) and Richard

Lloyd, Television's second guitarist (0051). For some reason there are a lot of drummers in the list. The most intriguing are the two 'mould failures', Eric Burdon (0008) and Pete Shelley (0048), from whose penises no cast was made. In 2000 she started also casting women's breasts, as an egalitarian move.

Wilko Johnson *(12 July 1947)*

The producers of *Game of Thrones* saw a documentary about the former Dr Feelgood guitarist and were impressed by his 'cold-eyed, thousand-yard stare'. So they hired him for the role of Ser Ilyn Payne, a mute executioner with a 'piercing, unsettling glare', without auditioning anyone else. 'He has not said much these last twenty years since the King had his tongue ripped out,' explained another character in the show. David Hepworth points out that, in real life, 'Wilko Johnson is literally the most talkative man in rock and roll.'

Brian May *(19 July 1947)*

The Queen guitarist likes to use an old sixpence as a plectrum, and told *Premier Guitar* magazine he is particularly devoted to pre-1956 coins. 'I can even feel the serrations,' he said. 'I can feel it in my fingers.' He described the sixpence sound as 'very clean, very nice – and if you angle it like this, to varying degrees, it gives you this kind of splutter, which in combination with the heel of the hand gives you almost the same kind of articulation as a human voice'. He has a thousand such coins. Other famous guitarists who use coins as plectrums include ZZ Top's Billy Gibbons, who favours the Mexican peso.

Don Henley *(22 July 1947)*

The lead singer of Eagles (never 'the' Eagles) is thought to have been the first person to use the phrase 'Love 'em and Lear 'em', bringing together, in a single pithy epithet, matters of the heart and executive jets. His former girlfriend Stevie Nicks said, 'It's something he would have said. He once sent a little cranberry-red Lear jet to pick me up from a Fleetwood Mac gig somewhere and fly me to New York.' Henley is thought to have first said this in or around 1977. The release a year later of fellow Eagle Joe Walsh's single 'Life's Been Good', about an egomaniacal rock star, can be no coincidence.

Linda Thompson *(23 August 1947)*

English folk singer, née Pettifer, former wife and collaborator of Richard Thompson, and mother of Teddy and Kamila Thompson. (They all recorded an album together in 2014, called *Family*, credited just to 'Thompson'.) Linda stopped singing in the early 1980s, afflicted by a vocal disorder called dysphonia, which everyone assumed was a psychological response to her break-up from her husband. Not true, it turns out. 'Linda Ronstadt was the first one who said to me, Don't listen to the doctors when they tell you it's all psychological,' Linda told Tracey Thorn. 'And now, NOW they have found out that it is akin to Parkinson's. So now, after all these years, I'm seeing a neurologist and having a MRI scan.'

Thorn talks of 'the plangent, weary resilience of that lovely, unadorned voice', which captures it perfectly. Happily, Linda can sing a little these days and she has recorded three very good albums, mostly in collaboration with son Teddy. Funnily enough, a friend of mine knew Teddy, who was over from the States one summer and fancied playing a bit of cricket for a team bad enough

to include him. As it happens I run such a team, and so it came
to pass that one day I sat outside a pub not far from Charlton-on-
Otmoor in Oxfordshire with the rest of my team, plus Teddy, his
mother and her second husband, who had come along to watch.
They were all delightful and unstarry and didn't want to talk about
music at all.

Meat Loaf *(27 September 1947)*

Mat Snow says the shortest interview he has ever heard of was
when a journalist (unnamed) asked Mr Loaf, as his first question,
'Is it glandular?'

Marc Bolan *(30 September 1947)*

Lead singer and primary songwriter of T. Rex and glam rock pioneer, who was the first man (in March 1971) to appear on *Top of
the Pops* wearing satin, glitter and a feather boa. Later that year
his song 'Jeepster' had to settle for being the Christmas number
two, kept off the top spot by Benny Hill's dairy fable 'Ernie (The
Fastest Milkman in the West)'.* Nick Coleman has described his
voice as a 'fey gurgle'.

   In September 1977, Bolan was killed in a car crash in Barnes.
The crash site has become a shrine to his memory. In 2013 it was
featured in the BBC Four series *Pagans and Pilgrims: Britain's
Holiest Places*. The site is owned and maintained by the T. Rex
Action Group.

---

* In 2006 David Cameron chose 'Ernie (The Fastest Milkman in the West)' as
one of his Desert Island Discs.

Greg Lake *(10 November 1947)*

Lead singer, guitarist and bassist from prog rock brontosauruses Emerson, Lake and Palmer, whose woeful albums were proudly brandished as status symbols by hairy people I knew at school. Lake always played concerts standing on a large Persian rug ('the size of Lincolnshire', according to Stuart Maconie). This was rumoured to have cost £2000, which was the average annual wage for men in 1972. In 2019 a rather battered and discoloured rug was sold by Lake's estate through the American auction house Julien's. They estimated it would sell for between $8000 and $10,000. The winning bid was $34,375.

Gregg Allman *(8 December 1947)*

Younger and better-looking of the Allman brothers, probably best known for marrying Cher in 1975. She decided to divorce him just two years later after an awards dinner, when he passed out face-first into a plate of spaghetti.

David Crosby also once passed out face-first into a plate of spaghetti, while dining with his friend Cass Elliot of the Mamas and the Papas. They had been up for three days on psychedelics. Eliott left him there without paying the bill.

Irving Azoff *(12 December 1947)*

Another manager famed for his tantrums and poor behaviour, who ended up managing (at various times) Dan Fogelberg, Steely Dan, Don Henley, Boz Scaggs, Warren Zevon, Jackson Browne, Stevie Nicks, Guns N' Roses, Billy Corgan and Nicky Minaj. Azoff stood 5 feet 3 inches and even his friends called him the Poison Dwarf. Frederic Dannen said he was 'one of the most loathed men in the music business'. Azoff once tore a television from the wall of a hotel and threatened to hurl it through the window unless the staff silenced building workers down below. At a posh Beverly Hills restaurant in 1974, Azoff found the service a little slow, so he set his menu on fire. A former friend of his, now a mortal enemy – this was a common narrative to his relationships – was celebrating his fortieth birthday, and Azoff wasn't invited. Azoff sent round a cardboard box with a live boa constrictor inside it.

As one blogger wrote, 'It's Irving's world. We just play in it.'

Pop Star Encounters

In 1990 my younger brother was married, and I went to his combined stag-and-hen night. We're very different people and I don't really know his friends, so it was a case of grabbing a bottle of beer and looking for someone to chat with. I fell into conversation with this lovely fellow, very quiet, unassuming, modest, rather small, no one you'd ever notice, and we got on famously. What do you do? I asked. I'm a musician, he said, but I also take a lot of photographs. I said I'm a writer and we talked happily about life in the arts, making ends meet, the freedom from bosses and office life, all that sort of stuff. After forty minutes or so he said he had to go, and I realised I hadn't asked his name. Bryan Adams, he said.

I was born in 1960 and most of my friends over the years have been around the same age. Many of us live in London, work in similar kinds of worlds and are quite sociable, and it was a while before I realised that surprisingly many of my male friends each had a rock star acquaintance or even a really good rock star friend. My Glaswegian friend and quizmate George knows Feargal Sharkey, who I met once in a pub in East Finchley. No one recognised him, even though he looked *extraordinarily* like Feargal Sharkey. My writer friend David knows Howard Devoto of Buzzcocks and Magazine, and invited me round to dinner to meet him. He was, again, a small, unassuming, terribly friendly and clearly highly intelligent man, then working as a librarian. When my friend Russell got an MBE he had a lunch to celebrate and I sat next to Hugh Cornwell. You try your hardest to be cool in these situations, but there is a part of me, and I think almost everyone, that remains the most abject teenage fan and worshipper, and although they are people just like you and me, on another level they are not. They remain rock stars, even if they were actually only rock stars for a short time thirty years ago.

So one day I had an idea. I put something up on Facebook asking my friends there if they had had any strange encounters with rock stars at any time in their life. The thread went bonkers. It wasn't just me, then. It was pretty much everyone.

'In 1977 I was at the Marquee with a friend who was in a punk band from Plaistow called the Tickets. He introduced me to Paul Weller, saying, "Paul, this is Stella. She wants to marry you so she can be called Stella Weller." With a look of disdain, he turned aside. Bruce Foxton bought me a consolatory pint.' S.K.

'While dining in a smart Hampstead restaurant, my companion remarked that George Michael appeared to be dining near the door. Confirming this with a backward glance, in a world-weary voice I replied, "Ah, George, let's chat to him when we leave." She seemed suitably impressed that I knew him (even though I obviously didn't). On the way out I immediately established an easy rapport with my comment, "Thank you for the music." To which I added, as the great man took my extended hand, "And we all had a laugh when you got stoned and put your car through a shop window." George chuckled and shook my hand, while his dinner companion, a sultry-looking geezer, gave me a death stare.' F.P.

'When I was on my gap year I climbed into the garden of Jimmy Page's Tudor mansion at Plumpton, Sussex, in the hope of hearing some mean guitar licks. He wasn't in.' N.N.

'Backstage with Pixies. Kim was knitting.' S.H.

'I nearly got run over by Eric Clapton in the early 90s, outside UCL. I stepped into the road not looking where I was going, and his car screeched to a halt before hitting me. Being an obstreperous student at the time I was about to the thump the bonnet when I realised there was a very annoyed guitar hero at the wheel . . . ' A.M.

'When I edited Wilko Johnson's book, he left a message on my phone asking if I thought he didn't know what a semi-fucking-colon was. Well, he was an English teacher in a previous life. A friend of mine was taught by him. He said he was brilliant, if a bit menacing.' R.B.

'I met Robert Plant on a train platform at Birmingham International station in 1989. I was returning from my first term at university, he was waiting to meet someone. I got off the train, put down my guitar and amplifier, looked up and there he was. Big hair (blond tinges), leather jacket, full-on rock star look. The words "I've got the same birthday as you" came out of my mouth. With a complete absence of "rock star", he broke into a broad smile and said, "Oh, have you, loike? Well, happy birthday for next August the twentieth." I replied, "And you", picked up my stuff and walked off. It was several minutes before I realised I'd left my tape deck and speakers on the train.' M.M.

'My then girlfriend met David Gilmour at a party and asked him what he did. "Um, I'm in music, I suppose." "Oh! Opera?"' N.L.

'My gynae was once Hank Wangford. But I suspect his side of the story is more interesting than mine.' A.B.

'Yes, mine too!' P.T.A.

'YES ME TOO!' G.B.

'A guy I knew looked remarkably like Kevin Godley of 10cc. One day he was walking through Soho with someone he wanted to impress, and Paul McCartney waved to him across the street (in error, obvs). My friend was delighted.' J.M.

'I once went dry-slope skiing with one of the blokes out of Climie Fisher. Even I don't find this interesting.' R.W.

'I chatted to the Red Hot Chili Peppers in Pizzaland on Oxford Street in about 1986. I had no idea who they were or why London's yoot kept coming in and asking them to autograph their skateboards, but they were very nice.' M.W.

'A bit drunk in the kitchen at a friend-of-a-friend's party in Clapham in the mid-1980s, I passed a bottle of wine to some bloke, and told him, "Hey, you look just like Neil Arthur, the singer out of that electronic band, Blancmange." "Yes, I get that a lot," he replied, "mainly because I am Neil Arthur, the singer out of that electronic band, Blancmange." We shared a couple more bottles, and he was a very affable chap.' G.P.

'I was in Miami Beach in the early 1990s with my dear friend Della. We were strolling down the beach when I spotted a young man I recognised. I said "Hi" and we started chatting. I mentioned that I'd seen him in the Fridge nightclub in Brixton. "Yes," he said, "I go there", so Della said, "Do you work behind the bar?" He said, "No, I'm in Take That." Della let out a mini scream. "Come and meet the lads," said he. We walked over to where the other members of the band were sitting, and we had a nice chat. Jason Orange actually offered me a piece of his orange. They told us where they were playing later, so we arranged to go and see them. They were trying to break into the US market. They were all really friendly and lovely. We said our goodbyes and carried on walking up the beach, when we suddenly remembered we were topless. Take That have seen my boobs.' G.B.

'I almost slept with Freddie Mercury in the Munich Hilton in 1979. But my cousin wouldn't let me, saying, "What would I tell your mother?" Now she says balefully, "I saved your life."' R.Y.

'I met Steve Diggle at a party and was charmed by him. After a while he said, "Pete Shelley's over there, do you want to say hi?" and I said, "No, I don't think I could handle it."' N.L.

'My former employer sponsored a client cricket reception/ dinner at the Café Royal in 2001. Ian Botham introduced me to Eric Clapton, who muttered something inaudible and shuffled off. "But isn't he surprisingly small?" I said. Botham remarked that many others said the same.' F.P.

'I was travelling with my friend to his workshop when he said, "Someone from U2 is coming to see my work." I said, "Which one?" He didn't know, he just knew it wasn't Bono. When we got there, this guy who looked like a rock star was there and we chatted to him and he had a look around, and we never had a clue who he was." W.J.

'Poly Styrene jumped fully clothed into the swimming pool at our small rural Welsh comprehensive school.' M.A.

'It was, if I recollect, just before Christmas 2009 and BBC Four had recently run an excellent series on the phenomenon known as progressive rock, rife with footage of men in steeple hats hunched over banks of keyboards and bearded types warbling hobbity tosh above a maelstrom of complex time signatures. Bumping into David Gilmour at a party, I enquired: what did he make of it all? Gilmour looked unexpectedly cross. "I've got two things to say," he said. "One, the Floyd were never prog. Two, it was all Emerson, Lake and Palmer's fault." After which he stalked off.' D.T.

'Loved interviewing pop/rock stars. I remember taking a flight very early one morning with Cliff Richard to some island in Denmark, where he was giving a concert. He was utterly charming – sat next to me on the plane, plonked me in his dressing room and took me out to dinner in the early hours. There was the usual fencing over questions about girlfriends, both of us knowing it had to be done for the publication in question. Best moment? When he turned to me in some god-forsaken airport lounge and asked a million eager questions about which face cream he should use.' C.H.

The Records That Time Forgot

Bee Gees: 'Spirits (Having Flown)'

In a book already replete with embarrassing confessions, I have
another one for you now: I have always loved the Bee Gees. And
not the fashionable early part of their career, but their disco stuff
onwards. For me, 'Stayin' Alive' is one of the greatest of all records
by anyone, and it sparked off what Neil Tennant has called their
imperial phase, when they really could do no wrong. After that
ended abruptly in 1981, they recorded many more albums without noticeably troubling the charts, but not one of those albums
is entirely without interest. Listen to their last recording (before
Maurice died of cancer), 2001's *This Is Where I Came In*, which is
baggy, overlong and often mediocre, and has one of the best songs
they ever wrote, 'Sacred Trust'. It was covered abjectly by some
winners of an ITV talent show, who reached number two with
it, but the Brothers Gibb's original version is a wonder you have
almost certainly never heard before.

And yet, despite their record sales and remarkable melodic gift,
no one takes them remotely seriously and few music fans would
admit publicly to enjoying their music. I have often wondered
why, until I read what Barry Gibb once said, while researching
this book:

'We never completely do a song just to please ourselves. We bring everybody we can into the studio, even the receptionist, so that we can get their opinions. We put about 30 per cent of what we consider to be art into our records, and about 70 per cent of it is writing for the public.'

If there's one thing a serious music fan doesn't like, it's groups who so clearly make commercial success their main priority. Except, isn't that what they all do anyway? A group like Manic Street Preachers pretend to be great artists, but listen to their records and you can always hear bits filched from other records that did well in the charts. They are brilliant magpies, and the Bee Gees were too. One of their albums, 1991's *High Civilisation*, is a straight rip-off of Prince: they even brought his engineer along for the ride. Later on they had an Enya fixation, and on almost every album after their hit with Diana Ross, 'Chain Reaction', there's a cod-Motown song with a four-to-the-floor beat. Done it before, it might work again.

There are only a couple of exceptions to this, and they occur during the aforementioned imperial phase. One is a song that Barry wrote for his brother Andy in 1977 or 1978, 'An Everlasting Love'. What a tune! It goes this way, it goes that way, and it's perfect in conception and execution. I can't believe Barry had to work at that, and I can't believe that he asked the receptionist his or her opinion about it. I imagine it came to him fully formed and he just wrote it down. The second is the title track of their first post-*Saturday Night Fever* album, *Spirits Having Flown*. The rest of the album is a little forced and over-polished, but this is completely perfect, a light Caribbean shuffle with an extraordinary melody that sounds like nothing else they, or anyone else, ever recorded. Neither of these songs were 30 per cent art; they were 100 per cent art. If only the rest of their career had been too. If the Bee Gees hadn't been so obsessed with selling records, I have a funny feeling they might have sold more records, whatever the receptionist might have said.

Quiz 2

1. The album version uses the name Coca-Cola and the single uses 'cherry cola' instead, to avoid a BBC ban. Who flew from Minneapolis to London just to sing the words 'cherry cola'?
2. Which former member of Buck's Fizz stood in the constituency of Kensington in the 2019 general election on behalf of the Brexit Party? She polled 384 votes and came fifth.
3. Between December 1964 and March 1965, who was a touring member of the Beach Boys, filling in for Brian Wilson, playing bass guitar and singing falsetto harmonies? He died in 2017, aged eighty-one.
4. Is it pronounced Lou-ee Armstrong, or Lou-iss Armstrong, according to the man himself?
5. The name of which female pop star is an anagram of PRESBYTERIANS?
6. The name of which American jazz pianist is an anagram of WATERFALLS?
7. The name of which guitarist and singer is an anagram of NARCOLEPTIC?
8. 'Who is the only winner of a Nobel Prize who has also won an Oscar?' For many years the answer to

this was George Bernard Shaw, but recently he has been joined by someone else who has also done both. Who?

9. The Arizona metal band Okilly Dokilly, whose debut album was entitled *Howdilly Doodilly*, claim to have been inspired by which character from *The Simpsons*?

10. When Barry Gibb of the Bee Gees became Sir Barry in the 2018 New Year's Honours List, the same three-word punning headline appeared in the *Daily Mail*, the *Daily Mirror*, the *Daily Star* and the *Sun* the following day. What was that headline?

Answers on page 247.

Answers to Quiz 1

1. James Blunt
2. Paul McCartney
3. The eighth
4. Named after instrumentalists rather than the singer
5. The United Kingdom
6. Stevie Wonder (for *Innervisions*, *Fulfillingness' First Finale* and *Songs in the Key of Life*)
7. Adele (*19*, *21* and *25*)
8. All are in 3/4 time
9. ABBA
10. 'We Built This City on Rock 'n' Roll' (as recorded by Starship)

1948–1950

Notable Births

4 February 1948:	Alice Cooper
12 March 1948:	James Taylor
26 March 1948:	Steven Tyler
12 May 1948:	Steve Winwood
15 May 1948:	Brian Eno
26 May 1948:	Stevie Nicks
31 May 1948:	John Bonham
20 August 1948:	Robert Plant
11 September 1948:	John Martyn
26 September 1948:	Olivia Newton-John
3 November 1948:	Lulu
6 November 1948:	Glenn Frey
3 December 1948:	Ozzy Osbourne
31 December 1948:	Donna Summer
9 May 1949:	Billy Joel
20 June 1949:	Lionel Richie
12 August 1949:	Mark Knopfler
20 August 1949:	Phil Lynott
23 September 1949:	Bruce Springsteen
22 December 1949:	Maurice Gibb, Robin Gibb
13 February 1950:	Peter Gabriel
2 March 1950:	Karen Carpenter
5 April 1950:	Agnetha Fältskog
13 May 1950:	Stevie Wonder
22 May 1950:	Bernie Taupin
14 September 1950:	Paul Kossoff
20 October 1950:	Tom Petty
9 December 1950:	Joan Armatrading

Alice Cooper *(4 February 1948)*

Alice Cooper was originally the name of the band, but everyone thought it was the pseudonym of lead singer Vince Furnier, and after a while he stopped arguing.

Frank Zappa saw the band perform in Los Angeles in the late 1960s when no one had heard of them. 'Everybody in the audience was on acid, of course, grooving on peace and love,' said Cooper, 'and then all of a sudden you hear this DA-NA-NAA-NAAA ... We scared the hell out of these people. That audience couldn't get out of the room fast enough. It was like somebody yelled "FIRE!" There were three people left standing: Frank Zappa, my manager Shep Gordon and one of [celebrated groupies] the GTOs. Frank said, "Anybody that can clear a room that quick, I've got to sign."' Alice Cooper ended up recording their first two albums for Zappa's various labels.

Cooper (the man) quickly became notorious for what became known as 'the chicken incident'. He says he thought 'chickens have wings, so they must be able to fly'. So he threw a live chicken into the audience, expecting it to soar into the heavens. As it was, the audience ripped it limb from limb. Shortly afterwards, Zappa rang him up and asked if the rumour was true, that Cooper had ripped the head off a live chicken and drunk its blood on stage. Cooper said no. 'Well, whatever you do, don't tell anyone you didn't do it,' was Zappa's sage response.

Livestock feature prominently in the Alice Cooper mythology. Since 1971 Cooper has frequently shared the stage with a large snake, usually a boa constrictor. The first was Kachina, who disappeared down a toilet drain in Tennessee and was never seen again. She was followed by Yvonne, Eva Marie Snake, Angel, Veronica, Mistress and Lady Macbeth. Since 2000 Cooper has generally made use of borrowed local snakes, which obviously saves on the cost of the live white mice they like to eat. One of the roadies has usually been deputed to look after the snake of the moment, and there is a custom-made metal case with a built-in heating pad for the snake to travel in between gigs.

The snakes actually caused very few problems for anyone, until a 1998 show at the House of Blues in Los Angeles, when the reptile of the moment did an enormous dump on the stage. 'It smelled so bad I was gagging,' said Cooper. 'I never expected there to be eight piles the size of a Doberman Pinscher, and this thing just kept going and going. Johnny Rotten was in the audience, and he said, "God, do you do that every night?" And I said, "Yeah, I know just where to touch the snake." He was very impressed.'

Steven Tyler *(26 March 1948)*

Sofa-lipped lead singer of Aerosmith these past fifty years, and father of actress Liv Tyler, who thought that Todd Rundgren was her father until she met Steven at the age of ten or eleven and noticed the physical similarities (lips like sofas). On their first Japanese tour, Aerosmith's promoter put turkey roll on the buffet table. 'I explicitly said "No turkey roll"!' screamed Tyler. The band went bananas and trashed the backstage area in a frenzy of heavy metal destruction.

In their druggy days – the 1970s and 1980s – Aerosmith scarcely knew what day it was, or month, or year. 'I'll tell you what's fun,' Tyler told a reporter while chemically enhanced. 'Finding the right stewardess and turning her upside down in the back of the plane. Ever done it? You come so fast, it's the greatest.'

In the late 1980s the band decided to clean up, possibly because there were no drugs left: they had taken them all. They met for a reunion dinner at a friend's house. Someone put on 'You See Me Crying' from their 1975 album *Toys in the Attic*.

'Hey! That's great!' yelled Tyler. 'We should cover this. Who is it?'

'It's us, you fuckhead,' said guitarist Joe Perry. 'Who the fuck do you think it is? It's that song you made us get a 109-piece orchestra for.'

Stevie Nicks *(26 May 1948)*

For forty years Stevie Nicks has been bashing a tambourine at the front of the stage for Fleetwood Mac. Only problem is that she has absolutely no sense of rhythm. So for forty years her tambourine has been discreetly taped up, so that it can be seen, but not heard.

John Bonham *(31 May 1948)*

According to Pamela Des Barres, 'The Bonzo I remember was a wide-eyed, sweet-faced prankster, a simple, adoring family man caught up in the maniacal rock 'n' roll maelstrom . . . I saw him as an overgrown teddy bear, unaware of his gargantuan force, ploughing through life with the unnatural grace only a rock drummer can summon up.' She then tells slightly too many stories of the Led Zeppelin skinsbasher getting wasted, trashing hotel rooms and shitting in girls' shoes. Linda Alderetti, one of his girlfriends, adds to the picture: 'John did not grow up with much sophistication, and he was not very bright. But he was a sweetheart with a soft, soft heart, and that was his weakness and he knew it, so he never showed that to anybody.' This, of course, has been the classic excuse for appalling behaviour by terrible men since the beginning of time.

Nick Drake *(19 June 1948)*

Sad, introspective and doomed singer-songwriter who recorded three albums in the late 1960s, none of which sold more than five thousand copies on first release. He wouldn't play live or be interviewed, which didn't help. After the failure of his third album, the stripped-back and coruscatingly gloomy *Pink Moon*, Drake gave up on music completely and retreated to his parents' home in Warwickshire, where he died of an overdose of antidepressants two years later. Whether he did so intentionally or not is unknown. Since his death his records have been critically reassessed, sales have been healthy, biographies have been written, reputations have grown. John Martyn was his contemporary and friend, and had this to say about him in an interview with *Word* magazine in November 2005:

'I never realised Nick Drake was ambitious until he confided to me that he was, and it took me greatly by surprise. Nicky was one of my favourite human beings in the world. It crushed him that he was ignored, because he was used to excelling at everything: as a student, as an athlete. It was the first time he'd ever failed at anything.'

John Martyn *(11 September 1948)*

There's a wonderful description of Martyn's madness in Allan Jones's book *Can't Stand Up for Falling Down*. Jones was writing for *Melody Maker* at the time.

'I knock on the door, provoking a great bellowing from inside. I push the door open and walk into the smallest dressing room I've ever seen, before or since. Martyn's slumped in a corner looking like he's been drinking since the dawn of time, or slightly earlier.'

Martyn says, 'Who the fuck are you?' but before Jones can answer, another maniac smashes him into a wall.

'If you're Chris Welch, I'm going to fucking kill you,' says Danny Thompson, Martyn's bassist. Martyn stands up and punches Thompson in the kidneys.

'Let him the fuck go,' he says. 'He's not the one you want.'

Thompson withdraws; Martyn offers Jones a drink; Jones accepts. Enter Paul Kossoff, who's playing guitar tonight.

'Who's this cunt?' he asks.

'He's from *Melody Maker*,' says Martyn, 'but he's not Chris Welch.'

Kossoff leaves, and fifteen minutes later reappears, bleeding from the nose and the lip.

'Fuck's going on now?' says Martyn.

Kossoff tells them he's been attacked by a gang of 'homicidal students'. Martyn's up like a flash, and Thompson too, breaking the arm off a chair to use as a club.

Kossoff takes them back to the bar and shows him a skinny little bastard who looks terrified.

'He's the one that hit me,' says Kossoff.

'He's not a fucking GANG, is he?' says Martyn. It turns out that Kossoff groped this bloke's girlfriend and the bloke gave him a bit of shove.

'You cunt!' shouts Martyn, and punches Kossoff in the face. Danny Thompson whacks him around the head with the arm of the chair he snapped off. Kossoff starts to cry. As Jones puts it, 'Martyn and Thompson stalk off, like people who are mad.'

After the show Jones is back in the dressing room to interview Martyn, when Paul Kossoff walks up to Martyn and smashes a beer bottle over his head.

'Everybody OUT,' Martyn shouts. 'I'm going to give this cunt the kicking he's been asking for.'

The room empties and everyone stands outside the door, listening to the mayhem within, 'a symphony of bone-cracking, head-banging, furniture-breaking, glass-shattering detonations'. Martyn finally opens the door with blood on his shirt, and deposits a now severely damaged Kossoff on the floor. 'Shall we finish that fucking interview now?' he asks Jones.

The music these people made that evening was recorded for Martyn's *Live at Leeds* album, and is sublime.

Olivia Newton-John *(26 September 1948)*

The Australian chanteuse's maternal grandfather was Max Born, a German-Jewish physicist who escaped to England with his family in the late 1930s from the Nazis. Born won the Nobel Prize in 1954 for his 'fundamental research in quantum mechanics, especially in the statistical version of the wave function'. Her father was an MI5 officer on the Enigma project at Bletchley Park during World War Two, and took Rudolf Hess into custody. The comedian Ben Elton is her third cousin.

Olivia Newton-John has recorded twenty-eight albums. Between 1998 and 2005, she was president of the Isle of Man Basking Sharks Society.

Ozzy Osbourne *(3 December 1948)*

In August 1969, Black Sabbath had been booked to play a series of dates at Hamburg's Star-Club, and guitarist Tony Iommi turned up at Ozzy Osbourne's home to give him a lift. Ozzy emerged in a T-shirt and jeans, holding a single shirt on a hanger. This, it transpired, was his entire touring wardrobe. You know we are going overseas, said Tony. Yes, said Ozzy. Are you sure you've got enough clothes for the trip? asked Tony. I am, said Ozzy, who got in the car and carefully hung up his single shirt.

Legend has it that Ozzy Osbourne once bit the head off a dove to enliven a meeting with record company executives in Los Angeles. In 1982, in Des Moines, Iowa, a teenager threw a dead bat on stage. Ozzy bit the head off that too.

'I honestly *did not know* it was a bat,' he told Allan Jones. 'You know, these kids are always throwing, like, plastic toys at me ...

so I just grabbed this *thing*, bit the head off and thought, *Fuck me!* The thing was *flapping*.'

Worried about the possibilities of infection, Ozzy got a rabies jab.

'Real bad news, man. Terrible. Imagine someone injecting a golf ball into your leg. The syringe was like a bicycle pump.'

Jones was interviewing Ozzy on tour in Texas, and *Melody Maker* photographer Tom Sheehan wanted to get some shots of the singer at the Alamo. So they hailed a cab. Unfortunately, during lunch, they had drunk enough to sink a battleship. Ozzy desperately needed a pee, and Jones was just looking around for somewhere sufficiently discreet when he heard a terrible scream. A woman was standing in mute horror, her mouth agape. She and her husband were staring at Ozzy, who had pulled down his trousers and was pissing noisily over the front wall of the Alamo.

At this moment the cops turned up, and told Ozzy that when you piss on the Alamo, you piss on the state of Texas. 'I mean, would you piss over Buckingham Palace?'

'Actually, I did once,' said Ozzy.

'What happened next?'

'I got arrested,' said Ozzy.

'Name?' shouts another cop, with his notebook out.

'John Osbourne,' said Ozzy. 'But me mates call me Ozzy.'

The cop gave him a closer look.

'You ain't the guy who eats bats, are you?'

Ozzy nodded keenly, thinking he might get away with this.

'Mister,' said the cop, 'we are taking you in.'

A few hours later, after his manager and future wife Sharon had shouted at everyone, Ozzy was released from the local correctional facility.

'They put me in a cell with a *murderer*,' he said with delight. 'He's just killed his wife. Bit her throat out. He was covered in blood, but seemed nice enough.'

Ozzy Osbourne's father used to have his milk delivered by Noddy Holder.

Ted Nugent *(13 December 1948)*

Wild man of rock, registered Republican loon and board member of the National Rifle Association who, in 2005, with his second wife Shemane, published a cookbook called *Kill It and Grill It*. Of President Barack Obama and his Secretary of State Hillary Clinton he said they should be 'tried for treason and hung'.* On Facebook he shared a video depiction of Hillary being shot by Bernie Sanders with the caption 'I got your guncontrol [*sic*] right here bitch.' In 2007, while wielding what appeared to be an assault rifle, but was probably only an assault rifle, he said that Obama could 'suck on my machine gun'. Of Senator Dianne Feinstein he said, while holding the same gun, 'Ride one of these, you worthless whore!' He called Obama 'a communist-educated, communist-nurtured subhuman mongrel'. In 2009 he told *Royal Flush* magazine, 'I'm stymied to come up with anything funnier than people who think animals have rights. Just stick an arrow through their lungs.' In 2012 Nugent pleaded guilty to illegally killing and transporting an American black bear in Alaska. In 2017 President Trump invited him for a 'long-planned' visit to the White House, in the company of fellow dementards Kid Rock and Sarah Palin. Nugent said the visit lasted four hours and was like 'a family reunion'. That would be the Addams family, presumably.

'Having a hundred girls isn't any different from one girl,' said Ted, in a more thoughtful mood, 'except I like it a whole lot better.'

---

* All pedants will now be crying ' "tried for treason and hanged", you idiot!'.

Billy Joel *(9 May 1949)*

In 1970, his lack of success made him attempt suicide by drinking furniture polish. 'It looked tastier than bleach,' he explained.

'I think of myself as a piano player and songwriter; my singing is all tied to my piano playing,' Joel said in 1982. 'I do all my vocals live while I'm playing, which results in leakage between the vocal and piano mikes. There's never the total separation you'd get with a first-rate mix, but that's become an aspect of my sound, a distinctive trait. And if I must overdub sometime, I'll literally sit at the closed piano and pound my fingers on the lid. Guess the piano bone is connected to the throat bone.'

Joel is unusual among songwriters, and rock stars generally, in that in the early 1990s, when he was barely into his forties, he simply stopped writing and recording new material. He had said what he needed to say, and there was no more gas in the tank. He has released just two songs since 1993.

Karen Carpenter *(2 March 1950)*

In 1976 she bought two flats in Century City and knocked them into one. Her doorbell chimed the first six notes of 'We've Only Just Begun'.

Tracey Thorn talks about her 'luxurious mink' of a voice. 'In the early days she sang from her position behind the drums, which I've always considered the coolest of musical accomplishments, but this wasn't allowed to last. It's obvious to us now, but it was a surprise to her at the time, that when people heard her sing they were overwhelmed ... Dragged out from behind the kit and made to stand centre stage, it was immediately apparent that she lacked the stage presence to do so, and wasn't a natural performer. Those around her felt that the drum kit was a security blanket, something she hid behind, and so they did her the great kindness of taking that security blanket away and throwing it in the bin.' Karen's tragedy (and I don't think that's too strong a word) was that she excelled at something, singing, that she didn't particularly want to do. She was an extreme introvert thrown into an extrovert world, a sheep in wolf's clothing, if you prefer. Says Thorn, 'maybe her love of playing the drums was really an act of self-knowledge, an understanding of what was good for her and where her limits, or her desires, lay'.

'She was so symbolic of a lot of women in America with bad self-image problems,' said Kim Gordon of Sonic Youth in 1994. 'And that meant her voice had this incredible vulnerability to it, in the midst of all that really schlocky music. In retrospect, in relation to her life, her lyrics were tragically profound.'*

Robbie McIntosh *(6 May 1950)*

Drummer for the Average White Band who made a fatal mistake at a welcome party for the band in Los Angeles in 1974. He and his fellow band-member Alan Gorrie thought the bowl of white powder contained cocaine. It was heroin. They each took an enormous snort, and McIntosh turned blue and died. Gorrie was saved by fellow partygoer Cher, who kept him conscious until the medics arrived. He is still playing with the Average White Band nearly fifty years later.

David Cassidy *(12 April 1950)*

Clean-cut teenybop pin-up of the early 1970s, who may not have been quite as pure as he made out. 'When the hall empties out after one of my concerts,' he told *Rolling Stone* in 1972, 'those

---

* Except that they weren't written by her. Dull brother Richard wrote most of them.

girls leave behind them thousands of sticky seats.' Bob Stanley said, 'He was a smooth article – five minutes with him and a girl had a past.'

Paul Kossoff *(14 September 1950)*

In November 1975, my friend Jim Lynch went to see Back Street Crawler at the Liverpool Empire. Paul Kossoff, formerly of Free, was their guitarist, and known to have been a heavy drug user, but he had announced that he was now clean, hence the tour. 'The concert was sparsely attended, maybe three hundred in a three-thousand-seat theatre, but they were really good,' says Jim. 'Lots of blues-based rock, with some outstanding guitar solos.' At the end of the gig the lead singer, as always, introduced the band. 'And on lead guitar, Paul Kossoff!' At which point Kossoff went stiff, bowed from the ankles and kept going until he hit the floor. Roadies rushed on, propped him against the speaker stacks and the band played an encore with their lead guitarist somehow managing to contribute even though he couldn't stand up. After the encore, four roadies carried him off.

He died a few months later.

Huey Lewis *(5 July 1950)*

More properly Hugh Antony Cregg III, the lead singer of Huey Lewis and the News had a grandfather who invented the red wax sealant you'll find on certain cheeses.

In 1984 there were only five number-one albums in the US, the fewest in history. Michael Jackson's *Thriller* was at the top for fifteen weeks, having spent twenty-two weeks at number one in 1983, and was the bestselling album of the year for the second year in a row. The soundtrack to the film *Footloose* spent ten weeks at number one, Bruce Springsteen's *Born in the USA* had four weeks there, and Prince's *Purple Rain* was number one for the last twenty-two weeks of the year. Which adds up to fifty-one out of fifty-two weeks. With just one week at number one, the fifth of those mighty sales behemoths was *Sports* by Huey Lewis and the News.

Songstories

'Werewolves of London'
(Warren Zevon, January 1978)

In 1975 Phil Everly was watching the 1935 horror film *Werewolf of London* on TV, when the idea came into his head that his friend Warren Zevon should write a song with that title. A little throwaway, which might even be a hit. Zevon, who was cynical but not that cynical, duly wrote it with his friends Leroy Marinell and Waddy Wachtel in fifteen minutes, and then forgot about it. But Jackson Browne read the lyrics and began performing the song during his live concerts. T-Bone Burnett also did it on the first leg of Bob Dylan's Rolling Thunder Revue in late 1975. 'Werewolves of London' was considered for Zevon's second, self-titled album of 1976 but rejected. They ended up recording it for the album afterwards, and despite Zevon's ferocious objections, Elektra chose it as the first single, and it became his biggest hit. On *The Larry Sanders Show* many years later, he said, 'Every show I do I play "Werewolves of London" and it's driving me fucking crazy.'

After Zevon's death in 2003, Browne said he thought the song described a posh English womaniser. 'It's about a really well-dressed ladies' man, a werewolf preying on little old ladies. In a way, it's the Victorian nightmare, the gigolo thing.'

'Grease'
(Barry Gibb, May 1978)

My friend Maxie was interviewing Bill Oakes, musical director of *Saturday Night Fever*, who immediately afterwards went on to work on the film of *Grease*. There was no title song, so Robert Stigwood suggested that Bill ring up Barry Gibb and ask him to write one. Barry was on his boat off the Miami shore, and couldn't quite hear what Bill was saying. 'You mean Greece, like the country?' asked Barry. 'No,' replied Bill. 'I said Grease, like the word.' Barry wrote down, 'Grease is the word ... '

'Are "Friends" Electric?'
(Tubeway Army, May 1979)

Gary Numan's first big hit, and possibly the only song about a man being serviced by an android prostitute ever to reach number one.* In 2006 Numan was interviewed in the *Guardian*:

'I was trying to write two separate songs and I had a verse for one and a chorus for the other ... but I realised they sounded all right stuck together. That's why it's five minutes long. Before I recorded it I was playing it back and I hit the wrong note and it sounded much better. That harsh note is probably the crucial note in the hook ... I didn't expect the success because you couldn't dance to it and it didn't have a definable chorus. My ambition at that point was to sell out the Marquee.'

---

* By the same token, 'December 1963' by the Four Seasons may or may not be the only song about premature ejaculation to reach number one. ('Oh my, as I recall it ended much too soon.')

'Angel Eyes'
(Roxy Music, 1979)

In the late 1970s Bryan Ferry was in trouble. Punk had arrived and his solo career had faltered, with low sales and vicious reviews from vengeful critics. So he re-formed Roxy Music and recorded a rather patchy and underconfident album called *Manifesto*. (What were his policies? We were never sure.)

But the second single, 'Dance Away', was remixed with a stronger beat and screechier guitars, and was a big hit, assisted by a memorable lyric: 'You're dressed to kill/And guess who's dying?' For the next single, Ferry went for broke. In its original form, 'Angel Eyes' had been a clumpy and drab thing, full of sludgy guitars and meat-and-potatoes drumming. Ferry didn't even attempt to remix it; he completely re-recorded it, but this time as pure joyous disco. It's still one of the cleanest recordings I have ever heard. The video captured the tone. There's a huge empty TV studio with three plinths in it. Ferry is on the highest plinth, miming away. Phil Manzanera is pretending to play the guitar on the next plinth down and Andy Mackay is on the lowest plinth, not really playing his saxophone. On the ground is a woman in a long dress playing a harp. There's nothing else in the studio at all, no leads, no microphones, and no sign of the helicopter you would have needed to get up onto that top plinth. The song is magnificent, a true critic-baiter. You didn't like that? Well, you'll absolutely hate this. Ferry made two more albums with the band before he had refined his sound sufficiently to go solo again. I doubt he has read a critic since. But 'Angel Eyes' was the crux on which all else rested.

'Another Brick in the Wall, Part II'
(Pink Floyd, November 1979)

Both the disco beat – sacrilege to all us long-term Pink Floyd fans, and disregarded within a week or so – and the school chorus of oiks from Islington Green School were producer Bob Ezrin's idea. I can probably still whistle every note of David Gilmour's guitar solo. The school received just £1000 for their contribution to a song that sold more than four million copies around the world; later they sued for more and won.

The song is a typically grim rendering of Roger Waters' dreadful experiences in a boys' grammar school in the 1950s. What I didn't realise (until I read Stuart Maconie's *The People's Songs*) was that Madness's 'Baggy Trousers' was, at least in part, a response to the Pink Floyd song.* As Suggs said, 'It sounded self-indulgent to be going on about how terrible schooldays had been; there was an inverted snobbery about it too. You went to a posh school? You wanna try going to my school ... So I tried to redress the balance a little bit with this song. The title refers to the high-waisted Oxford bags we used to wear with Kevin Keegan perms – the worst fashion known to humankind.'

'Baggy Trousers' was so popular with the schoolkids of 1980 that Madness subsequently embarked on a matinée tour, playing only to their younger fans.

'Careless Whisper'
(George Michael, July 1984)

Wham! were managed in the mid-1980s by Simon Napier-Bell. 'Everyone was convinced that "Careless Whisper" would one day

---

* In the same way that Joy Division's 'Love Will Tear Us Apart' was a slightly more barbed response to the Captain and Tennille's 'Love Will Keep Us Together'.

become Wham!'s biggest hit,' he later wrote. 'It was the song that had persuaded publisher Dick Leahy to sign the group in the first place, a song that George and Andrew had written together some years earlier.' At Napier-Bell's suggestion, they hired Jerry Wexler to produce it, and they flew out to his studios at Muscle Shoals to record it. 'We were staggered at the great musicians that Jerry had booked for us.' The version they recorded was perfect in every way ... too perfect. Bizarrely, it lacked soul. 'It was as stiff as a wooden spoon, yet it was impossible to fault it except by simply saying "we don't like it", which neither George nor I had the nerve to do.'

So the Wexler version of 'Careless Whisper' was quietly shelved and George Michael went back to work, writing 'Last Christmas' at his parents' house while Andrew Ridgeley watched *Match of the Day*. A few months later they had another go. Hugh Burns was playing guitar on the track, and says that George just made them play it over and over and over again. 'About the fourth or fifth time we went on for seven or eight minutes and got into a real solid groove. George suddenly stopped us and said, "That's it. That's the groove I want. Now start again and keep that groove right through." We did, and the next track was the backing track we used.'

Although Ridgeley co-wrote it, the performance was credited to George Michael in the UK and to Wham! Featuring George Michael in the USA. I doubt that Ridgeley minded; I'm sure he already knew the game was up. George had the talent and he, frankly, didn't. But that 50 per cent of 'Careless Whisper', which has sold six million copies around the world, was his ticket to a happy life in a restored fifteenth-century farmhouse in Cornwall with his delicious partner, Keren from Bananarama. Who needs talent?*

---

* I'm guessing at 50 per cent. But George Michael was, by all accounts, one of the good guys, and I can't believe he would try to fleece his best buddy from school. Even if he did end up with Keren from Bananarama.

The Records That Time Forgot

Electric Light Orchestra: *Out of the Blue*

I came of musical age in the punk era, but I was no punk. The Sex Pistols and the Clash seemed so grimly black and white, and I favoured music that had a little colour in it. Musical taste, I suspect, is a little like sexual preference: it is imprinted on us from an early age, and we can no more alter it than we can change the colour of the sky. My first musical memory is of an old Dansette my mother used to own, and the Beatles singles she bought every time a new one came out. I played them to death, including the B-sides. In 1977, not otherwise a good year for Beatles fans, an album came out that spoke subliminally to the moptop in us all. I heard the first single, 'Turn to Stone', and thought, that's for me. I went out and bought the album on the first day it was available, because even twenty-four hours later would have been too late.

Jeff Lynne was thirty when *Out of the Blue* was released, a good age to produce a masterpiece, although you are presented with the question of what to do with the rest of your life, because there's no way you can better this. His group, the Electric Light Orchestra, had arisen from the ashes of the Move, first in a slightly uncomfortable partnership with Roy Wood, and subsequently under Lynne's tight and, one has to say, absolute control. The original idea was to fuse rock 'n' roll with orchestral music: the seven-piece band included two cellists and a violinist. The first few albums were ugly and boring exercises in prog rock, with occasional bursts of orchestrated pop brilliance. By *Out of the Blue*, their seventh album, the prog had gone and the pop brilliance was everywhere. It could still lay claim to being one of the most sheerly tuneful albums ever made.

It was, though, out of its time. The Clash had declared Year Zero and decided that all music made before 1976, other than a bit of reggae, was essentially worthless. Least fashionable of all were the Beatles, especially their later, more complex works, and so a band like ELO, whose entire template was based on side two of *Abbey Road*, were never going to be music-paper favourites. But if punk was one response to the terrible dullness of most mid-1970s pop music, *Out of the Blue* was actually another. Recording technology had improved in enormous bounds over the previous ten years. With four or eight tracks it was easy: you just played the song all together, recorded it and that was that. With 24-tracks people started recording all the instruments separately, and that's why so much mid-1970s music sounds so flat and lifeless: technology had advanced more quickly than most people's ability to use it. Listen to ELO's albums of this time and you are listening to a band slowly learning how to use the studio as an instrument in itself. Joe Meek would have loved the late 1970s. Brian Eno, an avowed non-musician, made his best records simply by exploring what the studio would let him do.

The Electric Light Orchestra, meanwhile, had just had a biggish hit with *A New World Record*, a slightly anaemic album that is easy to admire but hard to love. Jeff Lynne went off to a rented chalet in the Swiss Alps to try to write the next one. He sat in his room for weeks, utterly bereft of ideas. The weather was awful throughout, but then one day the sun came out and 'Mr Blue Sky' came unbidden into Lynne's mind. He wrote an entire seventy-five-minute double album in three and a half weeks, and it took just two months to record.

What is extraordinary about *Out of the Blue* is its sheer profusion of musical ideas. It's an incredibly dense listen, packed with melodies and countermelodies. The DJ Kenny Everett, who had a two-hour show on Capital on Saturday morning, was so thrilled by the album he played every track but one on one of his shows. I was listening, and I was thrilled too. The album did suffer from Lynne's abiding weakness as a musician: poor lyrics. William, my friend who worshipped Dylan, shook his head with disgust. But as Trevor Horn once said, actually about ELO, no one worries about feeble lyrics when the music is this good.

Lynne never did anything as good again. The string players, increasingly supernumerary, were sacked and on the next album he included 'The Diary of Horace Wimp', one of the most abject songs ever recorded. I still bought everything he released and not a few albums he only produced, but there were only ever glimpses of genius in years of solid craft. That would be that, if time hadn't caught up with Lynne, as it has a tendency to do. Studio pop has become ever more complex and electronicised in the years since, but the sheer vibrant colour of ELO's best music has never dimmed, and Lynne, now in his seventies, plays live to adoring audiences worldwide. It's more than forty years since I first bought *Out of the Blue*, but it still gives me a rush every time I put it on. What else do we want pop music to do?

BILL'S SPOTIFY THE LINK

4.1

'Old Money'
by Lana del Ray

'All by Myself'
by Eric Carmen

'Little Me'
by Little Mix

'Grace Kelly'
by Mika

4.2

'Lady Lynda'
by the Beach Boys

'Plug In Baby'
by Muse

'If I Had You'
by the Korgis

'All Together Now'
by the Farm

4.3

'Could It Be Magic'
by Barry Manilow

'Minuetto Allegretto'
by the Wombles

'I Believe in Father Christmas'
by Greg Lake

'Can't Help Falling in Love'
by Elvis Presley

Answer

Each song contains (and in one or two cases is wholly based on) a well-known piece of classical music. 'Could It Be Magic' is based on Chopin's 'Prelude in C Minor, Opus 28, number 20', 'All Together Now' nicks the chord progression from Pachelbel's 'Canon', and the beginning of the riff in 'Plug In Baby' bears a notable resemblance to the toccata in Bach's 'Toccata and Fugue in B minor'.

1951–1958

Notable Births

30 January 1951:	Phil Collins
19 May 1951:	Joey Ramone
7 September 1951:	Chrissie Hynde
2 October 1951:	Sting
14 May 1952:	David Byrne
21 August 1952:	Joe Strummer
6 July 1953:	Nanci Griffith
10 October 1953:	Midge Ure
11 November 1953:	Andy Partridge
10 July 1954:	Neil Tennant
25 August 1954:	Elvis Costello
22 May 1955:	Jerry Dammers
31 January 1956:	John Lydon, a.k.a. Johnny Rotten
27 August 1956:	Glen Matlock
10 May 1957:	Sid Vicious
27 May 1957:	Siouxsie Sioux
22 September 1957:	Nick Cave
20 December 1957:	Billy Bragg
25 December 1957:	Shane MacGowan
8 March 1958:	Gary Numan
25 May 1958:	Paul Weller
7 June 1958:	Prince (formerly The Artist Formerly Known as Prince)
30 July 1958:	Kate Bush
13 August 1958:	Feargal Sharkey
16 August 1958:	Madonna
29 August 1958:	Michael Jackson

Joey Ramone *(19 May 1951)*

'Joey Ramone's voice was the cry of a fat baby seal stranded limbless on a floating ice shelf, abandoned by its mother. It was the most truly plaintive sound going that year [1976] and for many years after it, a sort of reproachful bark shading into a wail and a gulp.' (Nick Coleman in *Voices*.)

Steve Hillage *(2 August 1951)*

Slightly vanished from sight now, but I remember him as the lone vanguard of hippydom when punk swept the world in the late 1970s. Only Hillage still had long hair and played endless noodly guitar solos. You had to admire him, really.

He probably had no choice. Fashions change, but temperaments do not. 'Cauliflowers are a particularly pleasing example of the vegetable kingdom,' he told an interviewer in 1978. 'You can think of them as lumps of dirt that we stuff into our bellies. Or you can think of them as living beings who have minds and would very much like to communicate with us.'

John Deacon *(19 August 1951)*

Quiet-man bassist for Queen, who was the last of the quartet to join in early 1971. On Queen's first album he was credited as 'Deacon John', to make him sound more interesting. It didn't work, so they changed his credit to John Deacon from the second album on.

Chrissie Hynde *(7 September 1951)*

The lead singer and principal songwriter of the Pretenders, born in Akron, Ohio, came to London and worked at Malcolm McLaren's SEX shop alongside future members of the Sex Pistols. She asked both Sid Vicious and Johnny Rotten to marry her so she could get a work visa. She was kicked out of the band Masters of the Backside before they changed their name to the Damned and became famous. And she has enjoyed a longer and more productive career than any of her punk confrères.

In 1994, as a promo for one of her singles, Chrissie compiled her ten do's and don'ts for 'chick rockers', or 'How I Did It'. It included the following:

'Don't moan about being a chick, refer to feminism or complain about sexual discrimination ... No one wants to hear a whining female. Write a loosely disguised song about it instead and clean up ($).

'Do not insist on working with "females". Get the best man for the job, and if they happen to be female, great – you'll have someone to go to department stores with on tour instead of making one of the road crew go with you.

'Don't try to compete with the guys: it won't impress anybody. Remember, one of the reasons they like you is because you don't offer yet more competition to the already existing male egos.

'Shave your legs, for chrissakes!

'Don't take advice from people like me. Do your own thing always.'

Sting *(2 October 1951)*

In 1980 Allan Jones was accompanying the Police on a brief tour of India. He and Sting were on their way to a soundcheck for the evening's show, when they bumped into a guy Sting had known in South Shields who had sold up and gone to India, where he now passed his time lounging on beaches and smoking weed. In the taxi, Sting reflected on this encounter.

'It's strange talking to someone like that,' he said. 'That lifestyle he was talking about, sitting around all day getting stoned. It would satisfy absolutely none of my drives or ambitions. The whole hippy idea is something I find completely foreign. I was never attracted to it. I never understood it. I've only ever been interested in material success.'

Jones asked him what his ambitions were.

'If I was specific,' said Sting, 'I'd sound crass. I mean, basically I want gold records, money, fame and to enjoy being me.'

Roughly twenty-six years later I was pushing a book of mine* on *Loose Ends* on Radio 4, and who should also be in the studio that day but the former Gordon Sumner, promoting his album of John Dowland lute tunes. He was so breathtakingly handsome that several women audibly gasped when he walked in the room. He remains the only person I have ever seen who could rock a lilac tank-top. He sang his songs with an accompanist and we were all awed into silence. At the end of the show, after we had all done our bits, he was looking at my book and said, 'That looks interesting. Can I have it?' Because he's Sting, I said yes. I reckon he has enjoyed being him rather a lot.

New Musical Express (7 March 1952)

By the mid-1970s the *NME* had become Britain's bestselling inky rock magazine, but it was tired. Its best writers were either too old (Mick Farren, thirty-three), strung out on heroin (Nick Kent), burnt out after too much speed (Charles Shaar Murray), or had left altogether to go and freelance for classical music magazines (Ian MacDonald). An injection of youth was required, so Murray wrote an ad headlined 'Attention hip young gunslingers', offering a staff job on the magazine for the right candidate. 'Previous experience in either journalism or the music business is not essential,

---

* *The Prince of Wales (Highgate) Quiz Book* (Hodder & Stoughton), still available from all good charity shops.

but a good knowledge of rock and enthusiasm are, together with the ability to write lively and incisive prose.' They had twelve hundred applications. Among those who wrote in were Jonathan Coe, prog-obsessed schoolboy and future writer of comic novels including *What A Carve Up!* and *The Rotters' Club*; Neil Tennant, then an editor at Marvel Comics, later assistant editor of *Smash Hits*, and later still, one of the Pet Shop Boys; Sebastian Faulks, then a schoolteacher, later literary editor at the *Independent* and writer of novels including *Birdsong*; Paul du Noyer, later editor of *Q* and *Mojo*; and Paul Morley, then a bookshop assistant, later by some distance the most annoying regular face on BBC2's *Late Review*. None of them was hired.

In the end, the *NME* found room for two staff writers, Julie Burchill and Tony Parsons. I wonder what happened to them?

In 1978 Ian Penman joined the staff. 'I remember going to the *NME* offices for the first time,' he told Pat Long, 'expecting this glamorous, Algonquin Round Table-type of environment and instead it was a fucking dump full of people who were past their best and in some cases in very deep personal trouble hacking away on these metal typewriters which weighed a ton and had half the keys missing.'

'It was a psychedelic pirate ship,' said Danny Baker. 'A free-floating raft of misfits ... The kitchen at Carnaby Street was an absolute tip, absolutely filthy. Half-eaten ready meals with joints stuck in them everywhere. My wife Wendy was the editor's assistant and used to go and clean it up when it got too bad. She always says that the only person who'd help her was Paul Weller.'

Baker was, for a time in the late 1970s, the magazine's receptionist and switchboard operator. 'City Morgue!' he would cry into the phone. 'You stab 'em, we'll slab 'em.'

Joe Strummer *(21 August 1952)* and Mick Jones *(26 June 1955)*

'In Joe Strummer and Mick Jones, the Clash had punk's own Lennon and McCartney: Strummer, bilious and shouting through what seemed to be a mouthful of pebbles and rubbing alcohol, Jones, tuneful and slightly fey, with a voice as substantial as tissue paper.' (Stuart Maconie in *Cider with Roadies*.)

Tony Blair *(6 May 1953)*

When Mark Ellen was at Oxford there were only three bands, and he was in one of them, Ugly Rumours. All they lacked was a singer, and a friend knew Tony Blair, who had managed a band and appeared in revue shows, so they asked him to audition.

'The moment he arrived, wearing exactly the same boots as we had, he'd effectively got the job anyway. He had a folk-rock look about him – long hair with a fringe – and was keen, organised, quite posh, very funny and started a lot of sentences with the word "guys" ...

'"Any chance of doing "I Don't Want to Talk About It" by Crazy Horse?' Tony wondered. This was impressive: only the most insanely confident singer of a college rock band would dare suggest a ballad, let alone an obscure one. The audition got under way, two acoustic guitars, an unamplified bass, an upturned waste-paper basket and Tony emoting hard into a microphone that wasn't plugged in ...

'The new five-piece Ugly Rumours began appearing on the party circuit, Tony adopting a courageous hoop-necked top that revealed several square inches of bare torso. The only tensions were the endless do-you-tuck-your-flares-into-your cowboy-boots debates that panicked the ranks seconds before showtime, and the irritating sight of pretty girls in print dresses gathered around the central mike stand ...

'"Guys, guys," Tony called us together after one show. "We're OK and everything but we could be so much better if we rehearsed."'

Midge Ure *(10 October 1953)*

Scots singer for Slik, the Rich Kids and Ultravox who was actually christened James Ure and widely known as Jim. But his first band already had a Jim, so his bandmates suggested that he reverse Jim to make Mij, and that eventually became Midge.

Tito Jackson *(15 October 1953)*

The third child in the Jackson family, Tito now lives in Wolverhampton.*

Andy Partridge *(11 November 1953)*

Lead singer and main writer for the Swindon band XTC, and very possibly the only person (other than fellow band member Colin Moulding) to appear on *Top of the Pops* singing in a Swindon accent. 'When we started the band, we wanted to be rich and famous,' he said in 1989. '*Famous.* That was a requirement. I mean, what a stupid thing to want. We actually wanted fame, fortune and probably all to live in one house with a fire pole in the middle.' Although it's twenty years since they recorded any

---

* Desmond Dekker spent the last four years of his life living in Tunbridge Wells. Edwin Starr moved to England in 1973, opened a number of Starr Cafés in Essex and died, aged sixty-one, in Chilwell, Nottinghamshire. Kid Creole lived in Dinnington, South Yorkshire, for four years in the early 1990s. Bob Marley and the Wailers briefly lived in Neasden in north-west London. Nico spent most her final years living in the Prestwich and Salford area of Greater Manchester.

new material, their reputation seems to grow with time rather
than diminish.

Captain Sensible *(24 April 1954)*

For his book *Black Vinyl White Powder*, Simon Napier-Bell spoke
to the former Ray Burns, guitarist for the Damned and occasional
solo artist:
    'We thought up crazy names so we could keep signing on at the
DHSS. Mine came on the way to a festival in France. I'd bought
a second-hand shirt with epaulettes and I was pretending to be a
pilot. I shouted out, "Everything's under control. We're on autopi-
lot." Someone said, "Oh, it's Captain Sensible." Now I'm forty-six,
and I'm still stuck with the same name.'
    That was twenty years ago.

Neil Tennant *(10 July 1954)* and Chris Lowe *(4 October 1959)*

Dusty Springfield almost crashed her car the first time she heard
'West End Girls'.

Elvis Costello *(25 August 1954)*

'Virgin offered me a deal in 1979,' said Costello in an interview,
'and I turned them down. Offered me a lot of money. I asked
Richard Branson to name two songs off my last album, and he
couldn't do it. So I told him to fuck off.'
    In 1983 the Flying Pickets, a group of five old-school Marxist
actors and activists, formed an a cappella singing group and had
a huge Christmas hit with their version of Yazoo's 'Only You'.
Elvis Costello said he wasn't terribly keen on the music, but it was
always nice to have communists at number one at Christmas.

Stevie Ray Vaughan *(3 October 1954)*

'Boy, you could be the greatest guitar player that ever lived,' said B. B. King, 'but you won't live to see forty if you don't leave that white powder.' In one of music's more minor-key ironies, Vaughan did give it up, and then died in a helicopter crash aged thirty-five.

Adam Ant *(3 November 1954)*

In early 1980 Adam Ant was just another washed-up punk on an independent label. 'Cult,' he decided, 'is just another word for loser.' So he hired two drummers, started working with the clever tunesmith Marco Pirroni, slapped on the warpaint and relaunched himself as the first major teen idol of the 1980s. According to Dave Rimmer in his book *Like Punk Never Happened*, 'he mapped out all the moves for those who came after . . . He was the first to engineer a self-conscious move from margins to mainstream, from cult to conqueror. He didn't seem to have even the tiniest prick of conscience about "selling out", he just made damned sure someone was buying.' And yet, by the time this book was published in 1985, Ant's career was all but over. His last two solo albums (less pop, more dance) had been released to widespread indifference and he then parked his music career to concentrate on acting, which was a mistake. How can someone so sure-footed earlier in his career lose the plot so quickly and comprehensively? Two reasons, I think: no coherent Plan B; and pure demographics, for his fans did what all fans of teen idols do sooner or later: they grew up.

Jermaine Jackson *(11 December 1954)*

'Even though Michael is very talented, a lot of his success is due to timing and luck,' said Jermaine in the early 1980s. 'It could have

been him, or it could just as easily have been me.' It's his belief
that this is true that shows us how untrue it is.

Steve and Dan Peters *(birthdates unknown)**

Born-again Minnesotan brothers (and ordained priests) who in the
late 1970s began a bizarre but heartfelt crusade against rock music.
They believed that 'listening to rock music will be harmful to your
spiritual, emotional and mental health' and identified an 'epidemic'
of suicides among God-fearing teenagers who had been led astray
by the Prince of Darkness's own four-four beat. Their video *The
Truth About Rock* had some interesting claims:

- That Mick Jagger was 'an avowed homosexual'.
- That Barry Manilow was evil.
- That Janis Joplin would have died of venereal disease if
  the drugs hadn't got her first.
- That the cover of an album by the Alan Parsons Project had
  'girls with syphilis sores on their faces cloaked by veils'.
- That KISS stood for 'Knights in Service to Satan'.†
- That John Denver intended to become God.
- That Eagles' 'Hotel California' is about the Church of
  Satan. 'I mean, I don't know any other hotel where they'll
  let you check out but you can't leave!'

In their religious services they claim to have burned at least half
a million dollars' worth of records, tapes and memorabilia associated with rock performers. It seems to have run in the family. Their
mother Josephine identified secret Satanic messages on a Beach
Boys record, and refused to have a television in the house. The

---

* But they were both in their mid-twenties in 1979.
† In some interviews they say 'Kids in Service to Satan'.

Encyclopedia of American Loons (a real website) has described them as 'absolute legends of fundamentalist insanity'.

Green Gartside *(22 June 1955)*

Lead singer of Scritti Politti who, since their 1980s heyday, I had always assumed to have been born Green Gartside. But he wasn't. He changed his name from Paul Julian Strohmeyer. According to Stuart Maconie, he first got a subscription to the *NME* when he was eight and joined the Cwmbran Young Communist League at the age of twelve.

Interviewed by Tracey Thorn for *Naked at the Albert Hall*, Green discussed the difference between singing in the studio and singing on stage. 'I like singing in the studio,' he said, 'doing it until it's right. Singing live is like a complicated sporting event for the voice. A fiendish obstacle race. Over this hurdle, around this tricky bend, down for this horrible low note.'

'This is the most brilliant description of live singing I have ever heard,' said Tracey, 'and I relate to it one hundred per cent.'

John Lydon/Johnny Rotten* *(31 January 1956)*

John Lydon burned Sid Vicious's suicide note 'because that's what Sid would have liked'. In the early 1980s Lydon moved with his wife Nora to Venice, California. 'America's a fantastic country,' he told John Harris much later. 'It's new, it's undiscovered, it's undeveloped. They're mad, but they have a great openness to new things, which you don't get in England any more. Here, everything new is hated and resented. You're happy

---

* Rotten changed his name back to Lydon after leaving the Sex Pistols purely because Malcolm McLaren claimed he owned the copyright on the name Johnny Rotten.

with that scratchy toilet paper. I'm sorry, I like a bit of aloe vera on my bum now.'

In 1989 Andrew Mueller interviewed him in the conference room of a Sydney hotel. 'Lydon had installed himself at the far end, below a whiteboard on which he had inscribed the words "Go away". He was dressed in a luridly striped trousers-and-jumper combination over a multi-coloured polka dot shirt.' Possibly to break the ice, or because he was genuinely curious, Mueller asked him what the fuck he was wearing. 'He glared. It was an odd feeling. Lydon's glare was well known to me from Sex Pistols and PiL videos, and any number of magazine photos. Its power was not in doubt: John Lydon's glare had been punk's equivalent of Joshua's trumpet, an instrument of vengeance which had laid waste to everything that displeased it.' They had an anxious few seconds. 'Ridiculous, isn't it?' said Lydon in the end. 'Of course, only an Australian could have designed it.' From then on, the interview went swimmingly.

Glen Matlock *(27 August 1956)*

Credited as co-writer of ten out of twelve songs on the Sex Pistols' *Never Mind the Bollocks*, although by the time the album's recording sessions began, he had left the band.

Why did he leave?

Malcolm McLaren said he'd been fired for liking the Beatles too much.*

Steve Jones said he thought it bizarre that Matlock was always washing his feet, although that seems less than a sacking offence.

In his autobiography, Matlock says he resigned because he was 'sick of all the bullshit'. In Julien Temple's 2000 documentary *The*

---

* The American metal band Satanicide discovered that their bassist secretly liked Billy Joel's music. So they fired him.

Filth and the Fury, his former bandmates agreed that there had been tension between Matlock and Johnny Rotten. Matlock thinks this had been stirred up by McLaren, possibly for fun.

In his own autobiography, Rotten says that Matlock played bass on most of the album as a session musician. His replacement, Sid Vicious, only played on one track, and even that contribution was eventually overdubbed by someone else.

In 2002 Steve Jones admitted that pushing Matlock out of the band had been a mistake. 'We were what we were. Who cares if he washed his feet? That was him. I'm sure I had things that bugged him.'

Matlock has since pointed out that, after he left, the band only wrote two more songs.

Sid Vicious *(10 May 1957)*

One of very few pop stars to have been named after a pet rat belonging to Johnny Rotten. The former Simon John Ritchie had been bitten by Sid, and yelled 'Sid is really vicious!' He joined the Sex Pistols in February 1977, replacing Glen Matlock on bass. Their manager Malcolm McLaren said, 'If Johnny Rotten is the voice of punk, then Vicious is the attitude.' Allan Jones, interviewing the band in May 1977, described him as 'a loose-limbed pile of rags and leather and skin with the sheen of mildew'.

Poly Styrene *(3 July 1957)*

Here's Tracey Thorn writing about the lead singer of X-Ray Spex in *Naked at the Albert Hall*: 'I think of Poly Styrene as an example of someone who would probably never have got near a microphone in any other generation – almost the epitome of the non-singer, she could barely carry a tune, had no vibrato, nothing much to speak of in the way of range, and I absolutely loved her. Sheer force of will and strength of personality meant that she shone on stage, like a creature born to be there, delivering songs about modern society and its oppressive power over the individual with an irrepressible sense of joy.'

Jon Moss *(11 September 1957)*

I went to Highgate School, which is now an incredibly posh and expensive independent school in north London, where your parents need to be as rich as Sting for you to have any chance of getting in. In the mid-1970s, though, it was much, much cheaper and rather shabby around the edges, and they let in pretty much anybody, including me. Another such, a couple of years older than me, was a Jewish boy called Jon Moss, who was in my house (Southgate), looked hard and ran around with a rather lairy, girl-chasing crowd whose suits had wider lapels than anybody else's. What a surprise, then, to see him a year or so after he left as the drummer for punk group London: safety pins, torn T-shirts, rather more working-class accent than he had previously sported. (The band's singer called himself Riff Regan. His real name was Miles Tredinnick and his father had been a vice-marshal in the Royal Air Force.)

London got nowhere and Jon Moss vanished from sight until 1983, when he re-emerged as the drummer for Culture Club, who we later learned was having a hot affair with their singer Boy George. Jon Moss was gay! If you had told me that Sean Connery was a transvestite I couldn't have been more shocked. Of course, no one at Highgate had been gay, because no one was in those days, but even so. Jon Moss eventually settled down with an actual woman and had three children with her, and no one gives a hoot about his sexuality any more, or anyone's, come to think of it.

Sheila E *(12 December 1957)*

Percussionist and Prince protégée, real surname Escovedo, who like all Prince's protégées was very small indeed. (Watching them all play live together, you wondered when Snow White would show up.) 'I'm not trying to sell sex,' she once said. 'I just don't like wearing a lot of clothes onstage.'

Gary Numan *(8 March 1958)*

Born Gary Webb, the electronic pioneer and part-time android changed his name to Numan after spotting a plumber of the same name in the Yellow Pages. One wonders how he feels about the website numan.com, which claims to solve such quintessentially male problems as erectile dysfunction and hair loss. (Numan is famously as bald as a coot.)

One of my all-time favourite quiz questions is this: Who is older, Gary Oldman or Gary Numan? Answer below.*

Prince *(7 June 1958)*

In 2004, at the inductions for the Rock 'n' Roll Hall of Fame, an all-star band, featuring Tom Petty, Steve Winwood, Jeff Lynne and George Harrison's son Dhani, played a version of 'While My Guitar Gently Weeps'. Standing at the side of the stage for most of it, wearing a dinky red hat, stood Prince, who came on and played a guitar solo of such virtuosity and wild abandon that you can watch it over and over again (on YouTube) and never tire of it. The expression on Dhani Harrison's face as he sees what the Minneapolis munchkin is up to is a picture. At the end of the solo

---

* Gary Oldman was born on 21 March 1958. Which makes Gary Numan thirteen days older than Gary Oldman.

Prince throws his guitar straight up into the air and walks off the stage. The guitar doesn't land.

Kate Bush *(30 July 1958)*

One of pop music's terrifyingly few true geniuses, Kate Bush was born on exactly the same day as decathlete Daley Thompson, and 140 years to the day after Emily Brontë, whose novel *Wuthering Heights* gave her the theme and the title of her first hit. It was the first UK number one sung by a woman who had written the song herself. EMI wanted to release 'James and the Cold Gun' as the first single, but Kate insisted. 'I'm the shyest megalomaniac you're ever likely to meet,' she explained much later. Her vocal performance on 'Wuthering Heights' was completed in a single take.

Feargal Sharkey *(13 August 1958)*

When the Understones first started, Feargal Sharkey was the only member of the group with a job. He delivered and installed TVs for Radio Rentals.

Madonna *(16 August 1958)*

According to *Word* magazine in July 2005, her 'shag tree is more Escher than flow-chart'. There have been so many notches on the Ciccone bedpost it has probably crumbled into dust by now. In 1985 she married Sean Penn at Kurt Unger's $6.5 million house in Malibu to the theme from *Chariots of Fire*, while a dozen helicopters full of journalists and photographers circled overhead. Penn turned to the guests and shouted, 'Welcome to the remake of *Apocalypse Now*!' In 1987 there were rumours of an assignation with John F. Kennedy Jr; in 1988 she got very chummy indeed with comedian Sandra Bernhard; in 1989 she finally divorced

Penn; in 1990 she was reported to be an item with Lenny Kravitz, and may have shared bedclothes with Warren Beatty; and in 1991 had an eight-month fling with forgotten white rapper Vanilla Ice, which, by extraordinary coincidence, was roughly the length of his career. In 1993 it was supposedly the turn of fashion model Jenny Shimuzu, in 1994 cross-dressing basketballer Dennis Rodman,* in 1995 Tupac Shakur (a year before he was gunned down) and Anthony Kiedis of the Red Hot Chili Peppers, and in 1996 she had a child with not-wholly-unfit fitness instructor Carlos Leon. In 1998 she briefly dated box-fresh illusionist David Blaine before – WHOOSH! – he completely disappeared. In 2000 she married Mockney film director Guy Ritchie, whose 'friends' (i.e. probably Guy himself, on the phone) mischievously revealed to journalists that she would only let him eat smoothies for breakfast and steamed fish and vegetables for dinner, wouldn't let sunlight touch her skin, spent her nights smothering herself in anti-ageing creams at £500 a pot, and normally slept in a protective plastic body suit. 'By chance,' she once said, 'most of the men I have fallen in love with have turned out to be helpful to my career.' In 2007 she adopted a young boy, David Banda, from Malawi. Morrissey, in possibly his last recorded act of brilliance, commented thus: 'I wouldn't be surprised if she made that African boy she adopted into a coat and wore him for fifteen minutes, then threw it away.' David turned out to be rather good at football, and enrolled in Benfica's youth academy in 2017.

She also made a lot of records, but let's not worry too much about those, because I'm not sure she ever did. The credits, though, mattered a lot. In 1990 'Justify My Love' started out life as a poem by Prince's protégée Ingrid Chavez (who later married David Sylvian). Her boyfriend of the time, Lenny Kravitz, worked it up

---

* Rodman later recalled that their relationship began when she looked him up and down and said, 'You're staying with me. In my room.'

into a song, and Chavez recorded it. Madonna liked what they had done and wanted to have a go at it. She added nothing, other than changing a single line in the lyric. Her version, according to Chavez, was practically a heavy-breath-for-heavy-breath copy of the original demo tape. 'Lenny told me he was obsessed about getting it the same,' she said. So why didn't he use Chavez? 'Because Madonna can make more money,' said Chavez.

When 'Justify My Love' appeared as a single, it was credited to Madonna/Lenny Kravitz. Chavez had to sue to claim her credit, which she eventually received, as well as a healthy out-of-court settlement. But only from Kravitz's share of the proceeds. After the lawsuit had been settled, Chavez's lawyer confirmed that Madonna's writing credit had not been questioned by anyone.

In April 1994 a Chicago artist named Dwight Kalb constructed a sculpture of Madonna out of 180 lb of ham. Restaurateur Mel Markon had commissioned it, after Kalb successfully fashioned a statue of Brooke Shields from chopped liver.

Michael Jackson *(29 August 1958)*

Jackson had his first nose job as early as May 1979, when he was just twenty. He took home a keepsake, a purplish slice of his own nose cartilage in a small glass vial. Where did he keep it? There must have been so many of these vials by the end, you could probably now clone a completely new Michael Jackson from their grisly contents.

On 29 August 1984, Jackson was in Los Angeles to shoot a commercial for Pepsi-Cola. His team had made a deal with Pepsi after Coca-Cola had refused to cough up enough money. Because of his strict diet, Michael would never be seen to actually drink the stuff, and his face would be in the ad for just four seconds, but for that he would trouser a cool $5 million. The ad would be directed by Bob Giraldi, who had made the videos for 'Beat It' and

'Billie Jean'. Giraldi was near the dressing rooms when he heard a bloodcurdling scream. It was Michael, who had dropped one of his white gloves in the lavatory and needed someone to fish it out.

In the ad itself Michael had to emerge from a burst of flames, but a spark landed on his head and his hair caught fire. Possibly unaware of his increasing resemblance to a giant candle, he carried on dancing for a few seconds until minions covered his head with blankets and put out the flames. At hospital he was diagnosed with 'a palm-sized area of second- and a small area of third-degree burns' and prescribed Darvocet, a painkiller subsequently banned by the FDA. Slang terms for Darvocet include pinks, footballs, 65s and Ns. Physical and psychological symptoms of Darvocet abuse include confusion, hallucinations, skin rash, sudden changes in mood and delusions of grandeur. This, in short, is where it all started.

In 1987 Jackson tried to buy the remains of the 'Elephant Man', John Merrick. He was unsuccessful.

Jackson's friendship with his pet chimpanzee Bubbles came to a sudden end when Bubbles punched him. The hitherto cosseted primate was exiled from Jackson's Neverland Ranch and moved to an animal trainer's home in Sylmar, California.

In 2003 the Santa Barbara County District Attorney's Office and Sheriff's Department raided Neverland Ranch in search of evidence against the old child-abuser. They found many life-size mannequins of children, endless cardboard boxes that no one had bothered to unpack, an enormous crimson-and-gold throne for the King of Pop to sit in, several collections of photographs of teenage boys in various states of undress, and a secret cupboard hidden at the back of his bedroom and kept closed with three deadlocks. It was in here that he kept his most precious memorabilia, including a signed photograph of Macaulay Culkin, which included the message 'Don't leave me alone in the house.'

Pop Star Encounters 2

Although I spent two or three years as the *Daily Mail*'s pop corre-
spondent, reviewing albums and gigs, I have met very few pop stars
and am happy to keep it that way. I interviewed Mick Hucknall
once, which was a disaster, as I didn't ask him all the questions
my editors wanted me to ask, i.e. about his non-stop shagging. We
talked about music instead, and I was interested to note that despite
his roundy-round face, he was both taller and slimmer than I had
expected. I also went and introduced myself to Ricky Ross, lead
singer of Deacon Blue, after a particularly fine gig they had played
at the Town and Country Club in north London.

'Who did you say you were with again?' asked Ricky.

'The *Daily Mail*,' said I.

'Fuck off then,' said Ricky.

Here, then, are some more of the more inadvertent interactions
with pop stars experienced by some of my friends on Facebook.
There are some journalists here, but not dedicated music journalists, as I thought they might be a bit too blasé about meeting
famous musicians. The rest of us have collywobbles galore, and
sometimes do very silly things indeed.

'Our tennis club was a fifteen-minute walk from my school
in south Hampstead. There was a music rehearsal space, and

a band had arrived to work there. We were all standing about watching them unload their gear, when Phil Lynott saw us and shouted, "Put your hand up if you are a virgin!" Only one girl, an Orthodox Jew, put her hand up. The rest of us were also virgins.' K.R.

'Keith Moon once chatted me up in a Highgate pub. He was with Graham Chapman of Monty Python. I was only fourteen and he asked me to go back to Graham's house for a party. I asked if my star-struck boyfriend could come and the invitation was never mentioned again.' K.R.

'I once wet myself in front of Jerry Dammers, because I was too polite to say I needed to go to the loo. I was a bit drunk and thought no one would notice. But after the conversation had finished that there were streams of pee trickling across the floor from where I stood. What must people have thought?' K.R.

'Putney, SW London, October 1982. I'm setting off to work, and in my wallet is a ticket to see David Thomas in concert that night. He's the huge, lumbering frontman of very obscure US weird-rock band Pere Ubu, from Cleveland, Ohio. I'd seen them once, on impulse, at university in '78. I loved them immediately. My instant favourite band. Obviously, they broke up shortly afterwards. I had bought my ticket for his solo show early – my ticket was no. 001 – and I had been looking forward to the concert for weeks. As I leave the house, I see a huge, lumbering figure walk along the pavement, past my gate. "Ha! You're obsessed," I tell myself. "Now you think every random big guy you see looks just like David Thomas." Twenty seconds later, I draw level with the random big guy. It's David Thomas. "You're David Thomas!" He is even more surprised at being spotted than I am at spotting him. He has been living near by for a few months. We chat for a couple of minutes. "Well, I hope you enjoy the concert," he says. I ask if he'd mind giving me an autograph, and hand him my ticket. He signs it, saying, "Zero-zero-one? You are a big fan, eh?" Yes, I am. Thirty-eight years later, he and Pere Ubu are still going. And I still have the ticket.' G.P.

'I went to interview Jimmy Page once, and although he wouldn't show me his kitchen, he did tell me about his fancy oven and how he loved "whipping up" devilled kidneys. He also showed me a secret room, but I am SWORN to secrecy about that.' A.B.

'My rheumatologist was the junior doctor who pronounced Jimi Hendrix dead on arrival and signed the death certificate. Seifert's evidence says that he "was put on a monitor, but it was flat . . . as he was dead. I vaguely remember the clothes being flamboyant . . . [though] we didn't know he was Jimi Hendrix until later on".' L.G.

'Steve and I went to a gig at the Shepherd's Bush Empire and there was a support act, a bloke on a guitar. His set was amazing and I said to Steve, "This guy is going to be a big star, his music is really catchy." "Nah," said Steve, "he's nothing special." Before the main act came on we popped outside for a nifty fag and a ginger bloke asked us for a light and we got chatting. It was the support guy and he offered to play a gig in our garden for £250. I thought it was a cool idea, said I'd contact him and promptly forgot. A few weeks later I heard a familiar song on the radio which would become a huge hit . . . it was Ed Sheeran . . . the bloke who offered to play a gig in my garden . . . ' G.B.

'It was July 1963, in Weston-super-Mare. I was nine. My grandmother used to spend every summer there in a grand old

Victorian hotel on the seafront, and we sometimes joined her. We had just checked in, and sharing the lift up to our room were John Lennon and George Harrison. I knew immediately who they were – what starstruck nine-year-old wouldn't? – and when we got to our floor they helped carry our luggage to the door. My grandmother, whose knowledge of popular musicians started and ended with Frank Ifield, dipped into her purse and tipped John Lennon half a crown. John passed it to me, ruffled my hair and said, "Me laddo deserves it more than me." As he wandered off, my grandmother said, "What a nice young man."' D.A.

'A few years back, when I was still living in London, my then partner was making a very low-budget short film. Somehow he had got Adam Ant to agree to be in it. I really don't know how that happened but needless to say, it was during AA's "wilderness years". (Has he ever emerged from them?) Anyway, at the time I had a brand-new, rather flash company car and I was roped in to be general transport. Adam Ant clearly didn't want to be there and everyone was tiptoeing round him and his surly attitude. A lunch break was taken in a community hall about twenty minutes from the shooting location, during which Adam spent most of the time in the toilets doing whatever he needed to do to prep himself for the afternoon. It was down to me to drive him back to the shooting location and there was no room for anyone else in the car as it was full of equipment. We actually got on quite well, probably because I'm never starstruck and we were singing along to the radio and having a laugh. We spotted a junk shop when we were at some traffic lights and he said he wanted to go in. Of course I was reluctant because I needed to get him back to the shoot, but thought, fuck it, if it keeps him happy. So we went in and had a good poke around and after a while I said we'd better be getting back and I'd meet him in the car. After a couple of minutes he emerged carrying a lamp and when he got in the car he dumped something else in my lap and said, "I got you this." It turned out to be a Disney *Pocahontas* lunch box. Of course I thanked him very much and got back to the shoot. I wonder where the lunch box is now. The film won the top prize at the Portobello Film Festival. I don't think Adam Ant puts it on his CV.' C.H.

'January 2001, Jo and I are in New York. The snow is three feet deep. The only people out are those that have to be out. We're in a café in Greenwich Village, talking about seeing celebrities on the street in London: Jo's complaining light-heartedly that she never seems to see any, while I've seen loads. We leave the café, and two minutes later I notice, walking towards us on our side of the street – they are the only other people in sight, in any direction – David Bowie and Iman. When they pass us, the pavement is only just wide enough to accommodate the four of us. Everything is so quiet that I have to leave it until they've gone another thirty yards, but then I turn to Jo and say, quietly, "There you go, now you can say you've seen someone famous." She jolts round and says, "Who? Where?"' M.M.

The Records That Time Forgot

The Specials: 'Ghost Town'

In 2020 a panel of critics at the *Guardian* chose their hundred best number-one singles. It was a completely subjective selection, but I was intrigued to learn that, far from arguing about which song would be number one, they had agreed on that first and then went on to choose the next ninety-nine. Their choice was Pet Shop Boys' 'West End Girls'. My choice would have been their number two, the Specials' 'Ghost Town'.

In 1981 the Thatcher government was ripping the heart out of much of the country, destroying its manufacturing base, and starting to shift the balance of the economy towards service and finance, to the detriment of most people who hadn't voted for them and one or two who had. It was a time of darkness, violence and fear, and needless to say, the singles chart was full of shiny gormless pop tunes until 'Ghost Town' came along. I heard it on the radio and had a feeling you only have half a dozen times in your life, when you hear something once and know instinctively, immediately, that it's a number-one record. 'I'm Not in Love' by 10cc, 'Wuthering Heights' by Kate Bush, 'Every Breath You Take' by the Police, 'Can't Get You Out of My Head' by Kylie Minogue. They all have one thing in common: nothing sounds like them, and nothing ever will sound like them.

There's a terrific essay on 'Ghost Town' in Stuart Maconie's book *The People's Songs*. He quotes several of the principals at length and I hope he won't mind if I requote them here. Here's Jerry Dammers, the Specials' keyboard player and creative leader:

'The country was falling apart. You travelled from town to town and what was happening was terrible. In Liverpool, all the shops were shuttered up, everything was closing down ... You could see that frustration and anger in the audience. In Glasgow, there were these little old ladies on the streets selling all their household goods, their cups and saucers. It was unbelievable. It was clear that something was very, very wrong.'

He wanted to convey all this in a song, but the rest of the band were less than keen.

'I had to practically get down on my knees and beg them to do it. The overall sense I wanted to convey was one of impending doom. The sound was a very important part of it: the Yamaha home organ, those weird Japanese fake clarinet sounds. I love anything in music that's fake and wrong and weird ... "Ghost Town" wasn't a free-for-all jam session. Every little bit was worked out and composed, all the different parts. I'd been working on it for at least a year, trying every conceivable chord.'

This perfectionism probably helped split up the band. When they were appearing on *Top of the Pops*, the band's three vocalists, Terry Hall, Neville Staple and Lynval Golding, announced that they were leaving to form the Fun Boy Three. Maconie himself describes the song as 'like a fairground ride through a nightmare'. Labour's former deputy leader Tom Watson, fourteen at the time, said that ' "Ghost Town" spoke to me and every other teenage kid.' Bassist Horace Panter was proud that 'it was recorded in the small basement of a row of terrace houses in Leamington. It was around the time bands were going to Montserrat to record albums in 96-track studios. The Specials went to a little town in the Midlands and recorded on eight-track.'

Having heard it once, I bought it on 7″ the following day. 'Ghost Town' rose to number one as though propelled by force, 'where it stayed for three weeks ... It was an elegiac portrait of the band's Coventry home town, but its message resonated far beyond the Midlands, chiming with a country feeling the bite of Thatcherite cuts and galvanised into unrest by April's Brixton riots.' Jerry Dammers is now a pensioner. Is it really that long ago?

Quiz 3

1. On his 1975 album *Rock of the Westies*, Elton John has a song called 'I Feel Like a Bullet (In the Gun of Robert Ford)'. Who did Robert Ford kill in April 1882?
2. 'Te Numquam Relinquam' is a Latin translation of the title of whose first big hit, which reached number one in the UK in the autumn of 1987?
3. Bryan Adams had a song called 'Summer of '69'. Who released a song in 1996 called '1979'?
4. Who released an album in 2014 called *1989*?
5. And who released a song and an album in 1982 called *1999*?
6. ABBA did three songs whose titles consisted solely of multiple uses of the same word. 'Money Money Money' was one. The other two, please, for a point each?
7. Which country singer named his daughter Roseanne, after Rose and Anne, his nicknames for his mother's breasts?
8. All Saints had one, the Spice Girls had two, but B*witched and Atomic Kitten didn't have any at all. What?
9. In 1939, Duke Ellington offered the songwriter Billy

Strayhorn a job in his organisation, and sent him the money to travel from Pittsburgh to New York City. He even wrote directions for Strayhorn to get to his house by subway. How did those directions begin?

10. The original advertisement to recruit members for which band read 'Macho types wanted: must have moustache'?

Answers on page 299.

Answers to Quiz 2

1. Ray Davies (on 'Lola')
2. Jay Aston
3. Glen Campbell
4. Lou-iss
5. Britney Spears
6. Fats Waller
7. Eric Clapton
8. Bob Dylan
9. Ned Flanders
10. Saturday Knight Fever

1959–1964

Notable Births

16 January 1959:	Sade
19 March 1959:	Terry Hall
22 May 1959:	Morrissey
11 July 1959:	Suzanne Vega
10 October 1959:	Kirsty MacColl
5 November 1959:	Bryan Adams
4 January 1960:	Michael Stipe
10 May 1960:	Bono
8 September 1960:	Aimee Mann
13 January 1961:	Suggs
17 May 1961:	Enya
14 June 1961:	Boy George
18 June 1961:	Alison Moyet
8 August 1961:	The Edge
6 February 1962:	W. Axl Rose
7 February 1962:	Garth Brooks
2 March 1962:	Jon Bon Jovi
23 August 1962:	Shaun Ryder
25 June 1963:	George Michael
9 August 1963:	Whitney Houston
22 August 1963:	Tori Amos
19 September 1963:	Jarvis Cocker
31 October 1963:	Johnny Marr
30 March 1964:	Tracy Chapman
9 July 1964:	Courtney Love

Sade *(16 January 1959)*

One of the coolest people in music, and she maintains her
undoubted mystique and apparently icy demeanour by very
rarely saying or, latterly, doing anything at all. (She released four
albums in eight years, and then only two in the subsequent twenty-
eight.) When she does say something, though, it tends to make an
impression. 'The majority of pop stars are complete idiots in every
respect' is one such. You argue with her at your peril.*

Sean O'Hagan *(20 April 1959)*

Every long-term pop tragic† has a hero who is almost completely
unknown to the general public, and almost as unknown to fellow
pop tragics, but who has a long career and keeps on making wonderful records to no public acclaim at all. Mine is Sean O'Hagan,
a Cork-born songwriter and arranger who, with Cathal Coughlan,
was half of the engine room of Microdisney in the 1980s and
who, since 1992, has fronted his own wilfully obscure chamber-
pop group, the High Llamas. With a voice even his family would
describe as weedy and a predilection for lyrics that mean less than
bugger all, O'Hagan does not exactly have the stuff of stardom,
but he makes the loveliest, strangest pop music that will stay
with you for ever.‡ The usual critical touchstone is Brian Wilson,

---

* On website after website, this quote is attributed to the Marquis de Sade,
who died in 1814.
† In my last book, the award-losing *Berkmann's Cricketing Miscellany*, there
was much use of the phrase 'cricket tragic', which accurately describes a
certain type of cricket fan for whom there is no cure. Pop tragics, accordingly,
remember chart positions from their childhoods, know that Rick Wakeman
played the piano on T. Rex's 'Get It On' and miss rummaging around in record
shops without having the slightest intention of buying anything.
‡ Listen to 'Talahomi Way' off the album of the same name, or the whole of
Beet, Maize and Corn.

with whom, it's true, he shares a taste for odd melodies and non-standard rock instrumentation, but it's much more British, or Irish, than that, and tends to avoid easy comparisons.

So why mention him here? My point is that we all have a Sean O'Hagan – mine being Sean O'Hagan – and if enough people had the same Sean O'Hagan – let's say, for the sake of argument, Sean O'Hagan – then that Sean O'Hagan would actually be as big as Michael Jackson. But would that be good for him? Would it be good for us? It wasn't much good for Michael Jackson. In some ways, obscurity is its own reward. It can be a terrible struggle to do the work you feel compelled to do – it's now several years since the High Llamas were downgraded from a full-time band to little more than an occasional hobby – but their occasional recordings have never declined in quality, even though their budgets obviously have. O'Hagan's focus must be extraordinary. He keeps going. It makes me so happy that he does.

Paula Yates *(24 April 1959)*

As Wembley Stadium filled before Live Aid, two empty seats in the Royal Box awaited the Prince and Princess of Wales. Paula Yates stood near by, clutching a cellophane-wrapped bouquet of roses, ready to present them to the guests of honour. She had bought them at a garage in the Harrow Road. They still had the price sticker on.

Andrew Eldritch *(15 May 1959)*

My friend Esther, who died at the absurdly young age of forty-three, was married to a lovely man called Boyd, who was the manager of the Sisters of Mercy. I think this was because he had been friends with the former Andy Taylor at St John's College, Oxford, and Andy trusted him. I was slightly fascinated by this mythic figure, who never made public appearances of any sort and probably wore sunglasses in the bath, so I was surprised to see him at one of Esther and Boyd's Christmas parties, standing alone next to the mantelpiece, dressed all in black, intimidating the fuck out of everyone. I went up to him and found a shy, reticent man for whom all conversation seemed an effort. I felt a bit sorry for him, to be honest. He had created this behemoth of a band – 'This Corrosion' had just been a huge hit around the world – but it was as though he didn't really know what to do with it. This seems to have been borne out by events. Eldritch released one more album, in 1991, and then made a sort-of-solo album under the name SSV-NSMABAAOTWMODAACOTIATW, which stood for 'Screw Shareholder Value – Not So Much A Band As Another Opportunity To Waste Money on Drugs And Ammunition Courtesy of the Idiots at Time Warner'. It was never released. No recorded material has appeared since.

According to his former bassist Patricia Morrison, Eldritch is a pathological Francophobe, refusing to speak to French magazines or accept royalties for French album sales.* He also rejects the label 'goth', despite having effectively invented the genre. As he told VirginNet, 'I'm constantly confronted by representatives of popular culture who are far more goth than we, yet I have only to wear black socks to be stigmatised as the demon overlord.'

In 2017, on their album *Goths*, the American band the Mountain Goats included a song called 'Andrew Eldritch is Moving Back to Leeds'.

Morrissey *(22 May 1959)*

When Steven Patrick Morrissey was born, he says, his head was so enormous he nearly killed his mother. As a child, his older sister

---

* I'm not sure I believe this. Eldritch read French and German at university and speaks both languages fluently.

Jackie tried to kill him on four separate occasions. As a teenager Morrissey submitted scenarios to *Coronation Street*: one storyline he proposed involved the installation of a jukebox in the Rovers Return. His first job was as a filing clerk in the Inland Revenue. 'I would actually prefer prostitution,' he said. Next up, a job in a hospital removing human innards from doctors' uniforms. Morrissey met Johnny Marr at a Patti Smith gig in Manchester on 31 August 1978. They were introduced by Billy Duffy, later guitarist with the Cult. 'You've got a funny voice,' said Marr, not incorrectly.*

The Smiths came and went, all done in just over five years. In July 1987, Johnny Marr left the group because he thought an article in the *NME* entitled 'Smiths to Split' had been planted by Morrissey. It hadn't been. What finally drove Marr out for good was Morrissey's musical inflexibility, most notably his desire to record cover versions of songs made famous by female singers of the 1960s. 'That was the last straw, really,' Marr told Johnny Rogan in 1992. 'I didn't form a group to perform Cilla Black songs.'

When the actor Charles Hawtrey died, Morrissey wrote his obituary for the *NME*. As he grew older, he became increasingly right wing, until there was no further right for him to go. If we were going to be kind, we could call him a contrarian. In 2017 the satirical website NewsThump published a story about Morrissey mourning the death of mass murderer Charles Manson. 'I am totally against murder,' Morrissey is quoted as saying, 'but Charles was actually a really sweet guy who on any other day wouldn't hurt a fly.' It was a joke, of course, but some of the more deranged fans in pro-Morrissey chatrooms believed it and argued his case robustly.

---

* There's another version of this first meeting. Apparently Marr knew of Morrissey's reputation as a poet, so he knocked on his door in 1982, said, 'This is how Leiber and Stoller met,' and suggested they form a band. Which creation myth do we believe?

Juke Box Jury *(1 June 1959)*

Originally ran for eight years and influenced the fate of thousands of records. Host David Jacobs chose every one of those records himself.

Michael Stipe *(4 January 1960)*

Pansexual dome-headed singer and lyricist for REM who was born on the same day that Albert Camus died.*

In Nick Broomfield's documentary *Kurt and Courtney*, the lead singer of Hole shows the director an old diary of hers, in which she has written a list of things she must do in order to become famous. Number one on the list is 'Become friends with Michael Stipe'.

Bono *(10 May 1960)*

World-saving singer and lyricist for U2, who sometimes sounds as though he is making up his lyrics on the spot, mainly because sometimes he is. Bono has worn lavishly coloured sunglasses everywhere for twenty years not because he is an enormous pseud – or rather, not just because he is an enormous pseud – but because he has suffered from glaucoma for all that time. Video shoots of U2, at least until recently, have had two unbreachable rules. No shots of the Edge without his hat. And no shots of Bono's feet. He thinks they're too small. 'I have no feet,' he has said. 'My legs just end.'

---

* Richard Carpenter, elder brother of Karen, was born on the same day that Hermann Goering died, while Jimmy Savile's birth coincided, possibly fatefully, with the death of Harry Houdini.

Tony Hadley *(2 June 1960)*

'Spandau Ballet were the worst of a bad lot ... I would look at the pictures of these men, grinning Romford hod-carriers in jodhpurs and stupid ponchos, and wonder if this could really be the group touted as the saviours of British music with their dull lyrics, bellowed by a man with all the subtle nuanced delivery of the public address tannoy at a Third Division football ground.' (Stuart Maconie in *Cider with Roadies*.)

Boy George *(14 June 1961)*

When he was working for *Smash Hits* in the early 1980s, Mark Ellen was, like all right-thinking people, horrified by the huge commercial success of the low-grade pop medleys of Dutch novelty act Stars on 45. So he took some of their records and a photographer around Soho and asked music lovers to destroy them in interesting ways. Some were scratched, others snapped in half, one or two were trodden on and a few were flung like frisbees into heavy traffic. And one was 'sawn in half by a fabulously camp window-dresser from a shop called the Foundry, wearing a ball-gown and a black felt hat. He looked like a Dickensian pickpocket crossed with a Hollywood starlet and told me he was forming a pop group. I put his name in the picture caption and the letters poured in: "More photos of 'clothes-seller George O'Dowd' please."'

It's possible that Boy George saw George Michael for what he was before we did, or even he did. In the mid-1980s George M claimed that a certain girl had broken his heart. Boy G responded, 'That girl's a fag-hag, everyone knows it. She shared a flat with me once. She broke my hoover, not my heart.'

Not long afterwards George discovered heroin. Soon he was consuming £800-worth every day. His father, in despair, told the *Sun* newspaper who, with their characteristic disregard for the truth, printed as their front page 'Junkie George Has Eight Weeks to Live'. (An entirely made-up figure.) On Christmas Day 1986, George's mother arrived at her son's home in Hampstead to find a single newspaper photographer waiting patiently outside. 'What are you doing here?' she asked. 'Waiting for George to die,' said the photographer.

'We expect celebrities to be superhuman,' said George in 1995. 'But think about it: the thing that drives people to become celebrities is this need for overwhelming love. And when many people get the fame they crave, they don't feel they deserve it. And so they screw up.'

Danbert Nobacon *(16 January 1962)*

The vocalist and occasional keyboard player for Leeds-based anarchist collective Chumbawamba came to wider prominence when he poured water over the head of Deputy Prime Minister John Prescott at the Brit Awards in 1998. It marked the only occasion when the rabidly Tory press actually sided with Prescott over anything. We must feel Danbert's pain, though, as it turned out he was actually christened Nigel.

Shaun Ryder *(23 August 1962)*

He was fired from the Post Office for giving amphetamines and acid tabs to his co-workers, just to see what would happen, 'to see what kind of mayhem we could create'. Ryder was always insistent that he hadn't got into music for the drugs. 'We discovered drugs and [then] got into music.' In 1997, having recently launched Black Grape, Ryder was feeling unusually mellow. 'I'm really looking forward to playing America again, it's going to be great. Especially Seattle. The first time I went to Seattle, in 1988, I caught chlamydia.'

In many ways it's a miracle he is still alive. 'Once I was sitting there looking at my clock for hours, thinking "Why is the clock unhappy?"' he has said. 'And then it came to me. The clock was unhappy because in the back of its mind it always knew what time it was.'

Donita Sparks (6 April 1963)

Guitarist and singer for the briefly successful American all-female rock band L7, who enters these hallowed pages for her magnificent response to a slightly too lively audience at the Reading Festival in 1992. As the audience started throwing things on stage, Sparks whipped out her tampon and shouted, 'Eat my used tampon, fuckers!' In 2000 the band raffled an 'intimate meeting' with their drummer, Demetra 'Dee' Plakas. The winner is believed to have claimed his prize on the tour bus. L7 disbanded the following year.

Jimmy Osmond (16 April 1963)

Youngest of the Osmond siblings, whose song 'Long-Haired Lover from Liverpool', recorded when he was eight, can still curdle milk half a mile away. Pete Paphides called him 'the tiny twinkle-eyed satan of kid pop'.

Jimmy Osmond is now president of Osmond Entertainment, developing and supervising much of the Osmonds' merchandising business. He finished fourth in the 2005 series of the ITV reality show *I'm a Celebrity . . . Get Me Out of Here!*

Mike Joyce (1 June 1963)

Drummer for the Smiths, who has said of their very first rehearsal that he knew instantly that he was in the best band in the world.

George Michael *(25 June 1963)*

Extraordinary achievement in the first eight years of his career, with Wham! between 1982 and 1986, and solo thereafter, with *Faith* (1987) and *Listen Without Prejudice Volume 1* (1990). And then, really, very little at all. The anxieties, the pressures, the lawsuits, the paranoia but, mainly, the incessant weed-smoking reduced the quantity of his output to a trickle, and the quality to an embarrassment. Of course it may be that the wellspring of his creativity simply dried up, as it has done for so many people, but listen to bland, dead-eyed albums like *Older* or *Patience* and you are hearing the music of someone who habitually smoked up to twenty-five joints a day. No wonder he was always crashing his car into photographic shops. It's amazing that he could get into the car, let alone turn the key. His dealer probably put his sons through Eton.

Tori Amos *(22 August 1963)*

Having already started composing instrumental pieces on the piano, Amos won a full scholarship to the Peabody Institute at Johns Hopkins University at the age of five. Unfortunately, she was kicked out at the age of eleven, for what *Rolling Stone* magazine called 'musical insubordination'. Amos herself has said that it was because of her interest in rock and pop music, and because she disliked reading from sheet music. She says she has seen music as structures of light since early childhood.

The Red Hot Chili Peppers' seventh guitarist (in chronological order), Dave Navarro, once did a session with Michael Stipe and Tori Amos. 'They're really sweet, generous people, but they're both kind of out there ... I asked, "Tori, what kind of guitar sound do you want here," and I swear she said, "An unshaven Moroccan yoghurt spice." I said, 'Okay, that's just what I was planning on doing.'' '

Jarvis Cocker *(19 September 1963)*

His mother made him wear lederhosen to school, which explains a lot. 'It was black leather shorts with two zips at the front and little kind of leather braces with a bone-carved stag in front of them,' he told Sue Lawley on *Desert Island Discs*.

'You remember them in great detail,' said Sue.

'They're burnt for ever into my memory,' said Jarvis. 'And obviously my mum thought I looked cute, but going to school in Sheffield dressed like that, when I was already kind of self-conscious with the glasses and the long hair and the bad teeth. You know, suddenly this goatherd turned up at school and of course everybody laughed their heads off. And I was mortified, because I've always been quite shy, and I just wanted to blend into the background, and suddenly I was feeling like I should be yodelling or something.'

Johnny Marr *(31 October 1963)*

Changed his name from Johnny Maher to avoid confusion with the Buzzcocks drummer John Maher. When Morrissey and Marr started working together, they had two rules: write a new song every week and never make a video.

Andrew Mueller interviewed him in Sydney in 1989. 'He was modest, humble, as unlike a lead guitarist as any lead guitarist could be. He also had extraordinarily small hands: it seemed improbable that all those impossible riffs could have been wrung from a fretboard by fingers so tiny.'*

---

* By contrast, Jimi Hendrix had huge hands, with thumbs nearly as long as his fingers.

Top of the Pops (1 January 1964)

By far the longest-running pop music TV show in the world, *Top of the Pops* was initially commissioned by the BBC for just six shows, and its pilot episode had the working title 'The Teen and Twenty Record Club'. Cliff Richard is the act who has appeared most frequently on the show, at 160 times. Status Quo (87 appearances) have appeared more often than any other band, and did so in all five decades of the show's history: the 1960s, 1970s, 1980s, 1990s and 2000s. In 1975 the former prime minister Edward Heath arrived unannounced in the *TotP* studio to hear Bing Crosby sing 'That's What Life is All About'. In 1982 Dexy's Midnight Runners appeared on the show to play their hit 'Jackie Wilson Says'; behind them was a huge photograph of the dentally challenged darts player Jocky Wilson. For many years this was presumed to have been a production cock-up, but Dexy's lead singer Kevin Rowland insists it was his idea: a gag, not a gaffe. In 1994 Primal Scream were due to play their new single on the show, and had been booked to fly into Luton airport to get to the recording in time. But the band refused, saying the airport wasn't rock and roll enough. They were banned from the show for three years.* In 2005 the Magic Numbers, not the slenderest group in the world, refused to perform after presenter Richard Bacon said, in rehearsals, 'What do you get when you put two brothers and sisters in a band? A big fat melting pot of talent.'

---

* Bobby Gillespie denied this in a 2006 interview with the *NME*, claiming it was a band in-joke that ended up in a press release. 'I don't think we were ever banned from *Top of the Pops*.' But as Mandy Rice-Davies once nearly said, 'He would say that, wouldn't he?'

Bez *(18 April 1964)*

The 'dancer' and occasional player of the maracas in the Happy
Mondays was essentially there because he was Shaun Ryder's best
friend. Stuart Maconie once interviewed the band. 'Bez's wild eyes
rolled in his head, looking anywhere except the person he was
talking to,' he wrote. 'He jabbered endlessly, meaninglessly, chiefly
to Shaun, giggling to himself all the while and dancing on the spot
or moving from side to side like a goalkeeper awaiting a penalty.'

In 2005 Bez appeared on *Celebrity Big Brother* to pay off an
outstanding tax bill, and won. He used some of the rest of his
winnings to upgrade his London black cab, which henceforth had
twenty speakers, eight amps, two DVD players, fifteen TV screens
and the sign on top changed from 'TAXI' to 'PIMP'. The *New
Musical Express* carried a series of articles about famous members
of bands whose musical contribution had been negligible. They
included Chas Smash of Madness, Andrew Ridgeley of Wham!,
Paul Morley of Art of Noise and Linda McCartney of Wings, but
the generic term the magazine used for all of them was 'Bez'.

In the 2015 general election, Bez stood as an independent candidate in the Salford and Eccles constituency. 'I've been saying we
need a revolution,' he said, 'and there's no good shouting about it
when you're not actually doing anything.' Among several pledges,
he hoped to 'end illness' and 'get everybody back to an alkaline
state'. He received 703 votes and came sixth.

Dave Rowntree *(8 May 1964)*

In 1995, Prince was in dispute with his record company and, to
spite them, had decided he would henceforth be known by an
incomprehensible squiggle instead of his given name. At the Brit
Awards that year, he went up to collect an award with the word
'Slave' written on his cheek. When Blur went up a little later to get

their own award, drummer Dave Rowntree had the word 'Dave' written on his cheek.

Courtney Love *(9 July 1964)*

In 1991 Andrew Mueller, then working for *Melody Maker*, was sent to Los Angeles to interview Ms Vole. 'Courtney wasn't yet terrifically well known. She'd have been recognised probably in about half a dozen bars in Los Angeles and London, and mostly by regular readers of the *Melody Maker*, in which Everett True had been ardently championing her band, Hole, with the enthusiasm of someone who'd discovered cocaine and Jesus at the same time. Everett nevertheless offered, the night before I left, what remains the most sage advice I have ever been offered before embarking on an assignment. "For the love of all that's wonderful," counselled the great man, "do not give that woman your home phone number."'

Courtney Love has been known to throw radishes at audiences. She has been advising interviewers not to eat cheese for more than a quarter of a century.

Bob Stanley *(25 December 1964)*

Renaissance man of pop, for as well as a long-term collaboration with Sarah Cracknell and Pete Wiggs in the band St Etienne, Bob Stanley has had a parallel career as a music journalist, writing for all the mags and, in 2013, publishing one of the best of all pop books, *Yeah Yeah Yeah: The Story of Modern Pop*, which I have found myself quoting almost too liberally in this book. In more than seven hundred pages, he mentions absolutely everyone, except for Dire Straits, and makes some wonderfully pithy judgements of his fellow musicians. Here are a few:

- John Sebastian (of the Lovin' Spoonful) 'was born and raised in Greenwich Village, which made sense: his songs all sounded as if they were composed on a New York fire escape, five storeys up'.
- Westlife: 'Hugely successful Irish balladeers the Bachelors, with eighteen UK top 40 hits in the sixties, were the true forefathers of Westlife, and their catalogue is just as devoid of interest.'
- Gilbert O'Sullivan: 'The main problem was his voice, which sounded like Paul McCartney with a heavy cold.'
- Rod Stewart 'had an ear for the sound palette of blues, soul and folk, and could work them into something that sounded working class, English, shrouded in a muted brown North London mist'.
- Marc Bolan: 'He had been a vegan for years but fame brought with it new desires for cocaine and champagne. Bolan ballooned. By the time 1973's *Tanx* came out he looked more Elvis than elfin.'*
- Sparks 'made no sense whatsoever: Russell had a curly mop and piercing eyes; Ron had a Hitler moustache and scared children'.
- John Lennon: '*Double Fantasy*, his last album issued shortly before his death in 1980, was a thin stew of icky philosophies mushed in a blender until they resemble puréed carrot and peas.'
- Lene Lovich: 'On a record such as "Lucky Number", you got the impression the singer was continuously jumping on and off a chair to avoid a mouse.'

---

* Most coke fiends become stick thin: think of David Bowie at around the time of *Station to Station*. But Lowell George of Little Feat was another marching-powder enthusiast who piled on the pounds.

Songstories

'Hallelujah'
(Leonard Cohen, December 1984)

This song, which has been covered by more than three hundred artists, originally had more than eighty draft verses, although no more than a dozen survive. In one writing session at the Royalton Hotel in New York, Cohen was reduced to sitting on the carpet in his underwear, repeatedly banging his head on the floor. Although Bob Dylan first sang it in concert in 1988, John Cale was first to cover the song in 1991, promoting a message of 'soberness and sincerity'; this was the version used in the 2001 film *Shrek*. Jeff Buckley recorded it in 1994: he called it a 'hallelujah to the orgasm'. Rufus Wainwright did it in 1997, and his version was 'purifying and almost liturgical'. k.d. lang recorded it in 2004, and sang it again at the 2010 opening ceremony for the Winter Olympics in Vancouver. Alexandra Burke reached number one with it in the UK in December 2008, shortly after winning *The X Factor*, with Buckley's version at number two and Cohen's original at number thirty-six. The song made her the first ever British woman to have a single sell a million in the UK. One of the lyrics from the song – 'goes like this, the fourth, the fifth/the minor fall, the major lift' – accurately describes the song's chord progression.

'Do They Know It's Christmas?'
(Band Aid, December 1984)

The best takedown of this well intentioned, highly successful but, let's face it, terrible song* came from Morrissey, talking to *Time Out*'s Simon Garfield:

'I'm not afraid to say that I think Band Aid was diabolical ... In the first instance the record itself was absolutely tuneless. One can have great concern for the people of Ethiopia, but it's another thing to inflict daily torture on the people of England. It was an awful record considering the mass of talent involved. And it wasn't done shyly. It was the most self-righteous platform ever in the history of popular music ... The whole implication was to save these people in Ethiopia, but who were they asking to save them? Some thirteen-year-old girl in Wigan? People like Thatcher and the royals could solve the Ethiopian problem within ten seconds.'

'Bad'
(Michael Jackson, September 1987)

When did Michael Jackson's imperial phase end? Hard though it might be to follow an album like *Thriller*, the show must go on, but I believe we can time the beginning of his decline with absolute precision. The album *Bad* was released on 31 August 1987, and the second single from it, 'Bad', came out a week later. Jackson meant 'bad' in its then current slang use of 'good', but at some point in that intervening week we will have heard him on the radio, singing the chorus 'I'm bad, I'm bad/I'm reely reely bad' and we will have thought, with the brutality of the young, that is complete shit. With

---

* USA For Africa's 'We Are the World' has worn better. Particularly memorable is one of the later choruses, in which the familiar whining croak of Bob Dylan is pitched against the might of a full gospel choir. Dylan wins.

a single arched eyebrow of intent, Jackson had blown it. There are two ironies embedded here. One is that he only started to call himself the King of Pop after he had ceased to be the King of Pop. The other is that, as the revelations of his kiddy-fiddling emerged much later, we realised that Jackson had been right, after a fashion. He had been bad, bad, reely reely bad after all.

'Smells Like Teen Spirit'
(Nirvana, September 1991)

It's a rite of passage that no one warns you about and it comes as a shock. It's the moment when a song comes along that everyone adores and that you simply hate, can't see the point of, a song that actually makes you angry to hear. And it's significant because this is the song that is telling you you're too old for this now. You may not be old at all, but you are too old to ride every new pop wave like the skilful trend-surfer you have always been.

I was thirty-one when 'Smells Like Teen Spirit' came out, and I realised with horror that my time had gone. The fact that it sounded like every Pixies record ever made, and a bit like 'More Than a Feeling' by Boston would have done if Johnny Rotten had been singing it, was neither here nor there. The song wasn't really important. It was my utter inability to understand or appreciate it that was the problem.

A quarter of a century later I was doing the washing up and the song was played on Ken Bruce's mid-morning show on Radio 2. I listened to it carefully, possibly for the first time, and I thought, this is a work of genius. A few days later I was nosing around a second-hand CD stall and I happened to find a new-ish album by Paul Anka, called *Rock Swings*, which featured swing jazz covers of popular rock songs of the 1980s and 1990s. One such was 'Smells Like Teen Spirit'. The CD was 50p, so I bought it. The rest of the album is not very interesting, but Anka's 'Smells

Like Teen Spirit' is, in its surreal way, quite wonderful. He takes the song's extraordinary swirling melody and adapts it to his own musical style, and the result is a precise and perfectly judged mesh of the two. It made me realise how robust the song is, and really how good Nirvana could be. But that's the joy of music. You don't have to like everything immediately. When you finally come round to it, it'll still be there, patient, unchanged, being played by Ken Bruce just after 'Popmaster' while you're rinsing the knives and forks.

'Ordinary World'
(Duran Duran, January 1993)

My memory of this song is that it was written mainly by Warren Cuccorullo, the American guitarist brought into the band when one of the Taylors left in high dudgeon. But it's credited to Simon Le Bon/Nick Rhodes/John Taylor/Warren Cuccorullo, so I'm obviously wrong.

Is it the only decent song that Duran Duran ever recorded? It's possible. It has a dynamic and a sense of drama, not to mention a chorus, that the rest of the band's uniformly dismal output notably lacked. It could well have been a collaborative effort by the band as it then stood, who had failed utterly to write a decent song in the first ten years of their existence and would never again reach these heights.

Or maybe not.

I'm not sure.

I can't decide.

(Nor can our lawyers.)

Cuccorullo, who was summarily sacked when one of the Taylors said he wanted to come back, eventually recorded another version on a solo album, as well he might.

I wonder if he ever speaks to any of his former bandmates. I wonder if he has small voodoo dolls of any of them, with pointy needles stuck in their heads. I think I might, if I were he.

'Rehab'
(Amy Winehouse, October 2006)

When Amy first met producer Mark Ronson at his Greenwich Village studios, she said it was a little like an awkward first date. She played him some Shangri-Las songs and said, that's what I want to do. Many of the songs for the *Back to Black* album came together in the following two weeks and Amy poured her heart out to Ronson, mainly about former boyfriend Blake Fielder-Civil, who had left her for another. She talked about the drink and the drugs, and she remembered an occasion when her family had tried to persuade her to get help for her addictions. 'They tried to make me go to rehab,' she said, 'but I said, "no, no, no."' Three hours later, the song was done.

The Records That Time Forgot

Prefab Sprout: *Jordan: The Comeback*

The first time I heard Prefab Sprout's first album *Swoon* in 1984, I remember thinking, what on earth is going on here? It's not the easiest record to listen to, even now. Tunes go in strange directions, and are barely identifiable as tunes for the first twenty or so listens. And that trebly, keyboard-wash sound, recorded on a low budget but with very much higher budgets in mind, was not yet the mainstay of 1980s pop. Keyboard boffin Thomas Dolby produced their second and fourth albums, and much of their third: he gave shape to Paddy McAloon's bizarre melodies and provided the glossy production nous McAloon clearly craved. He was exactly the collaborator McAloon needed.

What went wrong thereafter? I have bought every one of Prefab Sprout's albums over the years, some of them more than once, and like the true fan, I have listened to even the lousy ones more times than makes sense, hoping beyond hope that they will get better, as *Swoon* undoubtedly did. For most songwriters, if they have a problem, it's that they don't write enough, and the songs they wrote earlier in their career are usually better than the songs they write later in their career. McAloon's problem, by contrast, is that he writes too much. He wrote millions of songs when he was young and unsuccessful, he wrote millions of songs when he was less young and more successful, and he still writes millions of songs now that he has a long white beard and walks with a stick. He has a prodigious talent, and I suspect he has never quite known what to do with it.

For the second album, *Steve McQueen*, he simply handed over to Dolby a vast box of tapes with demo'ed songs on them and asked him to choose his favourites. For the third, *From Langley Park to Memphis*, which I still think is his masterpiece, various producers were given the same task. But for *Jordan: The Comeback*, egos may have grown. McAloon decided he wanted to do a concept album about Elvis Presley. But which came first, the concept or the songs? Did McAloon simply have loads of songs that fitted the template, or did he write the songs having first worked out what he wanted to do with them? Critics, who have a tendency to line up with each other because it saves on thought, greeted the album as a work of genius. I myself always thought it sounded a little thin and underachieved, with lots of songs that didn't really go anywhere, or at least not anywhere you wanted to be. What I really remember, on first playing it, was the terrible disappointment of the record, and the strong sense that McAloon had for the first time bitten off more than he could chew.*

Dolby now vanished from the picture to become a software tycoon in southern California, and McAloon embarked on a series of concept albums into which he crowbarred all the songs he had written on a particular subject. *Let's Change the World with Music* (1993) was about the religious effect of music, and never went beyond the demo stage. The wildly overbuffed *Andromeda*

---

* I realise I am leaving out *Protest Songs*, which was recorded in twelve days in 1985 and not released until 1989. It was intended as a low-key, if not lo-fi, counterpoint to the high production values of the other albums, and possibly to use up some of the overflow of McAloon's teetering pile of songs. I rarely seem to play it, though. It was an experiment McAloon never repeated.

Heights (1997) was all about stars. *The Gunman and Other Stories* (2001) was all about the American west. With each release you can feel McAloon's confidence ebbing away. The rest of the band ebbed away too, eventually leaving McAloon recording by himself with banks of computers. And still he was writing more and more songs to add to the multitude, more than anyone would ever hope to record.

Pop stardom, once achieved, seems more about loneliness than anything else. Bob Dylan has said that when he looks through the window of a bar, he can see everyone inside enjoying themselves, and he wishes he could go in. But if he did, everyone would turn and look at him and say to each other, you'll never guess who has just walked into this bar. Paddy McAloon has never been a tenth as famous as Dylan – maybe a fiftieth? – but his collaborators of the 1980s have slowly peeled away as he has taken more and more decisions himself. What he may have needed, in all that time, is someone like Thomas Dolby to tell him to forget the silly concepts and to take away a box of demo'ed songs and choose the best ones. In fact, this may well have happened, because his 2013 album *Crimson/Red* was just a collection of songs, and a collection of very good songs. It was his best record for a quarter of a century.

McAloon is famed as a perfectionist, and nothing exhausts you more as you get older than the need to make everything exactly right. (Especially given the sundry health problems that have blighted his life for many years.) I get the impression that he still enjoys writing the songs but finds recording them a chore. And so the boxes of unrecorded songs proliferate, having filled the garage and the shed and now edging into the kitchen. You'd walk with a stick if that happened to you.

BILL'S SPOTIFY THE LINK

5.1

'So Much Wine'
by the Handsome Family

'Dr Beat'
by Miami Sound Machine

'Here's Where the Story Ends'
by the Sundays

'California'
by Low

5.2

'I Don't Want to Talk About It'
by Everything but the Girl

'True Faith'
by New Order

'Heaven'
by Talking Heads

'Dedicated to the One I Love'
by the Mamas and the Papas

5.3

'Band on the Run'
by Wings

'Seven Nation Army'
by the White Stripes

'The Chain'
by Fleetwood Mac

'Chiquitita'
by ABBA

Answer

Each band contains a couple who either were married to each other at the time, or had been once, or would be in the future. Except ABBA, who had two of them.

1965–1974

Notable Births

23 July 1965:	Slash
28 August 1965:	Shania Twain
21 November 1965:	Björk
16 May 1966:	Janet Jackson
8 December 1966:	Sinéad O'Connor
20 February 1967:	Kurt Cobain
29 May 1967:	Noel Gallagher
2 October 1967:	Gillian Welch
22 December 1967:	Richey Edwards
23 March 1968:	Damon Albarn
30 March 1968:	Celine Dion
28 May 1968:	Kylie Minogue
7 October 1968:	Thom Yorke
22 October 1968:	Shaggy
5 January 1969:	Marilyn Manson
27 March 1969 (or 1970):	Mariah Carey
24 July 1969:	Jennifer Lopez
4 December 1969:	Jay-Z
11 January 1971:	Mary J. Blige
20 January 1971:	Gary Barlow
23 July 1971:	Alison Krauss
6 September 1971:	Dolores O'Riordan
20 October 1971:	Snoop Dogg
6 August 1972:	Geri Halliwell
21 September 1972:	Liam Gallagher
17 October 1972:	Eminem
12 January 1974:	Melanie Chisholm, a.k.a. Mel C
13 February 1974:	Robbie Williams
6 March 1974:	Guy Garvey
17 April 1974:	Victoria Beckham

Slash *(23 July 1965)*

Born Saul Hudson in downtown Stoke-on-Trent, Slash used to own seventy-five snakes, but gave them all to 'respectable reptilian institutions' when his first son was born. 'I'd had some close calls with snakes eating my pet cats,' he told *Uncut* magazine in 2016, 'and had this sudden feeling that something terrible might happen to my kids.' The snakes, he added, are 'all doing very well', as are the kids.

Mike D *(20 November 1965)*

Founder member of the Beastie Boys, the former Michael Diamond is also credited with having come up with the name mullet for the ridiculous hairstyle, short at the sides and front, long and scraggly at the back, that every rock star on the planet had in the mid-1980s and Jason Donovan had a few years later. In 1995, Mr D wrote a piece for a magazine called *Grand Royal* in which he referred disparagingly to 'mullet-headed people', the Beastie Boys having recorded a song called 'Mullet Head' the previous year. Neither Billy Ray Cyrus nor Michael Bolton were available for comment.*

Janet Jackson *(16 May 1966)*

Possibly the sanest of the Jackson siblings, although obviously that isn't saying much. When she was young she had a small menagerie of pet animals, Jabar the giraffe, Louis the llama (who liked to chew gum), her four dogs ('They're the greatest listeners because

---

* The Beastie Boys could also be inventive and impressive liars. Among the claims they made in interviews were that as a sideline they manufactured bespoke digital watches, and that they recorded their album *Paul's Boutique* in the original Batcave from the 1960s *Batman* TV series.

they sit there and look at you and listen'), her fawn, her Mouflon sheep, her peacocks. She had always wanted a king cobra, but fate, or maybe the rest of her family, denied her.

In the mid-1990s Janet suffered a two-year bout of depression, which she cured with coffee enemas. The piping hot brew, she told *Newsweek*, helped wash away the 'sad cells' in her body. 'Your body cells hold emotions,' she explained. 'With the enema you can bring out the sad cells or – whatever it is – even stronger.' What was to blame for the melancholy mood? 'My childhood, my teenage years, my adulthood,' said Janet, which covers it pretty comprehensively. Janet has had her septum, navel, nipple and what she calls her 'down south' pierced, and presumably clanks when she walks. 'My friends and I have piercing parties. They'd all come over and there'd be no drinking or anything because you'll bleed more. So we'd sit and watch each other get pierced.' In an interview with *Ebony* magazine, she said she had had her nostril pierced for 'a spiritual reason which I don't talk about'.

Shirley Manson *(26 August 1966)*

Singer for Goodbye Mr Mackenzie and, since 1994, Garbage. Unlike Charles Manson and Marilyn Manson, Shirley Manson's real surname is actually Manson.*

Kurt Cobain *(20 February 1967)*

When he was young and hungry, Kurt played with Nirvana by night and cleaned dentists' offices by day, stealing nitrous oxide

---

* And her bandmate Butch Vig, who produced Nirvana's *Nevermind*, is genuinely called Vig. It's his forename that's made up. He is actually called Bryan.

from them to fund the band. In an early interview, he said that Nirvana had a 'gloomy, vengeful element based on hatred'. For much of his (brief) adult life he experienced constant agonising stomach pain, for which no doctor could ever discover the cause. Heroin seemed to calm his tortured stomach as well as helping him sleep. When Dave Grohl once offered him an apple, he replied, 'No thanks, it'll make my teeth bleed.'

In May 1991, as his band started recording *Nevermind*, Kurt ran into Courtney Love at a Butthole Surfers gig at the Hollywood Palladium. They demonstrated their mutual attraction by punching each other and wrestling on the floor. 'It was a mating ritual for dysfunctional people,' explained Courtney. Producer Butch Vig established that because Kurt sang so viciously hard, he could only do one or two songs a day before his voice was shredded. When the band went on tour to promote *Nevermind*, Courtney followed them and found them at a party in Chicago. She had brought a bag of sexy lingerie with her, and Kurt tried it all on for her. Kurt was enraged by the success of *Nevermind*. He had always viewed life as 'us' against 'them', and now he found that it was 'them' who were buying his music.

After Kurt and Courtney married, they would check into hotels as Mr and Mrs Simon Ritchie, Sid Vicious's real name. Neither of them were keen on housework. They let food go off and didn't get round to throwing it away. They tried to hire a maid, but when she walked into their Seattle home and witnessed the degradation, she fled, screaming 'Satan lives here!'

In August 1992 Courtney was in one wing of Cedars-Sinai Medical Center in Los Angeles, giving birth. Kurt was in another, undergoing rehab. At four o'clock in the morning, as the labour got harder, Courtney grabbed her intravenous drip stand and wheeled it over to Kurt's room, shouting 'You get out of this bed and come down now! You are not leaving me to do this by myself!' Kurt followed her sheepishly back to the maternity ward, wheeling his own drip stand. When the baby's head appeared, he was violently sick and passed out. Fortunately, according to Nirvana's biographer Everett True, Kurt recovered enough to hold his newborn daughter shortly afterwards. The following day he left hospital to buy heroin.

When asked what the name Nirvana meant to him, Kurt said, 'Total peace after death.'

Noel Gallagher *(29 May 1967)*

The older and more intelligent of the two Oasis brothers, whose Mancunian swagger, excessive hairiness and foul-mouthed sibling rivalry have entertained the nation for many years. Their song 'Wonderwall', released in 1995, reached only number two, as it was consistently outsold by a double A-side, 'I Believe'/'Up on the Roof', by those actors-turned-crooners (-turned-actors-again-pretty-swiftly), Robson and Jerome. 'Wonderwall' remains the second largest selling single not to top the British charts.* Noel probably thinks it's Liam's fault. Liam probably thinks it's Noel's fault.

Richey Edwards *(22 December 1967)*

Rhythm guitarist and primary lyricist of the early Manic Street Preachers, who was once challenged by the journalist Steve Lamacq to prove how much he lived out the music he played. Anyone at the peak of mental health would just have said bugger off, but Richey rolled up his sleeve, took out a razorblade and

---

* After 'Move Like Jagger' by Maroon 5 featuring Christina Aguilera, which spent seven weeks at number two, beaten to the top spot by six different songs, and which eventually became the second biggest selling single of 2011.

carved '4 REAL' in his arm. Only in pop music is this considered admirable, even rational behaviour. Richey disappeared on 1 February 1995, somewhere in the region of the Severn Bridge, and is believed by many to be living out the rest of his life as a quantity surveyor in Neath.

Damon Albarn *(23 March 1968)*

The perennially adventurous lead singer of Blur and Gorillaz was born on the same day as onetime England cricket captain Michael Atherton. His father Keith is an artist, designer and writer who once briefly managed Soft Machine.

In 1988 Albarn was working as a barman in London's swanky Portobello Hotel, which Tina Turner liked so much she bought the house next door. 'One night Bono was rude to me and I've never really forgiven him,' he said later. 'The Edge, on the other hand, was always really polite.'

If two letters had been transposed in his surname, and he had been christened Damon Albran, would he have been so successful?

Kylie Minogue *(28 May 1968)*

The diminutive Australian chanteuse is almost exactly a year older than the British Tory politician Jacob Rees-Mogg.

Shaggy *(22 October 1968)*

Known to his parents as Orville Burrell, the Jamaican reggae musician took his stage name from the proto-bearded waster in the TV show *Scooby-Doo*. In 1988 Shaggy enlisted in the US Marine Corps and served with a field artillery battery in the 10th Marine Regiment during the Gulf War. He reached the rank of lance corporal, although he was busted down in rank twice. 'I'm a guy with a big mouth, and I mouthed off a lot,' he explained later. In 2015 he released a single called 'Go Fuck Yourself', and the *Miami New Times* asked him who he'd like to go fuck themselves. 'ISIS can go fuck themselves. That's some crazy shit they're doing. If you're able to cut a man's head off, you're sick. But the right music evokes emotion. So if you're listening to Shaggy music or reggae music, they're not going to want to cut somebody's head off.' He diagnosed that an enormous bag of Jamaican weed would solve many of the world's more knobbly problems.

Shaggy's son Richard Burrell is a rapper who goes by the name of Robb Banks, but some wag on Wikipedia keeps changing his name to Scrappy Doo.

Marilyn Manson *(5 January 1969)*

As you might expect, the former Brian Warner has some unusual fans. Instead of asking for his autograph, some have asked him to cut them, or put cigarettes out on their faces. One asked him to sign his scrotum. 'He used a felt pen,' said the signee. 'It was, like, a turn-on.'

Mariah Carey *(27 March 1969 or 1970)*

'When I watch TV and see those poor starving kids all over the world, I can't help but cry. I mean I'd love to be skinny like that, but not with all those flies and death and stuff.' Did Mariah Carey really say that? In his book *Mind the Bollocks*, Johnny Sharp says it was a parody on a satirical website called Cupcake, which was then wrongly attributed to Carey by the music magazine *Vox*, the *Independent* and thousands of sniggering charlies on the internet. Lies are in the taxi on the way to the airport while Truth is still drinking its breakfast cup of tea.*

Sharp goes further. He unearths a whole load of stupid quotes attributed to female singers, none of whom actually said them. Here's Mariah again on the death of the King of Jordan in 1999: 'I'm inconsolable ... He was the greatest basketball player the world has ever seen.' Made up by an internet charlie, falsely quoted by CNN and *USA Today*.

And here's Britney Spears, interviewed by *Blender* magazine in April 2004: 'I get to go to lots of overseas places ... like Canada.' Except that she wasn't interviewed by *Blender* in April 2004. She was in the January issue of that year, but the quote wasn't. It's been attributed to her by IMDb and the *Sun*.

'I've never really wanted to go to Japan. Simply because I don't like eating fish. And I know that's very popular out there in Africa.' That's supposed to be Britney again, some time in the 2000s. Except that sushi is one of her favourite foods, and there's no evidence she ever said it.

You don't need to be Gloria Steinem to see some rather unpleasant sexism going on here, both from the purulent, malodorous computer nerds who made up the quotes in the first place and from the supposedly serious and thorough media outlets (and the *Sun*) that attributed them without bothering to check them. And all to

---

* That's not to say that Mariah isn't a bit of a diva. In her reality show, she wore sunglasses indoors and insisted that restaurants she was sitting in only played her music. In a 2018 interview in the *Guardian*, she quashed the myth that she preferred bathing in mineral water, but admitted she liked bathing in cold milk 'as a beauty treatment'. According to Alan Carr, who was working on a Channel 4 show called *The Friday Night Project*, she insisted on a dedicated 'staircase assistant' whose single task was to 'check the stairs for her to see if she could walk down them'. She will only be photographed on her right side, and for twenty years she pretended not to know who Jennifer Lopez was, because, she admitted, if she couldn't say something nice, it was better to say nothing at all.

make what point, exactly? That good-looking young women with singing and songwriting talent are not very bright? How deeply satirical.

Bernard Butler *(1 May 1970)*

'YOUNG GUITAR PLAYER NEEDED BY LONDON-BASED BAND. Smiths, Commotions, Bowie, PSBs. No musos please. Some things are more important than ability. Call Brett.' This is the ad placed in the *NME* by Brett Anderson as Suede starts to coalesce. Bernard Butler is the first to answer and is accepted into the band 'within fifteen seconds of him starting to play'.

Glenn Medeiros *(24 June 1970)*

After two enormous global hits in the late 1980s, 'Nothing's Gonna Change My Love for You' and 'She Ain't Worth It' (a US number one), Medeiros returned to his home state of Hawaii and became a teacher. He is now principal of St Louis School in Honolulu and, since 2017, its president/CEO.

Dolores O'Riordan *(6 September 1971)*

Although I never much liked the Cranberries' music, probably because of that irritating catch, or warble, in O'Riordan's voice, I was always struck by how small, thin and vulnerable she looked, as though she was carrying the weight of the world on those tiny shoulders. And it's not the actual smallness that was the problem. Dolly Parton is no taller and she is a powerhouse. Prince was only an inch or two taller and he ruled the world. But whenever I saw Dolores O'Riordan on the telly, she worried me, obscurely. Even her brutally overplucked eyebrows seemed like an unforced error. 'I . . . hated being on stage,' she said in

1994. 'I didn't care about singing to an audience but I didn't like people looking at my body.' In 2013 she revealed that she had been sexually abused by a family 'friend' between the ages of eight and twelve. She struggled with anorexia and depression, and was diagnosed as bipolar in 2015. Three years later she accidentally drowned in a hotel bath, having drunk rather a lot of champagne. It was quite a rock star way to go, after not a particularly rock star kind of life.

Snoop Dogg *(20 October 1971)*

Born Calvin Cordozar Broadus Jr, the rapper, actor and entrepreneur was born on the same day as Dannii Minogue.

Liam Gallagher *(21 September 1972)*

Magnificently thick and aggressive younger brother of Noel Gallagher and lead 'singer' of Oasis, whose main purposes in life are to get drunk on planes and to disagree with Noel on everything. Noel, for instance, believes strongly that aliens exist, so Liam does not. 'If I saw an alien, I'd tell him to fuck off, because whatever planet he came from, they wouldn't have the Beatles or any decent fucking music.'

On Wayne Rooney's hair transplant: 'I'm not having it. He looks like a fucking balloon with a fucking Weetabix crushed on top.'

There is a theory abroad that Liam is a comic genius, but I see him more as a kind of *idiot savant*, possibly without the *savant* bit.

Here's Liam on God: 'If a guy suddenly appears before me with a big beard and locks and all that caper and performs some fucking miracle, and then says to me, "Liam, I am God," I'd say, "Fair enough, it's a fair cop. I didn't believe in you but fair play, you've got me." But until that day comes he can fuck right off.'

He has strong opinions on where to go for his holidays: 'Fuck the sea. I ain't going in that. Fuck that, mate. That ain't meant for us. That's meant for the sharks, and the jellyfish, tadpoles and stuff.'

Like many people he has personal goals: 'I'm getting up earlier and earlier now, man. I try and beat the alarm clock. The alarm goes off at six and I try to get up at 5.59 just to do its head in.'*

He has worked out why Oasis never quite broke America: 'Americans want grungy people, stabbing themselves in the head on stage. They get a bright bunch like us, with deodorant on, they don't get it.'

His view of women is refreshingly up-to-date: 'If you want to see the opposite sex spout four heads, then exchange a couple of rings. You walk to the altar with a woman with one head and you walk back with a fucking monster.'

The best description of Liam comes, naturally enough, from his long-suffering older brother: 'He's like a man with a fork in a world of soup.'

Liam Gallagher admits to having read one book in his life. No one knows what it is, but I'd bet a lot of money it's *The Very Hungry Caterpillar* by Eric Carle.

Melanie Chisholm *(12 January 1974)*

Mel C is, as yet, the only Spice Girl I have spotted on the Edgware branch of the Northern Line reading a book. No one else recognised her, possibly because she wasn't wearing a tracksuit. She looked as contented and at peace as any celebrity I have ever seen.

---

* See Shaun Ryder for another prominent Mancunian who believes that alarm clocks are sentient.

James Blunt *(22 February 1974)*

A former reconnaissance officer in the Life Guards, who served in the 1999 Kosovo war, the former James Blount rose to fame in 2004 with the release of 'You're Beautiful', an emetic ballad inspired by a moment on the escalators on the London Underground, when Blunt spotted an old girlfriend on the up-escalator with her new boyfriend while he was on the down-escalator. 'It's always been portrayed as romantic, but it's actually a bit creepy,' said Blunt. 'It's about a guy (me) who's high and stalking someone else's girlfriend on the subway. And then the stalker kills himself.' 'Weird Al' Yankovic later parodied the song as 'You're Pitiful'.

A palpable posho in an ocean of proles, Blunt has long been an easy target for the humorously minded, but latterly, he has shown that rarest and most beautiful of things, a talent for Twitter. While others bluster and boast, Blunt responds with wit and self-deprecation. 'Can we all take a moment and remember just how terrible James Blunt was?' 'No need,' wrote Blunt, 'I have a new album coming soon.' 'James Blunt had his 15 min of fame and disappeared.' 'Even less than that!' wrote Blunt, 'The song was only 3 minutes and 30 seconds long.' 'James Blunt es lo peor que le ha pasado a la huminadad desde Hitler.' 'I'm guessing this is not good,' wrote Blunt. '@James Blunt why you only got 200k followers?' 'Jesus only needed twelve,' wrote Blunt. 'Is there one single James Blunt fan out there?' 'Most of them are single,' wrote Blunt. Only in Britain could this happen, for now the general impression of Blunt is that, OK, he did do that abysmal song, but he seems a decent bloke, don't you think?

Guy Garvey *(6 March 1974)*

There is, apparently, an Elbow tribute band who are so good at what they do that it's very hard to tell them from the real thing. They call themselves Arse.

Victoria Beckham *(17 April 1974)*

The former Victoria Adams, also known as Posh Spice, is the only former member of the Spice Girls not to have had a solo number-one hit. When the group were discussing a comeback tour in 2019, Beckham was originally intending to take part, but only if she wasn't miked up and could just mime along to all the songs.

Meg White *(10 December 1974)*

Drummer and vocalist for the White Stripes who wasn't Jack White's sister, as widely rumoured, but his wife. In 1997, on a whim, she played Jack's drums. Jack liked her 'primal' style, so they formed a band. By the time they made it big in 2002, they had divorced. Meg White describes herself as 'very shy', and in 2007 her acute anxiety caused them to abandon a US tour halfway through and cancel all remaining dates. They never played live again, and Meg White hasn't played a note since 2011. As a paid-up introvert myself, I admire anyone who can transcend their internal wiring, even for a while, because however enjoyable performing may be, it always comes at a cost, and the cost only ever mounts. Sooner or later there's only one thing you can do, and that's to stop.

The Records That Time Forgot

Yes: *Magnification*; **Stackridge:** *A Victory for Common Sense*;
Lindisfarne: *Promenade*

Bands still split up in the traditional fashion, but these days they
re-form as well. What marketing men would call 'the brand' is
unassailable. When Yes split up in the early 1980s, Chris Squire
(bass) and Alan White (drums) started working with the South
African guitarist Trevor Rabin and their old organist Tony Kaye
on a project they called Cinema. That didn't last long. Their former
vocalist Jon Anderson was brought into the fold and Cinema
swiftly became Yes again, although their material sounded nothing
like their old stuff: it included 'Owner of a Lonely Heart', which I
love, but is clearly a song by a completely new group. The brand,
though: the brand.

Yes have split up and re-formed more than most bands, with
Rick Wakemen alone having joined and left at least fifty-six times.
In 2001 he had left again, and the band were reduced to a four-
piece. Not that it really mattered: it had been many years since
they had recorded anything even halfway decent. But for their
next album they decided not to bring in a new keyboard player
but record with a full orchestra for the first time since their early
recordings in the late 1960s. *Magnification* was the result and,

although it's a little overlong, it is indeed magnificent: songs with actual tunes, great playing and a wonderfully broad dynamic range, using the orchestra to best effect. Unfortunately, the album sold poorly and no one heard it.

Stackridge were the first band on stage at the first Glastonbury festival in 1970, and it was pretty much downhill from there. Their utterly English, rural pop-rock with baroque tendencies never really found a substantial audience, but in the 1980s they morphed into the Korgis and had a big hit with 'Everybody's Got to Learn Sometime'. Then, after more skint years, they morphed back into Stackridge, played live, recorded albums, bickered constantly. The creative tension that every band needs but doesn't necessarily want was between their two main songwriters, James Warren and Andy Davis, who both left and joined the group uncountable times. But in about 2009, something seems to have clicked. The line-up of Warren, Davis, Jim 'Crun' Walter on bass and 'Mutter' Slater on vocals and flute, assisted by a top producer in Chris Hughes, recorded by far their best album, *A Victory for Common Sense*. It's a more mainstream record than any they had previous made, but it's so confident and full of invention you can only wonder why they hadn't tried doing something like this before. It's a joyously good piece of work. Unfortunately, the album sold poorly and no one heard it.

Lindisfarne, for decades the north-east's favourite band, also suffered a turbulent history, their low point being perhaps a re-recording of their biggest hit, 'Fog on the Tyne', with Paul Gascoigne on vocals, which seems to have obliterated the last vestiges of their reputations as serious musicians. By the time their main songwriter Alan Hull died of a coronary thrombosis, aged just fifty, in 1995, they hadn't made a listenable record in twenty years. But new players and singers were brought in and bassist Rod Clements, until then only an occasional songwriter, stepped up to lead the group and provide their material. Clements started writing with the folk-rock producer Nigel Stonier, and after a slightly tentative first album together, they produced an absolute beauty in 2002's *Promenade*. Produced by Stonier, it's harder-edged than almost all of Lindisfarne's records, with a wonderfully wry, droll, middle-aged take on life. Unfortunately, the album sold poorly and no one heard it.

There's something else these bands have in common: that after recording their best albums in decades and no one noticing, they all split up. Jon Anderson left Yes and has never returned, and the rest of the band did not reconvene to record again for another eight years. Stackridge crumbled into dust, while Lindisfarne never recorded again and only started playing live again a few years ago. All the terrible albums they had recorded could not rend them asunder, but the failure of a good album was something they could not recover from. It's the human condition in a nutshell.

Quiz 4: Pop the Question

This is all about philosophy and metaphysics. Here are some important questions of life, the universe and everything. Who asked them in these years? There's a point for each.

1. Why does my heart feel so bad? (1999)
2. Where did our love go? (1964)
3. What's love got to do with it? (1984)
4. Who let the dogs out? (2000)
5. How deep is your love? (1977)
6. Do you really want to hurt me? (1982)
7. Would I lie to you? (1992)
8. What's the frequency, Kenneth? (1994)
9. Now that we've found love, what are we going to do with it? (1978)
10. Why does it always rain on me? (1999)
11. What becomes of the broken-hearted? (1966)
12. How long has this been going on? (1974)
13. How soon is now? (1985)
14. How will I know? (1986)
15. Is that all there is? (1969)
16. Is this the way to Amarillo? (1971)
17. Who wants to live for ever? (1986)

18. Should I stay or should I go? (1982)
19. What's going on? (1971)
20. Wouldn't it be nice? (1966)
21. Wouldn't it be good? (1984)
22. Can we fix it? (2000)

Answers on page 313.

Answers to Quiz 3

1. Jesse James
2. Rick Astley ('Never Gonna Give You Up')
3. Smashing Pumpkins
4. Taylor Swift
5. Prince
6. 'Honey Honey' and 'Ring Ring' (pedants will have spotted that 'I Do I Do I Do I Do I Do' is a multiple use of two words. And 'Gimme Gimme Gimme (A Man After Midnight)' has that bit in brackets to foul everything up)
7. Johnny Cash
8. Melanies
9. 'Take the A Train' (Strayhorn's song of this title became the signature tune of the Duke Ellington orchestra)
10. The Village People

1975–present

Notable Births

29 May 1975:	Melanie Brown, a.k.a. Mel B
18 June 1975:	M.I.A.
14 October 1975:	Shaznay Lewis
21 January 1976:	Emma Bunton
2 February 1977:	Shakira
2 March 1977:	Chris Martin
8 June 1977:	Kanye West
8 September 1979:	P!nk
18 December 1980:	Christina Aguilera
25 January 1981:	Alicia Keys
31 January 1981:	Justin Timberlake
4 September 1981:	Beyoncé Knowles
2 December 1981:	Britney Spears
28 August 1982:	LeAnn Rimes
27 September 1982:	Lil Wayne
8 December 1982:	Nicki Minaj
25 October 1984:	Katy Perry
21 June 1985:	Lana Del Rey
8 October 1985:	Bruno Mars
28 March 1986:	Lady Gaga
20 February 1988:	Rihanna
5 May 1988:	Adele
13 December 1989:	Taylor Swift
17 February 1991:	Ed Sheeran
19 May 1992:	Sam Smith
23 November 1992:	Miley Cyrus
26 June 1993:	Ariana Grande
1 February 1994:	Harry Styles
1 March 1994:	Justin Bieber
22 August 1995:	Dua Lipa
18 December 2001:	Billie Eilish

Shaznay Lewis *(14 October 1975)*

Main songwriter and sole black member of the legendarily argumentative girl group All Saints. In *Word* in 2004, Andrew Harrison noted the extraordinarily rancorous nature of their break-up, and asked Shaznay when things had gone beyond no return. 'Truthfully, it was probably at the beginning,' she said. 'Before we were signed, the girls [Nicole and Natalie Appleton] had a meeting with London without telling me, and it was only when Tracey Bennett [then chairman of London Records] asked "Who wrote these songs?" that they admitted it was me. So I knew from then on that it wasn't going to last, before we had even had a hit.' The band eventually broke up after Shaznay and Natalie had a vicious argument about which of them would wear a particular jacket to a Capital Radio party.

And yet, sixteen years later, All Saints have re-formed, split up, re-formed again and are still together. The relative failure of their solo careers may have contributed to this state of affairs, but one imagines that their dressing room after a show is a bit like a rock 'n' roll restaging of Jean-Paul Sartre's play *Huis Clos*, whose most famous line is 'Hell is other people.'

Fiona Apple *(13 September 1977)*

Gifted but cripplingly sensitive singer-songwriter whose first album, *Tidal* (1996), sold three million copies and nearly ruined her life. Not that it had been in great shape before, exactly: one of *Tidal*'s songs, 'Sullen Girl', told of her rape aged twelve outside her mother's New York apartment. In interviews she talked of eating disorders and anti-anxiety drugs. She says that, while recording that album, her obsessive-compulsive disorder went off the scale. 'There was so much change all the time, because if you're OC you really need some kind of routine,' she told *Word*'s Craig McLean in 2006. 'And it was exhausting trying to maintain my routine for the nineteen months I was on the road. My best friend would come over and she'd find me in my room vacuuming and crying hysterically. I'd communicate with her via letters – like, I'd hand them to her!'

Her second album she called *When the Pawn Hits the Conflicts He Thinks Like a King What He Knows Throws the Blows When He Goes to the Fight and He'll Win the Whole Thing 'fore He Enters the Ring There's No Body to Batter When Your Mind Is Your Might So When You Go Solo, You Hold Your Own Hand and Remember That Depth Is the Greatest of Heights and If You Know Where You Stand, Then You Know Where to Land and If You Fall It Won't Matter, Cuz You'll Know That You're Right*, which got her into the *Guinness Book of Records*. You would probably pity her, if her music were not so daring, melodically rich and often quite glorious.

Johnny Borrell *(4 April 1980)*

Lead singer and frontman for Razorlight, who also went to Highgate School (where he was known as Jonathan). Renowned, for some reason, as a bit of a tool. Can't imagine why. 'I'm a genius. Musically, culturally, everything,' said Johnny in 2004. 'Compared to the Razorlight album, Dylan is making the chips. I'm drinking champagne.'

Lady Gaga *(28 March 1986)*

As well as being the only twenty-first-century pop star to name herself after a Queen song ('Radio Gaga'), the former Stefani Germanotta originally dyed her hair platinum blonde because people kept mistaking her for Amy Winehouse. What, there's only room for one big-nosed* strong-eyebrowed brunette pop star at any one time? But she obviously developed a taste for it. Immediately after finishing filming *A Star Is Born*, in which her hair was a more natural mousy brown, she told Ellen DeGeneres, she dyed her hair platinum again to 'let the character go'.

'I have this weird thing that if I sleep with someone they're going to take my creativity from me through my vagina,' she told *Vanity Fair* in 2010, not unreasonably.

Romy Madley Croft *(18 August 1989)*

One of the best interviews in Tracey Thorn's *Naked at the Albert Hall* is with Romy Madley Croft of the xx. Someone took a photo of them together, and when Thorn showed it to her children, they said, 'Mum, she looks more like you than we do.'

'And it's true: aside from any spiritual or musical connectedness, we look like mother and daughter. We have the same haircut, the same pale skin, the same-shaped pointy chin, and faces which, when we smile, form a slightly embarrassed or apologetic expression. On stage we stare at our shoes, off stage we stare up at you from under our fringes … We're polite, reticent, innately shy, and yet have both found ourselves inhabiting this least introvert-friendly of professions.'

Romy tells Tracey that, as a youngster, not only did she not dream of being a singer, she was actually so reluctant to sing, or be heard singing, that she would mime when people sang 'Happy Birthday'. 'That's hardcore shy,' comments Tracey, who nonetheless has an explanation. 'There is a type of singer, perhaps a minority but nonetheless a significant number, who sings almost against their will, and despite an instinctive aversion to all forms

---

* This is not an insult. I have always had a bit of a thing for women with prominent nasal appendages, and Gaga's is up there with the best of them.

of public display. These kinds of people sing because they need to more than they want to, because it offers an outlet for bottled-up feelings they sometimes don't even know they have, and in singing, they present an alternative model to the audience, a kind of anti-singer, or at least anti-performer, which is the antithesis of showbiz and showing off.'

Both Romy and Tracey admit that they have only sung kara-oke once, when extremely drunk. As it happens, the same is true for me. Romy sang Fleetwood Mac's 'Dreams'. Tracey did Will Young's 'Leave Right Now'. Fortunately, history does not record which song I murdered in my only brush with singing infamy. I have forgotten, and everyone else there has since met with an unfortunate end.

Harry Styles *(1 February 1994)*

The former One Direction singer particularly dislikes his girl-friends swearing or smoking. Before he became a singer his ambition was to be a lawyer. His hair hasn't always been curly: it was straight from when he was born until the end of primary school. Harry says he wouldn't date a girl if she didn't get on with his family. He celebrated reaching number one in America with 'Up All Night' by buying a mattress.

The X Factor (4 September 2004)

What do One Direction, Jedward, Olly Murs and JLS have in common? They all came to public prominence through the prism of Simon Cowell's godawful TV show, and not one of them won it. JLS and Olly Murs came second, One Direction third and Jedward sixth.

This is what Nick Coleman has to say about the show in *Voices*: 'Exhaustion is central to the *X Factor* experience, which defines singing as the sinew-straining, health-threatening, competition-shredding, life-changing exercise of supreme effort. But *X Factor* vocalisation is to true singing what keepy-uppies are to football. It is the exhibition of decontextualised skill; a measurement of the ability to show off.'

Bill's Spotify the Link

Warning: this one is brutally difficult,
so you'll get five songs each time.

6.1

'Star People'
by George Michael

'Somebody Told Me'
by The Killers

'She Drives Me Crazy'
by Fine Young Cannibals

'Does Your Mother Know'
by ABBA

'Take It Easy'
by Eagles

6.2

(Clue: this has nothing to do with the artists, although the ones who wrote their own songs could ultimately be held responsible.)

'Be Bop a Lula'
by Gene Vincent

'The Best Things in Life are Free'
by Superstar

'Brilliant Disguise'
by Bruce Springsteen

'Used to Love U'
by John Legend

'Real Gone Kid'
by Deacon Blue

6.3

(Second clue: this is about the lyrics of each song.)

'Come On'
by the Rolling Stones

'All Right Now'
by Free

'Papa Don't Preach'
by Madonna

'Angie Baby'
by Helen Reddy

'Only Yesterday'
by the Carpenters

Answer

Each of these songs features the rhyme maybe/baby.

Answers to Quiz 4: Pop the Question

1. Moby
2. The Supremes
3. Tina Turner
4. Baha Men
5. Bee Gees
6. Culture Club
7. Charles and Eddie
8. R.E.M.
9. Third World
10. Travis
11. Jimmy Ruffin
12. Ace
13. The Smiths
14. Whitney Houston
15. Peggy Lee
16. Tony Christie
17. Queen
18. The Clash
19. Marvin Gaye
20. The Beach Boys
21. Nik Kershaw
22. Bob the Builder

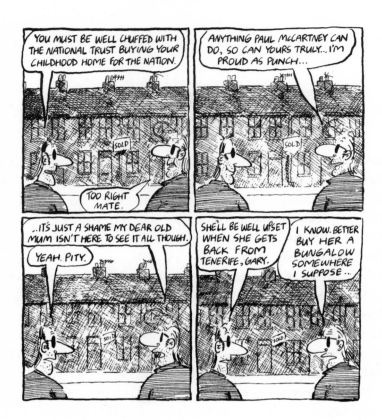

Acknowledgements

Myfanwy Alexander, Maxie Allen, John Ash, Dave Aylott, Tom Bannatyne, Annalisa Barbieri, Louis Barfe, Mike Barfield, James Berkmann, Martha Berkmann, Jean Berkmann-Barwis, Paula Bingham, Gaynor Bond, Tim Cooper, Sam Craft, Linda Grant, Martin Griffiths, Mel Griffiths, Sarah Hesketh, Corinna Honan, Jon Hotten, Claire Hume, 'Big' Dave Jackson, David Jaques, Wendy Jones, Stella Kane, Nick Lezard, Jim Lynch, Steven Lynch, John Morrish, Andrew Mueller, Nick Newman, Ged Parsons, Francis Peckham, the late Chris Pollikett, Lucy Reese, Kerstin Rodgers, Dorcas Rogers, Bill Saunders, Mat Snow, Boyd Steemson, D. J. Taylor, Russell Taylor, Pat Thomas, Mick Wall, Patrick Walsh, Robin Welch, Roland White, Roderick Young.

Celeb cartoons appear courtesy of Charles Peattie and Mark Warren. © Peattie & Warren. First published in *Private Eye* magazine.

Selected Bibliography

Viv Albertine, *Clothes, Clothes, Clothes. Music, Music, Music. Boys, Boys, Boys* (Faber & Faber, 2014)

Nick Coleman, *Voices: How A Great Singer Can Change Your Life* (Vintage, 2017)

Frederic Dannen, *Hit Men: Power Brokers and Fast Money Inside the Music Business* (Vintage, 1990)

Tim de Lisle (ed.), *Lives of the Great Songs* (Penguin, 1994)

Pamela Des Barres, *Rock Bottom: Dark Moments in Music Babylon* (Abacus, 1996)

Mark Ellen, *Rock Stars Stole My Life!: A Big Bad Love Affair with Music* (Coronet, 2014)

Simon Garfield, *The Nation's Favourite: The True Adventures of Radio 1* (Faber & Faber, 1998)

John Harris, *Hail! Hail! Rock 'n' Roll: The Ultimate Guide to the Music, the Myths and the Madness* (Sphere, 2009)

David Hepworth, *Uncommon People: The Rise and Fall of the Rock Stars 1955–1994* (Black Swan, 2017)

David Hepworth, *Nothing is Real: The Beatles Were Underrated and Other Sweeping Statements About Pop* (Black Swan, 2018)

David Hepworth, *The Rock & Roll A Level* (Bantam Press, 2019)

Gary Herman, *Rock 'n' Roll Babylon: 50 Years of Sex, Drugs and Rock 'n' Roll* (Plexus, 1994)

Allan Jones, *Can't Stand Up for Falling Down: Rock 'n' Roll War Stories* (Bloomsbury, 2017)

Hanif Kureishi and Jon Savage (ed.), *The Faber Book of Pop* (Faber & Faber, 1995)

Pat Long, *The History of the* NME*: High Times and Low Lives at the World's Most Famous Music Magazine* (Portico, 2012)

Stuart Maconie, *Cider with Roadies* (Ebury Press, 2004)

Stuart Maconie, *The People's Songs: The Story of Modern Britain in 50 Records* (Ebury Press, 2013)

Mark Mason, *The Importance of Being Trivial: In Search of the Perfect Fact* (Random House, 2008)

Margaret Moser and Bill Crawford, *Rock Stars Do the Dumbest Things* (Renaissance Books, 1998)

Andrew Mueller, *It's Too Late to Die Young Now: Misadventures in Rock and Roll* (Foruli Codex, 2014)

Simon Napier-Bell, *Black Vinyl White Powder* (Ebury Press, 2001)

Lucy O'Brien, *She Bop: The Definitive History of Women in Rock, Pop & Soul* (Penguin, 1995)

Raymond Obstfeld and Patricia Fitzgerald, *Jabberrock: The Ultimate Book of Rock 'n' Roll Quotations* (Canongate, 1997)

Johnny Sharp, *Mind the Bollocks: A Riotous Rant Through the Ridiculousness of Rock 'n' Roll* (Portico, 2012)

Bob Stanley, *Yeah Yeah Yeah: The Story of Modern Pop* (Faber & Faber, 2013)

Mitchell Symons, *That Book* (Bantam Press, 2003)

Mitchell Symons, *This Book* (Bantam Press, 2004)

Mitchell Symons, *The Other Book* (Bantam Press, 2005)

Tracey Thorn, *Naked at the Albert Hall: The Inside Story of Singing* (Virago, 2015)

Notes

1: 1901–1926

9   *'possibly the most significant cultural event in post-war America'*: Stanley, *Yeah Yeah Yeah*.

9   *a tell-all book by his son Gary*: Gary Crosby and Ross Firestone, *Going My Own Way* (Doubleday, 1983).

10   *'I've always been into ragtime...'*: Stephen Fortner, 'Keith Emerson interviewed by you', *Keyboard* (December 2010).

12   *'Things were so confused...'*: Justine Picardie, 'The first cut is still the deepest – lives of the great songs: "The First Time Ever I Saw Your Face"', *Independent*, 12 December 1993.

12   *'The intensity of it quite frightened me'*: Ibid.

12   *'He didn't like baring his emotions...'*: Ibid.

12   *'almost stripped naked'*: Ibid.

13   *'a twenty-dollar call girl...'*: Billie Holiday, *Lady Sings the Blues* (Doubleday, 1956).

15   *'Neither do I...'*: Peter J. Levinson, *September in the Rain: The Life of Nelson Riddle* (Taylor Trade Publications, 2005).

15   *'Thank you...'*: Timothy White, 'Ravi Shankar: gala 75th for the godfather of world music', *Billboard*, 18 March 1995.

16   *'Judy was an unusual child...'*: Quoted in David Shipman, *Judy Garland* (Hyperion, 1992).

16   *'The childlike lyrics were delivered...'*: Mary Harron, 'Lives of the great songs – when the pink bubble bursts: "Over the Rainbow"', *Independent*, 22 August 1993.

17   *'it only happened because Freddie Mercury...'*: Stanley, *Yeah Yeah Yeah*.

17   *'Dinah had the ego of an ox...'*: Quoted in O'Brien, *She Bop*.

17   *'her distinctive vocal style...'*: Richard S. Ginell, 'Artist Biography: Dinah Washington', AllMusic.com.

17   *'Long John Blues'*: Lyrics by Tommy George. © Warner Chappell Music, Inc.

17   *'Though ebullient and robust...'*: O'Brien, *She Bop*.

18   *'There was a large ashtray on the table...'*: *Mr Rock 'n' Roll*, Channel 4, 19 September 1999.

18   *'It was only one floor'*: Ibid.

18   *'Sorry, Miles...'*: Colin Larkin, *The Encyclopedia of Popular Music* (Omnibus Press, 2011).

18   *'I've changed music four or five times'*: John Szwed, *So What: The Life of Miles Davis* (Simon & Schuster, 2002).

19   *'He had the look of a card sharp...'*: Stanley, *Yeah Yeah Yeah*.

19   *'that Rolling Stones guy'*: Moser and Crawford, *Rock Stars do the Dumbest Things*.

19 *'Every time him and me got in contact . . . '*: Quoted in David Remnick, 'Chuck Berry lives!', *New Yorker*, 19 March 2017.
19 *'a stage I've been thrown off many times'*: Bryan Wawzenek, 'When Chuck Berry kicked Keith Richards off his stage', Ultimateclassicrock.com, 21 January 2017.

2: 1927–1934

23 *'David Bowie had invented . . . '*: Maconie, *Cider with Roadies*.
25 *'I Put a Spell on You'*: Lyrics by Jay Hawkins. © Song/ATV Music Publishing LLC.
25 *'a masterpiece of tortuous simplicity'*: Quoted in Tim De Lisle, *Lives of the Great Songs* (Pavilion, 1994).
26 *'If Larry likes the look of them . . . '*: Napier-Bell, *Black Vinyl White Powder*.
26 *'chimney sweep music'*: Adrian Deevoy, 'Stop the band, I wanna get off!', *Q* (March 1996).
26 *'Well, I do have a big Oliver! problem . . . '*: Ibid.
27 *'A blind man playing chess . . . '*: Bobby Womack with Robert Ashton, *Midnight Mover: My Autobiography* (John Blake, 2006).
28 *'the English Elvis . . . '*: Quoted in Ellen, *Rock Stars Stole My Life!*
28 *'He really was at the very cornerstone . . . '*: Quoted in '"Skiffle king" Donegan dies', BBC News, 4 November 2002.
29 *'but it seemed like a thousand'*: Jann S. Wenner, 'Lennon remembers, part one', *Rolling Stone*, 21 January 1971.
29 *'Let's jump out and play football'*: Ibid.
29 *In 1970 John Lennon was asked*: Ibid.
29 *'This is almost certainly an exaggeration . . . '*: 'How often did John Lennon do LSD during his peak of usage – really?', Reddit.com.
29 *'he had a wood-carved face . . . '*: Stanley, *Yeah Yeah Yeah*.
30* *Cash's biographer*: Robert Hilburn, *Johnny Cash: The Life* (Weidenfeld & Nicolson, 2014).
31 *'This is how he met . . . '*: Hepworth, *Uncommon People*.
32 *'They'd say, "Who's speaking" . . . '*: '"Real" Leonard Skinner saddened by crash', *Ocala Star-Banner*, 22 October 1977.
32 *'arguably the most influential . . . '*: David Itzkoff, 'Leonard Skinner, namesake of rock band, dies', *New York Times*, 20 September 2010.
33 *'The onus is on the viewer to interpret'*: Ray Coleman, *John Ono Lennon: Volume 2 1967–1980* (Sidgwick & Jackson, 1984).
34 *'James is indeed our number-one ambassador'*: 'Lawyer for wife of James Brown withdraws diplomatic immunity motion', AP News, 3 June 1988.
34 *'She had black and blue marks . . . '*: Steve Dougherty and Victoria Balfour, 'After allegedly beating his wife and shooting her car, James Brown may have to face the music', *People*, 25 April 1988.
35 *'the most beautiful woman I'd ever seen'*: Leonard Cohen, *Leonard Cohen on Leonard Cohen* (Chicago Review Press, 2014).
35 *'Look, I like young boys . . . '*: Justin Chandler and Andrea Warner, 'Leonard Cohen, the women he loved, and the women who loved him', CBC, 11 November 2016.
35 *'Yes,' said Janis*: Andy Greene, 'Flashback: Leonard Cohen stuns with "Chelsea Hotel #2" in 1985', *Rolling Stone*, 21 February 2017.
36 *'I went down there and did my first scene . . . '*: Adrian Deevoy, 'Porridge? Lozenge? Syringe?', *Q* (1991).

3: 1935–1939

41 *'He was pure instinct'*: Stanley, *Yeah Yeah Yeah*.
41 *'I'm going to mash this'*: Stephen Pile, *The Ultimate Book of Heroic Failures* (Faber & Faber, 2011).
41 *'I don't know anything about music'*: Raymond Obstfeld and Patricia Fitzgerald, *Jabberrock: The Ultimate Book of Rock 'N' Roll Quotations* (Canongate, 1997).

42 *'his bodily fluids'*: Hepworth, *Uncommon People.*
42 *'the power of fear'*: Tom Leonard, 'Wildest man of rock', *Daily Mail*, 8 November 2018.
43 *'one of [promoter] Bill Graham's guards ... '*: Steven Rosen, 'Led Zeppelin's 1977 Tour – A Tragic Ending!', Classic Rock Legends.
43 *'He was always good to me'*: Des Barres, *Rock Bottom.*
44 *'would argue with a signpost'*: Hepworth, *Uncommon People.*
44 *'born feet-first with a hard-on'*: Quoted in ibid.
45 *'I'm Jerry Lee's wife'*: Ibid.
45 *'Go home, baby snatcher'*: John Clarke, 'Great ball of ire: the day that shook Jerry Lee Lewis', *The Times*, 19 May 2008.
45 *'I was a young fool ... '*: Kureishi and Savage (ed.), *The Faber Book of Pop.*
45 *'Myra grew up ... '*: Hepworth, *Uncommon People.*
46 *'the day the music died'*: 'American Pie, Pt 1' lyrics by Don McLean. © Songs of Universal Inc., Benny Bird Co. Inc.
46 *'it's always the funny-looking ones'*: *Word* (July 2005).
46 *'a man who thinks with his dick'*: Ibid.
47 *'Since the band had started ... '*: Bill Wyman, *Stone Alone: The Story of a Rock 'n' Roll Band* (Viking, 1990).
47 *'There was a brief, very sixties, flicker ... '*: Ellen, *Rock Stars Stole My Life!*
47 *'died ten years ago'*: Jay Cocks, 'The Everly Brothers in arms', *Time*, 24 June 2001.
47 *'In the whole fourteen-year period ... '*: Stanley, *Yeah Yeah Yeah.*
48 *'Everyone has the feeling ... '*: Herman, *Rock 'n' Roll Babylon.*
48 *Don, interviewed by the* Los Angeles Times, *said*: Randy Lewis, 'Don Everly on death of brother Phil: "I think about him every day"', *Los Angeles Times*, 3 April 2014.
49 *'an almost monstrous level of control ... '*: Maconie, *The People's Songs.*
49 *'a powerful and vindictive man ... '*: 'Late Bay City Roller Alan Longmuir: Tam Paton depravity "ran deeper than we know"', *Edinburgh Evening News*, 13 November 2018.
49 *'the victim of a set-up ... '*: Ibid.
49 *'I'm delighted he's dead ... '*: Quoted in Maconie, *The People's Songs.*
50 *'half goddess, half icicle'*: Richard Goldstein, 'A quiet night at the balloon farm', *New York* (October 1966).
50 *'the sound of a body falling downstairs'*: Morrissey, *Autobiography* (Penguin, 2013).
50 *'I want to be a blues singer'*: O'Brien, *She Bop.*
51 *'There were no traces of black ... '*: Lucy O'Brien, *Dusty* (Sidgwick & Jackson, 1989).
51 *'All I know is that I have a distinctive voice ... '*: Quoted in ibid.
51 *'reclusive, lazy, petulant and totally charming'*: Napier-Bell, *Black Vinyl White Powder.*
51 *'a bit like a master and his dog ... '*: Quoted in Chris Lycett, 'Obituary: John Walters', *Guardian*, 1 August 2001.
53 *'Your daughter must not go to school today'*: Garfield, *The Nation's Favourite.*
53 *'There is always some speculation ... '*: Ibid.
54 *'I think that a very strong case could be made ... '*: Ibid.
54 *'Benign, sarcastic, confident ... '*: O'Brien, *She Bop.*
54 *'I don't like old people on a rock and roll stage ... '*: Alex Witchel, 'Flashing back with: Grace Slick', *New York Times*, 18 October 1998.
55 *'As long as we are locked up ... '*: Ira B. Nadel, *Various Positions: A Life of Leonard Cohen* (Pantheon, 1998).
55 *'I wasn't in the right kind of condition ... '*: Sylvie Simmons, '*Mojo* presents ... An introduction to Leonard Cohen', *Mojo* (2001).
55 *'I love you, Leonard'*: Nadel, *Various Positions.*
55 *'but he had a licence to carry ... '*: 'Marky Ramone: "Phil Spector didn't hold a gun to us"', NME.com, 2 December 2008.

4: 1940–1941

66   *a fascinating and in-depth interview*: Maureen Cleave, 'How does a Beatle *live*? John Lennon lives like this', *Evening Standard*, 4 March 1966.
66   *'Imagine'*: Lyrics by John Lennon. © Lenono Music.
68   *'You can't appreciate what a jail is . . . '*: Quoted in Joe Taysom, 'Frank Zappa once got arrested for making a fake sex tape', *Far Out Magazine*, 23 April 2020.
68   *'I love your hat'*: Albertine, *Clothes Clothes Clothes*.
69   *'buying porn from the little concession stand . . . '*: John Harris, 'Mission: unlistenable', *Guardian*, 4 August 2006.
69   *in his book about Laurel Canyon bands*: David McGowan, *Weird Scenes Inside The Canyon: Laurel Canyon, Covert Ops & The Dark Heart of the Hippie Dream* (Headpress, 2014).
70   *'I am going to be bigger than Elvis Presley'*: Hepworth, *Nothing is Real*.
70   *'scything misanthropy'*: Stanley, *Yeah Yeah Yeah*.
70   *'Bobby invented a character to deliver his songs'*: Quoted in Hepworth, *Nothing is Real*.
71   *'Just because you like my stuff . . . '*: *Bob Dylan: Inspirations* (Andrews McMeel, 2005).
71   *'playing like a bunch of cunts'*: Tom Pinnock, 'Deep Purple: "We were dangerous, unpredictable . . . it wasn't cabaret', *Uncut*, 6 November 2015.
71* *'He didn't think much of it'*: *Word* (May 2005).
72   *'radiating hippie allure and authenticity'*: Richard Williams, 'Crosby, Stills, Nash & Young reviews – two books, four highly developed egos', *Guardian*, 25 July 2019.
72   *'As a metaphor for the destiny . . . '*: Ibid.
72   *'Crosby, Stills, Nash and Young have spent . . . '*: Peter Doggett, *Crosby, Stills, Nash & Young: The Biography* (Bodley Head, 2019).
73   *'he was the guitar hero of the boys . . . '*: Hepworth, *Uncommon People*.
73   *'it is impossible to overstate . . . '*: Stanley, *Yeah Yeah Yeah*.
73   *'a living myth . . . '*: Quoted ibid.
73   *'I'm precise. I think in proportions . . . '*: Nigel Farndale, 'Art Garfunkel on Paul Simon: "I created a monster"', *Daily Telegraph*, 24 May 2015.
74   *'he was recruited because drummers . . . '*: Hepworth, *Uncommon People*.
78   *'literally miraculous'*: Stanley, *Yeah Yeah Yeah*.
78   *'You can go directly to the bank'*: 'You've Lost That Lovin' Feelin' by The Righteous Brothers', Songfacts.com.

5: 1942–1943

94   *'I would never have gone public . . . '*: Des Barres, *Rock Bottom*.
94   *'Be careful swimming in the coming year'*: Ibid.
94   *'We're in Sweden, right . . . '*: Jones, *Can't Stand Up for Falling Down*.
96   *'It was too destructive'*: Richard Goldstein, 'A quiet night at the balloon farm', *New York* (October 1966).
97   *'[The band] has been our home . . . '*: David Gans, 'Dead end', *Rolling Stone*, 25 January 1996.
98   *'Did you take any dope . . . '*: Dave Lifton, 'When the Allman Brothers Band's road manager killed a club owner', Ultimteclassicrock.com, 29 April 2015.
99   *'The Pretenders'*: Ellen, *Rock Stars Stole My Life!*
99   *'I think I'll go and get a job . . . '*: Des Barres, *Rock Bottom*.
99   *'Finally in New York'*: Raymond Obstfeld and Patricia Fitzgerald, *Jabberrock: The Ultimate Book of Rock 'N' Roll Quotations* (Canongate, 1997).
100 *'Every time I saw Janis . . . '*: Des Barres, *Rock Bottom*.
100 *'so my friends can get blasted . . . '*: Joe Taysom, 'Janis Joplin's will include a special party fund for an "all night" wake', *Far Out Magazine*, 22 October 2020.
100 *'If I had all the money I've spent . . . '*: *Sir Henry at Rawlinson End* (Charisma Records, 1978).

100 *'Of course we're doing it for the money as well'*: David Fricke, 'The Rolling Stones: Mick Jagger and Keith Richards' uneasy truce', *Rolling Stone*, 7 September 1989.

100 *'the good time that's been had by all'*: *Word* (July 2005).

100 *'He's always looking for it'*: Dylan Jones, 'Men of the Year – 1999: Keith Richards', *GQ* (October 1999).

101 *'there were maybe ten other women'*: Quoted in Dave Swanson, 'Mick Jagger's wife and girlfriends through the years', Ultimateclassicrock.com, 16 July 2016.

101 *In her autobiography*: Ronnie Spector with Vince Waldron, *Be My Baby: How I Survived Mascara, Miniskirts, and Madness, Or, My Life as a Fabulous Ronette* (Harmony Books, 1990).

102 *After he beat her to the ground*: See O'Brien, *She Bop*.

102 *'own failure of nerve'*: Ibid.

102 *'Yesterday'*: Lyrics by Lennon–McCartney. © Sony/ATV Tunes LLC.

103 *'My father was a schoolteacher ... '*: 'Pink Floyd and Company – Roger Waters interview', *Penthouse* (September 1988).

103 *'If I had written ... '*: Randy Lewis, 'The long and the short of it is, Newman's thinking big', *Los Angeles Times*, 21 April 1995.

104 *in Ray Manzarek's words*: See Sterling Whitaker, 'How Jim Morrison got arrested onstage in New Haven', Ultimateclassicrock.com, 9 December 2015.

105 *'We had this group which we all knew ... '*: Obstfeld and Fitzgerald, *Jabberrock*.

105 *'common-law widow'*: Des Barres, *Rock Bottom*.

105 *'The words that go with this ... '*: Philip Norman, *Symphony for the Devil: The Rolling Stones Story* (Simon & Schuster, 1984).

105 *'I must say, in fairness to the poppy ... '*: Harris, *Hail! Hail! Rock 'n' Roll*.

106 *'I don't know if I've been lucky ... '*: Ibid.

106 *'There was a knock on our dressing-room door ... '*: Ibid.

112 *'to bring attention to the end of the American dream'*: Interview with Much Music, 1982.

113 *'We just thought it was funny'*: Joel Keller, 'Spouting', *New Jersey Monthly*, 19 December 2007.

114 *'I haven't even told my mum ... '*: Interview with *Billboard*, 2013.

117 *'the least annoying'*: 'How did the band get their name? British edition', UpVenue.com.

120 *'Rex Stardust'*: *Monty Python's Contractual Obligation Album* (Charisma Records, 1980).

120 *'nonsensical near-homophone'*: 'The 30 worst names for bands', *Word* (September 2005).

121 *'It's Raining Again'*: Lyrics by Richard Davies and Roger Hodgson. © Universal Music Publishing Group, Sony/ATV Music Publishing LLC.

6: 1944–1945

129 *'No matter how muted or quiet the radio ... '*: Stanley, *Yeah Yeah Yeah*.

130 *'I threw a Guinness bottle against the wall'*: Thomas M. Kitts, *Ray Davies: Not Like Everybody Else* (Routledge, 2008).

131 *'Whatever he did'*: Michael Goldberg, 'Dennis Wilson: The Beach Boy who went overboard', *Rolling Stone*, 4 July 2017.

131 *'Dennis was a sex fiend ... '*: Ibid.

132 *'seen more sex than a policeman's torch'*: Ellen, *Rock Stars Stole My Life!*

132 *'He was always a very selfish lover'*: Caroline Graham, 'Britt mocks "sex god" Rod', *Mail on Sunday*, 21 July 2002.

133 *'Sex at one point ... '*: Benjy Potter, ' "I'll fade away": Celtic-daft Rod Stewart says sex with Penny Lancaster "is still great but they're having NO more kids" ', *Scottish Sun*, 30 May 2019.

133 *'Dolenz looked at the producers ... '*: Stanley, *Yeah Yeah Yeah*.

134 *'a gloomy, troubled person ... '*: Napier-Bell, *Black Vinyl White Powder*.

135 *'I didn't take the song as seriously as all that'*: Nick Hasted, 'Carly Simon: The making of "You're So Vain"', *Uncut* (April 2010).

135 *'Our needs are different'*: Timothy White, 'Carly Simon: fathers and lovers', *Rolling Stone*, 10 April 1981.

135 *'a slightly chubby, red-headed . . . '*: Long, *The History of the* NME.

136 *'It's all very hazy to me now'*: '70 facts you might not know about Neil Young', Tidal.com, 17 June 2016.

137 *'Just starting to rain, it was'*: Quoted in Harris, *Hail! Hail! Rock 'n' Roll.*

137 *'I watched the Beatles from the side of the stage'*: Gerald Nachman, *Right Here on Our Stage Tonight!: Ed Sullivan's America* (University of California Press, 2009).

139 *'I am the Walrus'*: Lyrics by John Lennon and Paul McCartney. © Sony/ATV Music Publishing LLC.

139 *'the most beautiful line . . . '*: Stanley, *Yeah Yeah Yeah*. 'Wichita Lineman' lyrics by Jimmy L. Webb. © Canopy Music, Inc.

140 *'Lily the Pink'*: Lyrics by John Henry Gorman, Roger Joseph McGough and Michael McGear. © Noel Gay Music Co. Ltd.

141 *'What Garfunkel made from the bones of the demo . . . '*: Giles Smith, 'Lives of the great songs: "Bridge over Troubled Water"', *Independent*, 11 September 1994.

143 *'We played it, and you know . . . '*: 'Toni Visconti on recording Bowie's "Heroes"', YouTube.com.

145 *'in the area of being the greatest pop group ever'*: Paul Morley, 'Showing off', *Observer*, 14 June 2009.

7: 1946–1947

155 *'You sleep in sunlight . . . '*: Nik Cohn, 'Be happy, don't worry! On tour with The Who', *Cream*, 21 (February 1973).

155 *'sycophantic friends would dose . . . '*: Des Barres, *Rock Bottom*.

156 *'We staggered on stage . . . '*: Ibid.

156 *'Now look up there'*: Ibid.

156 *'Perhaps we could make the middle darker . . . '*: Ibid.

156 *'full of dust and guitars'*: 'Syd Barrett: The madcap who named Pink Floyd', *Rolling Stone*, 23 December 1971.

157 *'the kid under the tree by himself'*: Jimmy McDonough, *Soul Survivor: A Biography of Al Green* (Hachette, 2017).

157 *'His brothers were real manly'*: Ibid.

157 *'We were having dinner one night . . . '*: Ibid.

159 *'Retarded artistically . . . '*: Des Barres, *Rock Bottom*.

159 *'Later, he heard the record . . . '*: Napier-Bell, *Black Vinyl White Powder*.

160 *'Keith showed me the way to insanity'*: Tony Fletcher, *Dear Boy: The Life of Keith Moon* (Omnibus Press, 2010).

160 *'Nothing seemed to quell the fact . . . '*: Des Barres, *Rock Bottom*.

160* *According to David Hepworth*: In *The Rock & Roll A Level*.

161 *'They flipped out . . . '*: Sam Kashner, 'Fever pitch: when Travolta did disco; the making of *Saturday Night Fever*', in Nelson George and Daphne Carr (ed.), *Best Music Writing 2008* (Da Capo, 2008).

162 *'Freddie, nobody should go on after you'*: Peter Sands, in Alexis Petridis, '"This is a very good question, Bob Dylan": Elton John, interviewed by famous fans', *Guardian*, 12 October 2019.

163 *'I slept with three . . . '*: Quoted in Alexis Petridis, 'Marianne Faithfull: the muse who made it on her own terms', *Guardian*, 23 October 2018.

163 *'She walked through the whole thing . . . '*: Ibid.

164 *'I've got all the stories'*: Ibid.

164 *'I have never seen a girl who looks like this'*: Albertine, *Clothes Clothes Clothes*.

164 *'There's an authority to her singing . . . '*: Thorn, *Naked at the Albert Hall*.

165 *'I do appreciate being slightly well known . . . '*: Clinton Heylin, *No More Sad Refrains: The Life and Times of Sandy Denny* (Omnibus Press, 2011).

165 *'There was a lovely assortment of backstage munchies . . . '*: Chris Frantz, *Remain in Love: Talking Heads, Tom Tom Club, Tina* (White Rabbit, 2020).
166 *'Warren Zevon is a poet . . . '*: Hunter S. Thompson, 'Patrick Roy and Warren Zevon – two champions at the top of their game', ESPN, 28 May 2001.
166 *'I was so short-sighted . . . '*: Napier-Bell, *Black Vinyl White Powder*.
167 *Elton John's pseudonyms may be the best*: Rebecca Lewis, 'These are the dirty fake names Elton John uses to check-in at hotels', *Metro*, 6 February 2016.
167 *the* Guardian *asked various celebrities*: Petridis, '"This is a very good question, Bob Dylan": Elton John, interviewed by famous fans'.
168 *'At the end of the show, of course . . . '*: Raymond Obstfeld and Patricia Fitzgerald, *Jabberrock: The Ultimate Book of Rock 'N' Roll Quotations* (Canongate, 1997).
168 *'Thirteen inches long'*: Rock Babylon, Rapido TV, 1998.
170 *'cold-eyed, thousand-yard stare'*: GQ (April 2014).
170 *'He has not said much . . . '*: Hepworth, *The Rock & Roll A Level*.
170 *'Wilko Johnson is literally the most talkative . . . '*: Ibid.
170 *'I can even feel the serrations'*: Jason Shadrick, 'Rig rundown: Queen's Brian May', Premierguitar.com, 23 July 2014.
171 *'It's something he would have said . . . '*: In Harris, *Hail! Hail! Rock 'n' Roll*.
171 *'Linda Ronstadt was the first . . . '*: Thorn, *Naked at the Albert Hall*.
172 *'fey gurgle'*: Coleman, *Voices*.
173 *'the size of Lincolnshire'*: Maconie, *Cider with Roadies*.
173 *'one of the most loathed men in the music business'*: Dannen, *Hit Men*.
174 *'It's Irving's world. We just play in it'*: 'Azoff's Power', The Lefsetz Letter, 8 May 2008.
182 *'We never completely do a song . . . '*: 'Bee Gees write '70s songs to the tune of big money', *Detroit Free Press*, 27 July 1979.

8: 1948–1950

189 *'Everybody in the audience was on acid . . . '*: 'Alice Cooper and Noel Fielding talk rock'n'roll, drink, drugs and golf', *Guardian*, 21 January 2012.
190 *'It smelled so bad I was gagging'*: 'The snakes', Sickthingsuk.co.uk.
190 *'I explicitly said . . . '*: Moser and Crawford, *Rock Stars do the Dumbest Things*.
190 *'I'll tell you what's fun'*: Ibid.
190 *'Hey!'*: Ibid.
191 *'The Bonzo I remember . . . '*: Des Barres, *Rock Bottom*.
191 *'John did not grow up . . . '*: Quoted in ibid.
192 *'I never realised Nick Drake was ambitious . . . '*: Graeme Thomson, 'Booze is fuel', *Word* (November 2005).
194 *he told Allan Jones*: Jones, *Can't Stand Up for Falling Down*.
196 *'I'm stymied to come up with anything . . . '*: 'Inside the mind of Ted Nugent – RF6 exclusive', *Royal Flush*, 29 December 2009.
196 *'Having a hundred girls . . . '*: Raymond Obstfeld and Patricia Fitzgerald, *Jabberrock: The Ultimate Book of Rock 'N' Roll Quotations* (Canongate, 1997).
197 *'It looked tastier than bleach'*: Hank Bordowitz, *Billy Joel: The Life & Times of an Angry Young Man* (Billboard Books, 2005).
197 *'I think of myself as a piano player . . . '*: Ibid.
197 *'luxurious mink'*: Thorn, *Naked at the Albert Hall*.
198 *'She was so symbolic . . . '*: In Liz Evans, *Women, Sex and Rock 'n' Roll: In Their Own Words* (Pandora, 1994).
198 *'When the hall empties out . . . '*: Robin Green, 'David Cassidy: naked lunch box', *Rolling Stone*, 11 May 1972.
199 *'He was a smooth article . . . '*: Stanley, *Yeah Yeah Yeah*.
201 *'Every show I do I play . . . '*: Quoted in Hepworth, *The Rock & Roll A Level*.
201 *'It's about a really well-dressed ladies' man . . . '*: 'Browne remembers Zevon', *Rolling Stone*, 19 September 2003.
202 *'Grease (Is the Word)'*: Lyrics by Barry Gibb. © Crompton Songs.

202 *'I was trying to write two separate songs . . . '*: Dorian Lynskey and Dave Simpson, '"Born Slippy was a greyhound we bet on"', *Guardian*, 24 February 2006.
203 *'Dance Away'*: Lyrics by Bryan Ferry. © Universal Music Publishing Group.
204 *'Everyone was convinced . . . '*: Napier-Bell, *Black Vinyl White Powder*.
205 *'About the fourth or fifth time . . . '*: Ibid.

9: 1951–1958

217 *'Cauliflowers are a particularly pleasing . . . '*: Sharp, *Mind the Bollocks*.
218 *'Don't moan about being a chick . . . '*: Quoted in Lorraine Ali, 'The grrl who heads the jet set', *Los Angeles Times*, 18 June 1994.
218 *'It's strange talking to someone like that'*: Jones, *Can't Stand Up for Falling Down*.
220 *'I remember going to the* NME *offices . . . '*: Long, *The History of the* NME.
220 *'It was a psychedelic pirate ship'*: Ibid.
221 *'The moment he arrived . . . '*: Ellen, *Rock Stars Stole My Life!*
222 *'When we started the band . . . '*: Steve Pond, 'XTC ninjas of the mundane', *Rolling Stone*, 20 April 1989.
223 *'Virgin offered me a deal in 1979'*: Interview with David Wild, *Rolling Stone*, 1 June 1989.
224 *'Boy, you could be the greatest . . . '*: Kerri Leigh, *Stevie Ray: Soul to Soul* (Taylor Publishing, 1993).
224 *'Cult'*: Dave Rimmer, *Like Punk Never Happened: Culture Club and the New Pop* (Faber & Faber, 2011).
224 *'Even though Michael is very talented . . . '*: Quoted in Randall Sullivan, 'Curse of Michael's millions: How Michael Jackson's family preyed on his wealth and took it by the vanload after his death', *Daily Mail*, 10 November 2012.
225 *'listening to rock music . . . '*: Quoted in Herman, *Rock 'n' Roll Babylon*.
226 *'because that's what Sid would have liked'*: 'Q Awards 2001: "Inspiration Award" – John Lydon: The dirty rotten scoundrel', *Q* (November 2001).
226 *'America's a fantastic country'*: John Harris, 'I'm a Sex Pistol, get me out of here', *The Times*, 6 February 2004.
227 *'Lydon had installed himself at the far end . . . '*: Mueller, *It's Too Late to Die Young Now*.
227 *'sick of all the bullshit'*: Glen Matlock, *I Was a Teenage Sex Pistol* (Reynolds & Hearn, 2006).
228 *'We were what we were . . . '*: *Classic Albums: Never Mind the Bollocks, Here's the Sex Pistols*, 26 October 2002.
228 *'a loose-limbed pile of rags . . . '*: Jones, *Can't Stand Up for Falling Down*.
230 *'I'm not trying to sell sex'*: Daisann McLane, 'The glamorous lie', *Spin* 2.11 (February 1987).
231 *'shag tree is more Escher than flow-chart'*: 'The love unlimited orchestra', *Word* (July 2005).
231 *'Welcome to the remake of* Apocalypse Now*!'*: Wendy Leigh, 'Madonna can't stop loving Poison Penn – he's a dead ringer for the dad who broke her heart', Mail online, 27 September 2013.
232 *'By chance'*: *Newsweek*, 1985.
232 *'I wouldn't be surprised . . . '*: 'Morrissey slates Madonna during US gig', *NME*, 16 July 2007.
232* *Rodman later recalled*: Dennis Rodman with Tim Keown, *Bad as I Wanna Be* (Bantam Doubleday Dell, 1996).
233 *'Lenny told me . . . '*: Ron Givens, 'Controversy over "Justify My Love"', *Entertainment Weekly*, 1 February 1991.
234 *'a palm-sized area . . . '*: Hepworth, *Uncommon People*.
242 *'"Ghost Town" spoke to me . . . '*: @tom_watson, Twitter, 22 October 2019. Quoted in Maconie, *The People's Songs*.

242 *'it was recorded in the small basement . . . '*: Hugh Montgomery, Paul Bignell and Mike Higgins, 'Ghost Town: The song that defined an era turns 30', *Independent*, 3 July 2011.
243 *'where it stayed for three weeks . . . '*: Ibid.

10: 1959–1964

253 *'I'm constantly confronted by . . . '*: Interview with Alexa Williamson, Virgin.net, 1997.
254 *'I would actually prefer prostitution'*: Morrissey, *Autobiography* (Penguin, 2013).
254 *'You've got a funny voice'*: Ibid.
254 *'That was the last straw, really'*: *Record Collector* (November/December 1992).
254 *'I am totally against murder'*: Pete Redfern, 'Charles Manson was actually a pretty nice guy, insists Morrissey', NewsThump.com, 20 November 2017.
254* *another version of this first meeting*: See Maconie, *The People's Songs*.
255 *'I have no feet'*: '99% true', *Word* (January 2005).
256 *'sawn in half by a fabulously camp window-dresser . . . '*: Ellen, *Rock Stars Stole My Life!*
256 *'That girl's a fag-hag . . . '*: Quoted in Napier-Bell, *Black Vinyl White Powder*.
257 *'We expect celebrities to be superhuman'*: Raymond Obstfeld and Patricia Fitzgerald, *Jabberrock: The Ultimate Book of Rock 'N' Roll Quotations* (Canongate, 1997).
257 *'to see what mayhem we could create'*: In Harris, *Hail! Hail! Rock 'n' Roll*.
257 *'We discovered drugs . . . '*: Ibid.
257 *'I'm really looking forward to playing America . . . '*: Ibid.
258 *'Once I was sitting there . . . '*: In Sharp, *Mind the Bollocks*.
258 *'the tiny twinkle-eyed Satan of kid pop'*: Pete Paphides, *Broken Greek* (Quercus, 2020).
259 *'musical insubordination'*: Steven Daly, 'Tori Amos' secret garden', *Rolling Stone*, 26 June 1998.
259 *'They're really sweet, generous people . . . '*: Joe Gore, 'Inside the peppermill: Dave Navarro and Flea reinvent the Chilis', *Guitar Player* (April 1995).
260 *'It was black leather shorts . . . '*: *Desert Island Discs*, BBC Radio 4, 24 April 2005.
260 *'He was modest, humble . . . '*: Mueller, *It's Too Late to Die Young Now*.
261 *'What do you get when you put . . . '*: Genevieve Roberts, 'Magic Numbers walk out after fat "jibe" by "Top of the Pops" presenter', *Independent*, 29 April 2013.
262 *'Bez's wild eyes rolled in his head . . . '*: Maconie, *Cider with Roadies*.
262 *'I've been saying we need a revolution . . . '*: Emily Heward, 'Bez to join fracking protest as he launches plan to run as Salford MP in 2015 general election', *Manchester Evening News*, 14 March 2014.
263 *'Courtney wasn't yet terrifically well known . . . '*: Mueller, *It's Too Late to Die Young Now*.
265 *'soberness and sincerity'*: *The Fourth, The Fifth, The Minor Fall*, BBC Radio 2, 1 November 2008.
265 *'hallelujah to the orgasm'*: Ibid.
265 *'purifying and almost liturgical'*: Ibid.
265 *'Hallelujah'*: Lyrics by Leonard Cohen. © Sony/ATV Music Publishing LLC.
266 *'I'm not afraid to say I think Band Aid . . . '*: Simon Garfield, 'This Charming Man', reprinted in Paul A. Woods (ed.), *Morrissey in Conversation: The Essential Interviews* (Plexus, 2017).
266 *'Bad'*: Lyrics by Michael Jackson. ©Mijac Music.
269 *'Rehab'*: Lyrics by Amy Winehouse. © Sony/ATV Music Publishing LLC.

11: 1965–1974

281 *'respectable reptilian institutions'*: Tom Pinnock, 'Slash: "I felt very proud that I was part of this grand lineage of English piss-heads"', *Uncut*, 8 January 2016.

281 *'I'd had some close calls ... '*: Ibid.
281 *'They're the greatest listeners ... '*: Tom Hibbert, 'Janet Jackson: "I've always wanted to own a king cobra because they're so dangerous', *Guardian*, 29 July 2015. Originally published in *Smash Hits*, 27 August 1986.
282 *she told* Newsweek: 'Rhythm and the Blues', *Newsweek*, 16 November 1997.
282 *'My friends and I have piercing parties ... '*: 'Janet Jackson's piercing parties', *National Enquirer*, 9 May 2001.
282 *'a spiritual reason which I don't talk about'*: Laura B. Randolph, 'Janet', *Ebony* (December 1997).
283 *'gloomy, vengeful element based on hatred'*: Phil West, 'Hair swinging neanderthals', *The Daily*, February 1989.
283 *'No thanks, it'll make my teeth bleed'*: Dave Thompson, *Never Fade Away: The Kurt Cobain Story* (St Martin's, 1994).
283 *'It was a mating ritual ... '*: Poppy Z. Brite, *Courtney Love: The Real Story* (Touchstone, 1999).
283 *'Satan lives here!'*: Melissa Rossi, *Courtney Love: Queen of Noise* (Pocket Books, 1996).
283 *'You get out of this bed ... '*: Michael Azzerad, 'Territorial Pissings: The battles behind Nirvana's new album', *Musician* (October 1993).
284 *according to Nirvana's biographer*: Everett True, *Nirvana: The True Story* (Omnibus Press, 2006).
284 *'Total peace after death'*: Thompson, *Never Fade Away.*
285 *'One night Bono was rude to me ... '*: Adrian Deevoy, 'Stop the band, I wanna get off!', *Q* (March 1996).
286 *'I'm a guy with a big mouth ... '*: 'Hot shot: Shaggy talks about his time in the Corps and his new CD, "Summer in Kingston", *Military Times*, 1 September 2011.
286 *'ISIS can go fuck themselves ... '*: Dyllan Furness, 'Shaggy shares his strategy for defeating ISIS', *Miami New Times*, 6 July 2015.
286 *'He used a felt pen'*: Moser and Crawford, *Rock Stars do the Dumbest Things.*
288 *'I ... hated being on stage'*: In Liz Evans, *Women, Sex and Rock 'n' Roll: In Their Own Words* (Pandora, 1994).
289 *'If I saw an alien ... '*: 'Ten things you might not know about Liam Gallagher', Rize Festival.
289 *'He looks like a fucking balloon ... '*: Luke Leitch, 'Liam Gallagher: "Clothes are important, man"', *Telegraph*, 1 August 2012.
289 *a theory abroad that Liam is a comic genius*: Alessia Armenise, '100 Liam Gallagher quotes that prove he's a comic genius', ShortList, 15 March 2020.
290 *'He's like a man with a fork ... '*: *Q* (April 2009).
291 *'It's always been portrayed as romantic ... '*: Dave Simpson, 'James Blunt: How we made "You're Beautiful', *Guardian*, 14 January 2020.
291 *Blunt responds with wit and self-deprecation*: '25 times James Blunt well and truly won Twitter', Music + Sport, 2017.

12: 1975–present

303 *'Truthfully, it was probably at the beginning'*: Andrew Harrison, 'Facetime', *Word* (August 2004).
303 *'There was so much change ... '*: Craig McLean, *Word* (March 2006).
304 *'I'm a genius ... '*: *NME*, 27 January 2004.
305 *'let the character go'*: *The Ellen DeGeneres Show*, 27 September 2018.
305 *'I have this weird thing ... '*: Lisa Robinson, 'Lady Gaga's Cultural Revolution', *Vanity Fair* (September 2010).